D1522868

LEE AND ME

Art direction, cover and layout
Paola Gallerani

Managing Editor
Jayleen Lawler

Co-editors
Helen A. Harrison, Eugene V. and Clare E. Thaw
Director, Pollock-Krasner House and Study Center
Barbara A. MacAdam, critic and editor-at-large Art News

Fact Checker
Saskia Flower

Editor
Wendy Keebler

Color separation
Premani s.r.l., Pantigliate (Milano)

Printed by
Monotipia Cremonese, Cremona

Officina Libraria
Via Carlo Romussi, 4
20125 Milan
Italy

ISBN: 978-88-3367-016-4
© Officina Libraria, Milano, 2020

Printed in Italy

officinalibraria.net   Officina.Libraria   officinalibraria

Ruth Appelhof

LEE AND ME

An Intimate Portrait of Lee Krasner

OFFICINA
LIBRARIA

Ruth Appelhof
and Lee Krasner
in front of
Night Watch
(1960), Pace
Gallery, New
York, 1979.

To my husband, Gary Adamek

Contents

Acknowledgments

My deepest thanks go to the Pollock-Krasner Foundation and the Pollock-Krasner House and Study Center for the generous support they provided with a fellowship that has allowed me two years of research and writing. In particular, I would like to thank Ronald Spencer, Samuel Sachs II, Kerrie Buitrago, and Caroline Black from the Foundation and my dear friend for many years, Charles Bergman, who, sadly, died in 2018. It was Sam Sachs who first discussed with me the value of my old reel-to-reel tapes of interviews with Lee Krasner and how it was my intellectual duty to transcribe them for future research. This led me to the Belfer Sound Laboratory at Syracuse University, my alma mater. The laboratory agreed to take the old tapes and transcribe the interviews into digital format. As a token of my appreciation, I donated the tapes to the Arents Research Library at Syracuse.

I remain deeply grateful for having had Lee Krasner's support, which began in 1974 and continued through the rest of her life. Even now, in doing research for this book, I feel her penetrating and insightful gaze over my shoulder. Since my retirement in 2017, I seem to have fallen back under Krasner's watchful presence. After discussing her with more than one hundred people from the art world, many of whom I had known from my Guild Hall days, and reading the work of critics, curators, and art historians, including Barbara Rose, Robert Hobbs, Gail Levin, Ellen Landau, Jennifer Landes, Joan Marter, Phyllis Braff, Christina Strassfield, and Amei Wallach, I have achieved a better understanding of Krasner's life and work. In addition, my interviews with her friends, colleagues, art-world associates, and neighbors yelded often surprising insights into her personal and artistic journey, as well as an understanding of how my own feelings about her evolved over the years.

In addition, I extend my appreciation to those at the East Hampton Library, the *East Hampton Star*, the Archives of American Art in New York and in Washington, D.C., the New York Public Library, the Museum of Modern Art Archives and Library, the Pollock-Krasner House and Study Center in East Hampton, and the Pollock-Krasner Study Center at Stony Brook University's library at the Southampton campus. It was a great joy to do research on your august premises. I also extend my deepest appreciation to the American Academy in Rome for inviting me to spend the spring of 2017 as a scholar in residence. There I made lasting friendships and wrote the first draft of this manuscript.

Of all the art historians who have devoted time to Krasner, it was Barbara Rose who made the greatest difference in her life. She curated a 1983–1985 retrospective exhibition that was organized at the Museum of Fine Arts, Houston, and traveled to the San Francisco Museum of Art, the Chrysler Museum of Art in Norfolk, the Phoenix Art Museum, and the Museum of Modern Art in New York. This revealed Krasner in a new light. Robert Hobbs followed with a comprehensive show that traveled from the Los Angeles County Museum of Art to the Des Moines Art Center, the Akron Art Museum, and the Brooklyn Museum in 1999–2001. And Eleanor Nairne, curator at the Barbican Art Gallery in London, and her team have mounted a spectacular exhibition that travels to Frankfurt, Bern, and Bilbao in 2019 and 2020. Of course, nothing can be written about Krasner without reference to Gail Levin's comprehensive biography and Ellen Landau's catalogue raisonné, from which I have sought guidance many times.

In 2016, when I contacted Rose about writing this book, she warned me, "So much has been written about Lee I don't think you could add anything." She was adamant that there had already been more than a sufficient number of art historians writing about Krasner, all of whom had explored every inch of the artist's life. Of course, I persevered, and Rose became my first and strongest ally. My deepest thanks go to her for the way she responded to my many questions and for writing her insightful preface to the book. I am also grateful to Robert Hobbs, who gave me wonderful leads on roads I delighted in exploring.

I am grateful to the "Krasner Team": Helen A. Harrison, the Eugene V. and Clare E. Thaw Director of the Pollock-Krasner House and Study Center, who on a daily basis supplied me with valuable information and, as my mentor, reviewed the manuscript before publication and wrote a moving foreword; Jayleen Lawler, a young writer who resolved my many roadblocks, acting as my assistant and loyal friend; Barbara A. MacAdam, critic and editor-at-large with *ARTnews*, whose editing was critical to the project; and Saskia Flower, a recent Courtauld graduate, who assisted with the Krasner exhibition at the Barbican and combed through this manuscript to ensure accuracy.

I wish to thank the people I contacted for information and those I interviewed. Your time and knowledge were all critical to the insights I derived in writing this book. So many of you provided fascinating and beautiful stories. I am sorry not to have been able to include all of your valuable contributions, but I encourage those interested in pursuing this information further to contact the Pollock-Krasner House and Study Center for access.

Finally, I am grateful to my children, Gregory Appelhof, who shared his computer expertise, and Lee Ann Earle, who researched a multitude of topics, from the feminist movement to the psychic meaning of the number eleven, and to my husband, Gary Adamek, for his constant attention and moral support. You all helped in so many ways to make my dream a reality.

Ruth Appelhof

Foreword

History, it's said, is memory. And memory, at its root, is mindful recall. The very act of remembering is a conscious process that is essential to the appreciation of history, whether personal or collective. Individual memories, in the form of first-person testimony, can enlarge and enrich historical knowledge, and that is what Dr. Ruth Appelhof's reflections on her experience with Lee Krasner have done.

We may already know a lot about Krasner; however, as Ruth has shown, this iconic artist is an especially fertile subject for such recollection. Outspoken, articulate, and opinionated, she has related her own story eloquently and at length. There have been many scholarly articles, monographs, catalog essays, and a comprehensive biography devoted to her, and her work has been widely exhibited and analyzed. But as we all know from experience, the private person may differ greatly from the public persona. The dynamics of a relationship reveal aspects of character and personality that are unique to that interaction, even as they confirm or refute widely held assumptions or so-called common knowledge.

Ruth is refreshingly frank about her own assumptions and perceived limitations in coming to terms with a woman widely regarded as a formidable, even adversarial, interviewee. Intensely protective of her late husband's legacy and skeptical of the motives of those who approached her for information, Krasner was well fortified long before Ruth came on the scene. But the fact that Ruth was interested in her, rather than in Jackson Pollock, was clearly a decisive factor in her submitting to being interviewed. No doubt, Ruth's warm temperament and maturity enabled her to gain some measure of Krasner's trust, yet she was aware that some of what Krasner told her raised more questions than it provided answers, at least to her satisfaction. In other words, history according to Krasner was a version of the past edited to suit the needs of the present.

Those unanswered questions, lying dormant for decades, are the impetus for Ruth's candid, insightful meditation on her singular interaction with a woman who could be remarkably forthcoming while, at the same time, controlling the narrative. That the woman is a key figure in the development of American art gives Ruth's story even more depth and resonance, although it's her personal perspective that brings it vividly to life.

It has been a privilege to follow Ruth on this journey and a joy to find it concluded so brilliantly.

Helen A. Harrison
Eugene V. and Clare E. Thaw Director,
Pollock-Krasner House and Study Center

The Many Faces of Lee Krasner

When Ruth Appelhof, a young and curious aspiring art historian, met Lee Krasner, the latter was a well-known, if not world-famous, painter, celebrated not so much for her own highly original work as for being the widow of Jackson Pollock. She and Pollock had worked for the WPA during the Depression, but their work took different directions when Lee was exposed to Cubism and began studying with the outstanding teacher of modern art in America Hans Hofmann. She, in turn, passed on Hofmann's lessons, not only to Pollock but also to Clement Greenberg, who championed Krasner's husband as the greatest American painter. Greenberg acknowledged her work in private but did nothing for her in public.

These are stories Appelhof came to know when she was invited to interview Krasner for her master's thesis. It was the summer of 1974, and Appelhof was staying with Krasner in the modest house she and Pollock had occupied since moving to East Hampton from Manhattan in 1945. Her stories of life with Krasner are both humorous and illuminating, exposing aspects of the artist yet to be explored. This portrait of Krasner renders her more human and complex than many thought her to be, because Appelhof actually lived with her and spent decades researching and constructing the story of her life and experience based on dozens of interviews and documents gleaned from friends and critics alike.

As a firsthand, intimate, and human view of Krasner and the art world she lived in, this new study is indispensable.

Barbara Rose

CHAPTER ONE

Driving Miss Krasner

I recall standing over the kitchen sink in our always-freezing Skaneateles, New York, house (heated with a wood-fired Jøtul stove), washing the remnants of some makeshift supper off my plate. I wasn't a great cook; I never consulted recipes, so our meals usually consisted of hot dogs and hamburgers or, for special occasions, chicken and dumplings. My children often took part in the kitchen activity. Making cookies out of bran meal was one of our favorite culinary pastimes—it was the communal activity more than the taste or nutrition that excited us. Finally drying the last dish, I was, as usual, fighting off the exhaustion of managing my responsibilities as a thirty-four-year-old college professor, mother, and graduate student when the phone rang. I wiped my hands on my jeans and picked up the receiver of the avocado-green wall phone next to my 1974 wall calendar.

Fig. 1
Ruth viewing
Combat (1965)
at Whitney
Museum,
New York, 1973.

A harsh, gravelly female voice with a distinct Brooklyn accent greeted me and asked, "Do you ever come to New York? Would you come by and say hello?"

My world changed in that instant, a culmination of months of research. Earlier that year, I had been assigned to write a final report for a graduate class taught by Professor Antje Lemke of the Library Science Department at Syracuse University.[1] The subject was supposed to be someone I admired. I immediately thought the perfect project would be a bibliography devoted to Lee Krasner. I not only appreciated her work, but beyond that, I also found there was something utterly intriguing about her personality—and I was eager to know more. Krasner became my role model, a feminist paradigm who seemed indebted to no one but herself. She was a symbol of artistic power, who had achieved respect among the cultural elite and was one of the most talented painters of her time but had not received the level of attention she so obviously deserved.

My passion for Krasner had been aroused by the 1973 exhibition "Large Paintings," curated by Marcia Tucker at the Whitney Museum of American Art.

I ended up sending Krasner the extensive body of information I had compiled on her, resulting from many hours spent thumbing through volume after volume of the *Art Index*. I mailed the bibliography to the world-renowned Marlborough Gallery, which represented Krasner, with a note that began, "Hello, I'm Ruth Appelhof." I'm not sure I had any expectation of receiving a reply, just hoping she would see it and be pleased. But what ultimately transpired was something I had certainly never anticipated.

Her call would lead me to an adventure of a lifetime, filled with humor and some sadness.

Early Encounters

Arriving at Krasner's New York City home—a high-rise building at 180 East 79th Street that she had occupied since 1967—I was duly impressed. The apartment was enormous, at least from my small-town upstate New York perspective, and every wall was covered with Krasner's powerful paintings.

I had been told not to ask her about Jackson Pollock, her late husband, whom she simply called Pollock. She let it be known that she had grown tired of talking about him and now wanted the art world to pay attention to her. For me, it was "crystal clear," as Krasner used to say, that she wanted my full attention. But most important, she craved that from the art world.

Krasner was more than hospitable, and I felt we hit it off immediately. She and I sat at the dining-room table, sipping tea and talking about the research I had done on her. The apartment had an artsy look, with unmatched chairs and tables—one chair was of beautifully woven wicker, while another had curved animal tusks as armrests. Overall, it looked like a gathering of treasures you'd find at an exotic Parisian flea market, as if the space itself were a Surrealist work of art.

On one wall of the apartment hung a gorgeous "emblem" painting, *Rising Green* (1972), one of a series of canvases Krasner painted in the early 1970s that were hard-edged and minimalist. I recognized this 82-inch-by-69-inch painting from the Arnold Newman portrait of Krasner sitting in front of it. Somewhat out of character, Krasner looks directly into the camera, relaxed and smiling slightly, yet still daring the viewer to challenge her authority as the "master" of the work.

The budding curator in me was digesting her oeuvre as I settled in to chat. Certainly, as much of Krasner's late work suggests, she made a measured effort to paint in the style of the period—in this case, like minimalists Ellsworth Kelly and Frank Stella—while still clinging to the vibrant green leaf shapes and the soft mauve flower buds of Henri Matisse. Striking in this canvas, are the two white ovals that anchor the image. They act as both background and foreground, while demonstrating the "push-pull" effect that her teacher Hans Hofmann often advocated. *Rising Green* (1972) is a classic composition in Krasner's mature style, referencing both the human body and the forms of nature with which, as I was soon to learn, she had surrounded herself in the Hamptons.

Krasner seemed pleased with our conversation and was forthcoming in inviting me to return and stay with her in the future. Of course, I was thrilled and visited her often, sleeping in her tiny maid's room, which I adored; it had a womblike effect on me.

My visits, though brief—on weekends, for a day or two—were always very intense. Krasner occasionally discussed the logistics of an exhibition she was planning. She rarely indulged in serious "art talk," but I nonetheless hung on her every word. Other than reading art periodicals and occasionally traveling to New York City to see an exhibition, my upstate life had been completely devoid of art-world news. To my delight, while I was at Krasner's, a few of her admirers would stop by, including Cynthia Navaretta, Cindy Nemser, Francis V. O'Connor, and the preeminent feminist art historian Linda Nochlin. Nochlin's candid conversation with Krasner would precipitate one of the most horrifying experiences I'd have with Lee, relating to the recent publication of the memoir by Pollock's beautiful lover, Ruth Kligman, obviously an open wound.[2] (Details in chapter five.)

Finally, during one visit, Krasner invited me to come out to East Hampton in the summer so I could interview her for my master's thesis. Summers were always lonely and difficult for me because my children would join their father, from whom I was divorced, in Minnesota. The invitation seemed too good to be true.

It was easy to say yes. Of primary importance, of course, would be spending time interviewing Krasner, learning what made her and her work so significant at this time and place. I knew there would be some logistics to overcome, but I also realized this might be the next step—the first real one—toward my career in the arts. It was the new beginning I had wished for.

Hitting the Road

I'm not sure how or why I would have purchased an orange Ford Pinto. I do remember flirting with the owner of the car dealership and telling him my sad but true story of what I had learned was "middle-class poverty." The shocking color stood out as freakishly ugly, and certainly this must have been the cheapest car on the lot.

Krasner came out of her high-rise apartment, the doorman carrying her bags, and gasped at the vehicle parked at the front curb. But to her credit, she didn't say a word.

Off we went to Long Island. Surprisingly, neither of us had a clue about where we were going. Since Krasner didn't drive, she didn't really know the way, and I hadn't bothered to get directions, assuming there would be clear signs and that she could help navigate. There were many confusing moments during which Krasner, obviously lost, maintained her "in control" demeanor, pointing at signs and gesturing to turn left or right. We did finally make it—a three-hour drive that took more like five.

East Hampton had not really been on my radar. There was much I didn't know about it—most notably, the relationship the area had with so many artists, including Robert Motherwell, Willem de Kooning, and Pollock and also historical icons like Winslow Homer, who visited in 1874, and Thomas Moran, who came a few years later and built a beautiful Queen Anne–style house on Main Street, where he gathered his entire family for the summers. The community was filled with writers, painters, musicians, and other creative people, who treasured the beautiful natural landscape, the sandy beaches and salt water, the fresh corn and tomatoes, and the peace and quiet of country living.

In a remote wooded setting called Springs, we pulled up to a three-bedroom cedar-shingled farmhouse with a barn, about the size of my own little home and barn in Skaneateles. There were a few cottages and clapboard homes in the area, but it was mostly woods and fields full of straggly weeds.

We parked the orange Pinto in the driveway. There had been little attempt to landscape the property the way we did then in the upstate suburbs. Here there was nothing but a stray lilac bush at the corner of the back porch. I was horrified to realize my lack of taste was in clear view of friends and neighbors, and I quickly carried our bags into the house. I did not pack lightly, as I needed a large IBM Selectric typewriter and an even bigger reel-to-reel tape recorder, along with a suitcase full of books and, of course, some pretty clothes for the festivities to come.

The air inside was a bit stuffy, since the house had been closed all winter. I caught my breath as I stepped into a beautiful, spacious, and rustic kitchen. It was not fancy—all the appliances were along the southern wall, and there were two gorgeous six-foot-long, thick slabs of marble resting on a Spanish

Fig. 3
Pollock-Krasner House, 1974.

Fig. 4
Kitchen window,
Pollock-Krasner
House, c. 1975.

sideboard. It served as the island countertop, a gift from new neighbors Valentine and Happy Macy, who were from Westchester.

What I loved was the pantry. It was full of treasures—spices, pots and pans, and a huge array of condiments, all meticulously lined up and exuding delicious aromas. Krasner's six-sided marble breakfast table was set in the back doorway so that she could see the view to the water every morning as she sipped her coffee. On the wall next to the back door was a framed silkscreen poster she had just finished for the 1974 Springs Invitational held annually at Ashawagh Hall. This poster was a thing of pride for Krasner. She was one of two dozen important American artists to be invited to create the announcement for the Springs exhibition, an honor she cherished. At the end of the summer, upon my departure, Krasner would hand me one of them as a gift—but she refused to sign it, explaining that signed copies were only allotted to paying customers.

Eventually, I learned that some of the other East Hampton artists invited to create posters, including de Kooning, Ilya Bolotowsky, Perle Fine, and Ray Parker, had previously set the bar high for artistic excellence at this community event which was part of the Fisherman's Fair celebration held every July. Knowing this gave me an understanding of the significant artistic community I had come to visit. To my surprise, there was a second framed poster, also in the kitchen, of *Blue and Black* (1953–1954), announcing Krasner's 1973 exhibition at the Whitney, her first major museum show in America.

On one wall stood an English pre-Jacobean court cupboard from the seventeenth or eighteenth century, another gift from Valentine and Happy Macy. Krasner would eventually give one of her mosaic tables to the Macys as a thank-you for their generosity.

The dining room had a massive round wood table that seated ten. Scattered around the center of the table and throughout the house were the shells and fossils that Krasner collected.

A huge white polar-bear rug was set off by an impressive bay window, with sunlight pouring in to warm the interior, which Krasner used as a greenhouse for her hanging spider plants and ferns set out on the floor. These huge plants reminded me immediately of those in her New York apartment.

A seven-foot-tall wooden "found object" sculpture, originally exhibited as an outdoor fountain at Guild Hall in 1968, stood in the corner of the room. This work, the single one in the house created by an artist other than Krasner, was made by her next-door neighbor and nephew, Ronald Stein, who came to Springs in 1963 and moved in next to Krasner into what had been planned as her studio. He was to be her companion in later years. His presence also added difficulties to her already anguished life story.

On the side wall next to the bay window stood Krasner's seven-foot-tall work *Lame Shadow* (1954), a huge collage of rich earth tones that Gene Baro would select for the Washington, D.C., Corcoran Gallery of Art exhibition the following year. And of primary importance, on the wall above the monumental table, was one of Krasner's magnificent "Umber" paintings, *Cosmic Fragments* (1962), with its ten-foot-long clash of brushstrokes, dominating

Fig. 5
Kitchen interior,
Pollock-Krasner
House, 1974.

the space. Adding to the drama, as a transition piece from the dining area to the living room, was an elegant hand-woven wicker rocker.

The small living room, facing the porch and the road beyond, was sparsely furnished, with, as the centerpiece, an exotic horned red Victorian settee that had been a gift from Krasner's close friends Alfonso Ossorio and Ted Dragon, who also owned the matching side chairs at their famous East Hampton estate.[3] Krasner would return the gift. In her will, dated January 10, 1979, she states, "I give and bequeath my horned love seat to my friend, Ted Dragon."[4]

A few odd chairs were scattered around the room, including a handsome Boston rocker. Along the walls were shelves of books that had belonged to both Pollock and Krasner, as well as a record player and a stack of well-worn album covers. I had to assume there were records in the sleeves, but we never tried to take them out and play them. A curio shelf was set between the floor-to-ceiling window and the door looking out onto the front porch, which displayed more shells and memorabilia. One of Krasner's most important early paintings, an abstract still life with fruits resting on a table, *Untitled* (1940), hung over a desk. A tightly designed Cubist composition, it is defined by heavy black outlines that isolate the forms against a gray background.

On the front porch, a huge round mosaic table took up most of the space. This 1948 table, one of two—the earlier one had been created the year before—was made with leftover tesserae that Pollock had brought with him when he and Krasner got married and moved to Springs in 1945. Krasner worked on the tables during the freezing winters huddled by the woodstove on the first floor, while Pollock painted in the barn.[5] These tables, made from the rim of a simple wagon wheel, became the touchstone for Krasner's constantly evolving art throughout her life.

Fig. 6
The Pollock-Krasner House living-dining room, c. 1975.

Fig. 7
Krasner's shell
collection in her
bedroom, 1974.

A staircase led up to three bedrooms and a bathroom with a clawfoot tub. My room was farthest in the back, small and bare. The only hint of her late husband's existence was a photograph by Hans Namuth showing Pollock sitting beside his Model A Ford and some huge exotic peacock feathers in a vase. A blond wood desk and bureau were on opposite sides of the room. The only other decoration was a patchwork quilt on the single bed. I later learned that Pollock used to paint in this room before he renovated the barn, and then Krasner went on to do her "Little Image" paintings here.[6] From the window, I could see a vast panorama of grass billowing in the breeze and in the distance a breathtaking view of Accabonac Harbor and Gardiners Bay.

Surprise Agenda

Looking back, I now realize that from the first day, Krasner expected me—in fact, needed me—to take care of her. Doing errands and taking her to appointments were all part of the unspoken "house rules." My twenty-four-hour presence was strictly enforced. But I also understood that I was to remain in the background—not interfering with the "adults"—in much the way the women of her childhood had been expected to behave. While I was the mother of two children and in my mid-thirties, in the sixty-five-year-old Krasner's mind, I was merely an intern or a studio assistant. It was only after I began interviewing others for this memoir that I uncovered the truth behind our presence as "summer sitters." We were, in effect, Krasner's summer servants and, to an even larger degree, guardians against her fear of being alone.

It is interesting that art historian and feminist Cindy Nemser, who was one of the first to write thoughtfully on Krasner and who inspired me to

reach out to the artist, had warned me to "be strong" in her presence. Nemser was worried that I might not be up to the challenge Krasner presented with her strident personality. Still, after seeing the 1973–1974 Whitney exhibition and reading articles on Krasner in the art magazines, I had longed to take the next step.

My Protestant family background had not prepared me for such a forceful and acerbic person. Without a father and with a mother who was loving yet afraid of life, I learned always to rely on my outward appearance and soft voice. I was a "nice" girl. Few people, I assumed, would challenge someone with such a modest demeanor. While I was sure I could win Krasner over with kindness and openness, as I had done with difficult people my entire life, her battle to eradicate my dignity and self-respect was unrelenting.

Soon enough, I was made aware that there were a number of additional house rules. The most shocking was "No baths." It seemed, she said, that "two guys had stayed on the property the previous year," and she was convinced that they had taken so many baths that the well ran dry.[7] The solution was to bathe in Gardiners Bay. Krasner promised to show me where the beach was located.

Early the following morning, we chatted about our upcoming work schedule and decided to do the interviews in the afternoon. That way, I could type them up at night and prepare questions for the next day. This being 1974, not much had been published on Krasner. My research turned out to have been seriously incomplete. Having read the few pieces written by Nemser and seen the "Large Paintings" exhibition at the Whitney, I knew I was walking into an art-historical gold mine. I had brought a suitcase with many of the most pertinent books and was looking forward to having a discussion with Krasner every day.

The Interviews

Interviewing Krasner was always like running across a minefield. She would challenge simple questions, and while I had tried to educate myself about the important stages of her life and work, I began to doubt my research. In addition, I began seeing unexplained anger in her, a rage that would erupt without warning. It was frightening. At first, I tried to dive into her childhood and early schooling, asking questions about her family and their backgrounds. From her point of view, it was important that her interviews be absolutely consistent. She had prepared answers for everything and seemed to have the same responses no matter who was talking to her.

Now, looking back, it may have been that Krasner withheld information to preserve her own personal myth, just as she had done with Pollock. She was firm in the telling of her life story and would not deviate in its details. So if there seemed to be a detour in her narrative, she would rectify it the next day. Often in the mornings, when I was reading to her the typed manuscript from the day before, she would start screaming and take out a huge black marker, holding it like a saber and striking out entire passages.

Reading was an issue for her. Art historian Robert Hobbs told me that she probably suffered from dyslexia. That Krasner didn't read much in her middle and later years is confirmed by the many people she called upon to read aloud to her, starting with the visit of Sanford Friedman and Richard Howard in 1958.[8] Yet in her high school years, she was deeply influenced by Edgar Allan Poe and Maurice Maeterlinck, as well as by the great Russian authors (Fyodor Dostoevsky, Maxim Gorky, Ivan Turgenev, and Nikolai Gogol). And of course, later, she was hugely moved by Arthur Rimbaud. As she enthusiastically stated to me, she was inspired by John Graham and his *System and Dialectics of Art*, a book she must have read on her own sometime between 1937, when it was published in New York, and 1942, when Graham put her in his exhibition at McMillen Inc. Gallery.[9]

Years later, when James Valliere was staying with her between 1963 and 1965, he was tasked to cataloguing the Pollock-Krasner library on the bookshelves in the living room. After doing so, he'd give the list to Krasner to identify which items had been owned by Pollock and which were hers. She'd return it to him the next day with no notes, saying they were all Pollock's. Valliere said, "This was a significant piece of information that took me several more weeks to fathom."[10] In my interview with him, I asked if it was possible that she might have not even read the list. He agreed that this could have been the case.[11]

Daily Chores

Once I got my bearings, Krasner began to trust me to do some errands on my own. I learned where butcher Rudy De Santi's store, Dreesen's, was located. He loved Krasner and told me she was more than friendly, delighting the locals when she wore her fur coat into his tiny store to buy fish or steaks. Just as Pollock and Krasner had done since they moved to East Hampton in 1945, I would shop for staples such as bread and eggs at the Springs General Store owned by Dan Miller, which was just around the corner from the house.

She explained that I would be doing some driving, since she didn't drive herself. I think she might have hoped that I would assist with the cooking and other household chores, but that didn't happen. I was, at best, a poor "sous chef," trying desperately to follow her directions. She discovered one of my foremost blind spots: I was lost in the kitchen.

Every morning when I came downstairs, Krasner would be sitting at the marble-topped kitchen table, sipping coffee. My job was to make toast. However, the toaster was like nothing I had seen before. It was not automatic and had to be monitored carefully. You'd place the toast in the open flaps and then close them to heat. No matter how hard I tried, I burned the toast every morning. For Lee, this was a disgrace. She screamed at my stupidity, and I was humiliated.

Krasner was known as a fine cook. In fact, her reputation was so good that many from the art world would come to the house in Springs looking forward to a delicious meal. She explained to me that her love for fish derived from the fact that her parents had run a vegetable and fish market in Brooklyn.[12] She often had vegetables from one of the village farm stands and cooked some sort of fresh local fish, usually cod or haddock.

In the pantry off the kitchen, I found a recipe in Krasner's handwriting. It was from "Loie," the nickname for Arloie, the wife of Sanford McCoy (Jackson's brother). It called for the fish to be covered by milk in a saucepan and cooked over very low heat for half an hour or so. You would then add flour, butter, more

Fig. 9
Dan Miller, owner of the Springs General Store, with Pollock, Krasner and Costantino Nivola, April 1949. On the wall is the untitled painting (1948) with which Pollock settled his grocery bill.

milk, cheese, and a grated onion and serve over boiled potatoes, garnished with parsley.

For dessert, it was lemon pudding made with egg yolks and beaten egg whites or a fruit compote. Unfortunately, my memory of our meals is less than her reputation purported.

I soon realized that my presence was more about Krasner's welfare than about my research. She needed a driver to get her to and from events and to do daily errands. The most fun was going to the beach at Louse Point and, certainly, attending exhibitions at Guild Hall and Ashawagh Hall in East Hampton. So the orange Pinto saw a lot of mileage. Of utmost importance, though we were in separate rooms, is the fact that I served as her overnight companion and protector. My interviews with so many other "summer sitters" revealed that they were as shocked as I at the enormity of her fear of being alone.

Dinner with the Littles

Other than fish, vegetables, and an occasional dessert, I don't specifically recall many of our meals. But I do remember one special evening when John and Josephine Little were coming over for dinner.

Soon after the Pollocks moved to Springs, they, in turn, had helped the Littles find a house. John had been a fellow student with Krasner at the Hans Hofmann School of Fine Arts and was one of the leaders of the loosely defined East Hampton Abstract Expressionists group. He also started the Signa Gallery, along with Alfonso Ossorio and Elizabeth Parker, located at 53 Main Street, East Hampton, which opened to a crowd of art-world celebrities (including Marcel Duchamp, and Harold Rosenberg) on July 13, 1957.[13] Like Hofmann, Little used flat, vibrant, abstract color areas, and less gesture than Krasner or Pollock, in executing his works.

Krasner sent me to Dreesen's to pick up a big sirloin steak while she was buzzing around the kitchen making preparations. The Littles were two of her oldest friends, and I could tell this evening meant a lot to her. I had various tasks assigned to me. First, I was to take Comet and a scrub brush and clean all the white plastic lawn chairs. There were quite a few of them, and it took most of the afternoon. As dinnertime drew near, I was asked to put the washed lettuce in a basket and go outdoors and swing it around to get out the

Fig. 10
Krasner and John Little in East Hampton, NY, 1982.

water. I had no idea what this was about but gave it a shot, swinging it back and forth. Krasner was furious that I didn't know how to do this. It worked best, she shouted, if you did full circles with the basket—and did it vigorously. This led me to think of some of her great paintings, such as *Portrait in Green* (1969), in which she had used the same gesture so brilliantly.

When the Littles arrived, I was introduced, and we talked briefly about John's paintings, as he and Krasner were strongly inspired by Hofmann's "push and pull" theory of painting. Mostly, however, it was just small talk, and then, after dinner, we had coffee in the living room. I brought up the subject of my new Nikon camera, as Little said he knew something about photography, and I was inching toward suggesting that I might take some pictures of Krasner (forbidden until then) and the guests. When I brought the camera down from my room and showed it to Little, Krasner started snarling and screamed at me to go up to my room. I was horrified to be disciplined in front of others; clearly, she'd wanted her friends to herself.

Bathing at Louse Point with the Rosenbergs

Fig. 11
Louse Point
Cottage, East
Hampton,
NY, 2019 Another evening, we drove to Louse Point, a beautiful piece of land jutting out into Gardiners Bay, just a few miles away from Krasner's house, to bathe.[14] The problem would be how to get clean in salt water while dressed in a bathing suit, but since house rules were strict and there wasn't even an outdoor shower at the house (a mainstay for most beach cottages), we'd have to accommodate ourselves.

Louse Point is one of the most beautiful spots in the Hamptons. It is covered with crooked old pine trees that have survived cold, windy winters and has a sandy shoreline ringed with thousands of seashells. In a tiny cabin at the bend of Louse Point Road is where Krasner and Pollock first stayed in the Hamptons.

While it was starting to get dark, we plunged into the chilly water, soap in hand. Just then, a car pulled up. In it were Harold and May Tabak Rosenberg. The Rosenbergs were old friends of Krasner and Pollock. Harold was a WPA artist with Krasner and then became a critic. His mature writings, identifying the criteria for "Action Painting," favored de Kooning over Pollock. Rosenberg never wrote about Krasner. May had been her best friend for many years and had been Pollock and Krasner's witness at their wedding in 1945.[15]

Greetings were exchanged, and I was introduced to the Rosenbergs. The atmosphere seemed strained, but I had no idea how difficult and convoluted the Rosenberg and Krasner relationship had become. As Krasner told me, it was a small community of artists, and clearly many dramas had arisen among them.[16]

Truth be told, very late at night, with soap and towel concealed under my pajamas, I occasionally tiptoed out of my room to take a warm bath in the little clawfoot tub—using as little water as possible. The small luxury was worth the risk.

Party at Victoria Barr's

Our routine was, on rare occasions, interrupted by friends, making calls or visits to the house, and I began to wonder when and if I would meet some of the great artists who lived out there. Unfortunately, that was not to happen. When I asked about visiting other artists, I was told it wasn't possible. Two of them were particularly important to my research: De Kooning and Ossorio. Krasner never told me why she refused to introduce me to them, but my more recent interviews, many with people she knew well, have revealed to me how difficult it was for her to maintain friendships.

I did have one exciting chance to hobnob with the Hamptons art world. Victoria Barr, daughter of Alfred H. Barr Jr., the director of the Museum of Modern Art in New York, invited Krasner to a gathering at her art studio in Bridgehampton. This time, I was included. The studio was located behind the Grange, a big Victorian house on Montauk Highway just east of the Founders Monument commemorating Bridgehampton veterans.[17] There were a few other outbuildings behind the main house. This one was previously the studio of Abstract Expressionist Grace Hartigan, who, somewhat younger than Krasner, was dating Bob Keene, the owner of this Victorian mansion, and proprietor of a Southampton book store.

Barr was welcoming people and making sure everyone had a drink. In an interview with her on May 14, 2018, she would remember these parties fondly, saying that she'd had them for at least four or five years in a row in the 1970s. Her guest list included close friends, people who had invited her to parties the previous year, and artists such as Jane Freilicher, Robert Dash, and Krasner, as well as the photographer Hans Namuth and gallerist John Bernard Myers. It was very casual, in the tradition of East Hampton. Most of the guests just mingled on the expansive lawn, drinking and nibbling on nuts.

In our 2018 conversation, Barr explained that she and Krasner first met when Marcia Tucker, who had organized the Whitney show in 1973, took her to Krasner's Springs home. Barr had warm memories of this meeting.

In contrast to what many considered Krasner's predominantly hostile attitude toward the women's movement, Barr said she found her relaxed and "very friendly with other women." In fact, she recalled Krasner telling her, "We're all in this together."[18]

At the party, as we walked into the studio full of strangers, Krasner turned and took off. I kept smiling and doing my best to move around, looking at the paintings by our hostess. Only one person spoke to me. It was Peter Namuth, the photographer's son. He was in his twenties, a bit too young for this crowd, and, like me, seemingly somewhat out of place. We chatted for a while. Although I knew that his father had documented so much of the artistic lives of Krasner and Pollock, I did not ask him to introduce me to his father or, for that matter, to anyone else—which I now regret.

He told me about Montauk and how beautiful it was there. He said it had the romance of a "foreign country, where the sea meets the sky." He added that his dad would be there the next day. I was thoroughly intrigued, and before we parted, he asked me if I would like to go with him to visit a famous beach resort best known by locals as the End. My gratitude was immense. I was invited into the hallowed arena of artistic genius. Of course, I agreed to go.

The following morning, I mentioned to Krasner that I had arranged to go to Montauk for the day. She knew Peter Namuth, and I was sure she would be fine with this idea. But no, she yelled that I was strictly not allowed to go anywhere.

I was again caught off guard. What was she afraid of, and how could I assure her that it would be fine? Nevertheless, when Namuth called to say he'd pick me up, I had to apologize and say no. After all, I was a guest of Krasner's and wanted, more than anything else, to build a strong and trusting relationship with her. My job was to explore her genius and write about it. I was totally unprepared for the events to come.

A Visit to an Oceanfront Home

One glorious day, Krasner was invited to have lunch at the oceanside home of Frank and June Noble Larkin. It was hot and sunny. I had donned my bathing suit under shorts and a shirt and grabbed a beach towel. I took a small Kodak Instamatic camera in case something caught my eye. Of course, I had not forgotten that I was forbidden to take pictures of Krasner. I wondered if this was perhaps because she considered herself a celebrity and wanted to avoid undue publicity or worse. She was self-conscious because people had called her "ugly."

We arrived at what was a unique Further Lane beachfront mansion, a combination of contemporary design with the shingle style of the Hamptons. It was one of the most beautiful homes in the area. Modernist lines supported unique "eyebrow windows" that undulated across the front of the deck, draped with ivy. It was discreetly tucked behind the double dunes. I learned later that the home, designated as the First Spaeth House, was built by art collectors Otto and Eloise Spaeth and designed by architects George Nelson and Gordon Chadwick in 1955. Eloise Spaeth was a very important member of the East Hampton museum and theater Guild Hall Board of Trustees for years, amassing a collection of significant American art for the institution. It was located on the ocean near Two Mile Hollow Road and was then known among locals as the gay beach.

Krasner suggested that I grab a towel and go to the beach. I quickly realized I was not there for lunch. So, camera in hand, I headed for the water, which was just over the crest of the double dunes. It was a wide-open vista, completely devoid of people. My first look at East Hampton's Atlantic beaches, famous for their white sands and shining waters and miles and miles of seascape, was thrilling. Far superior to the boardwalk in Ocean City, Maryland, where I'd spent my childhood summers, here I could see for miles in either direction, and there'd be still no one in sight.

After spreading out my towel on the sand, I began reading and relaxing. Not long after, I saw a man coming out from behind the dunes wearing a white terry-cloth bathrobe. He was stocky and seemed somehow menacingly athletic. He walked straight past me toward the water, dropped his robe, and dove in, completely naked except for a little white swim cap. Trapped like a spy with my camera in hand, I was shocked and afraid, concerned that he would think I was documenting his private activity. Suddenly, in my mind, I had become transformed into a salacious member of the paparazzi. And as the hours passed, more men arrived on the scene, many without swimwear. It was quite a sight for a young mother from the suburbs. I kept

Fig. 12
First Spaeth
House in East
Hampton, NY,
2019.

my head down and, camera under cover, dug in for the long run. They were putting their towels on the sand within a few feet of mine. Grabbing my few belongings, I gave up my post and walked back to the house. Krasner was just leaving, so it was pretty good timing. I later suspected that she may have anticipated the awkward situation in which I found myself.

I was to return to the house again in 2003, when I was the executive director of Guild Hall. The house was still owned by June and, Frank, active patrons of the arts in East Hampton as well as in New York City. They invited a number of art-world celebrities and Guild Hall trustees for cocktails one evening to celebrate the opening of an exhibition titled "Strangers in the Village," organized by Gary Garrels and two young curators from the Museum of Modern Art. June Larkin, who had helped arrange for the show, was a member of the board of MoMA and was one of my favorite trustees at Guild Hall. In fact, she and I had cooked up the show with Garrels over lunch in the MoMA trustees' dining room the year before.

Of all the hundreds, even thousands, of art-scene events I attended on the East End after I returned to Guild Hall in 1999, the one that most marked my full-circle experience with Krasner was this "Strangers in the Village" party. It was a glorious exhibition of the most challenging art of our time. Unfortunately, the community didn't take well to the idea of bringing "strangers," that is, New York City contemporary artists, into Guild Hall, which had, as a matter of policy, focused only on artists of the region.

In attendance were one hundred or so top luminaries from Guild Hall and the Museum of Modern Art, including Richard Oldenburg, Guild Hall trustee and retired director of MoMA; Richard Meier, architect of the Getty in Los Angeles; Paul Goldberger, architectural historian; Gary Garrels, curator of prints at MoMA; Mickey Straus, chair of Guild Hall; Rona Roob, retired chief of the MoMA Archives; and various other Guild Hall trustees. In stark contrast to 1974, when I was dismissed to the beach, I was now a reputable player, at last in the game.

CHAPTER TWO

The Tapes: Guarding Her Myth

Interviewing Lee Krasner in 1974 was a challenge unlike any I'd experienced before. I was thirty-four years old, and she was sixty-five, the same age as my mother, with whom I was very close. The 1970s were complicated for me. Newly single, I was teaching part-time, at SUNY Auburn, raising two kids on my own, and, thanks to the GI Bill, taking a course a semester at Syracuse University to earn my master's degree in art history.

As described in chapter 1, after a few face-to-face conversations in New York City that spring, Krasner invited me to spend the summer with her in East Hampton, researching her for my master's thesis and receiving my master's degree from Syracuse University that same year. I did some preliminary reading and packed a suitcase full of books to help inform my questions, seeking to discover insights into Krasner's psyche and to explore the underlying meaning of her paintings. The mystery to be unraveled was Krasner's artistic journey, trying to understand the forces that inspired her, the springboard to her unique form of Abstract Expressionism.

Fig. 13
Krasner in her
East Hampton
studio, 1974.

We made this taped interview while sitting around her small kitchen table during July and part of August, looking out on to Accabonac Creek. While I realized that Krasner might repeat herself from previous interviews with other critics and art historians, I had hoped to gain her sufficient trust to reveal more of her story. Rereading these interviews, I noticed nuanced variations in some of her comments, which made it a fascinating puzzle.

While she offered several candid responses and made a few contradictory statements, I began to see her motivations. It became clear that what she really wanted was to be linked with scholars, literary people, artists, museum professionals, and collectors—all those who could legitimize her efforts. Analyzing that summer from her perspective and combining that with discussions I had with more than one hundred people who knew her—including art historians, gallerists, and friends—helped open a window onto her personality, her thinking, and her art. However, while Krasner might share with me an occasional new glimpse into her creative process, she would also be ready to argue or, worse, to stop the exchange. I was confused by this kind of off-putting behavior, especially since it was she who had invited me to do the interview. My quest for an answer to this dilemma led me to write this book—the story of two women, who sometimes talked past each other yet still struggled to communicate, to understand, and to contribute to the world of art.

We spoke first about Krasner's "matriarchal" family. She confirmed that she was the daughter of Joseph and Anna Krassner and then spoke about her family's immigration to America.

RA: Your father was from Odessa, Russia. I was wondering about your mother. Where was she from?

LK: Both were from Russia. But they're not from Odessa. They're from a very small town.

RA: Near Odessa?

LK: Near. In that vicinity. Odessa would have been the closest. I am the first born in this country. My brother and four other sisters were born in Russia. And there is only one other sister born here following me. Two of us born here. And I'm the first born. That is to say, my father came here a few years or some time before he sent for the family. So there was a separation. He left my mother, four sisters, or three—one had died—and my brother in Russia. He came over here. And then sent for the family. And I'm the first born here after the family arrives with my mother. And they come over in one trip. And following that is my one other sister. And that constitutes the entire family.

RA: OK. Now, your father ran a small grocery store.

LK: Yes, the grocery shop was not a grocery shop. It was a combination of fruit and vegetable and fresh fish.

RA: Does this have anything to do with your love of fish now?

LK: I am Scorpio, who crawls, I'm late-October Scorpio. And Scorpio crawls at the bottom of the ocean, so maybe that's why I like fish and not because my father ran a fish market. No, I adore, I love fish, you know, mad for it till today.

RA: Did he run this shop alone even though he couldn't speak English?

LK: With my mother.

RA: Did your mother speak English?

LK: Well, they couldn't, there wasn't much, you didn't have to communicate an awful lot by way of tending the shop.

RA: Did you ever get involved in working there?

LK: Not really. Once or twice. I mean, that's all fuzzy and hazy. A tiny, little bit, like, to come over for a half hour. Never alone. Never in charge or anything, till somebody was going to deliver something or something like that. But hardly. I would say a tiny little touch of it. Not enough to have made a real impression.

RA: Do you remember getting dressed up and—

LK: Oh, yes, we had beautiful things. Oh, yes, divine things. I remember a sister, married sister, coming from someplace to visit and bringing a scarf and a muff set out of a heavenly magenta color, which is one of my things right up until today—not magenta but in that rose family. I remember that—beautiful, beautiful—and I can remember getting so excited, about a navy-blue cape and a rolling sailor hat and patent-leather shoes for Passover. You know, I have touches of things like that.

RA: Were you close to one or the other of your parents? Or do you remember any incidents that are particularly touching for you that were meaningful to you later in life?

LK: Yes, my mother very much gave the direction, but I adored my father. His image is as powerful for me as my mother's image, although she was the verbal one.

RA: And that's probably the reason you call your family "matriarchal."

LK: That's right, because she was the verbal one, so to speak. She was the one that said what had to be done. However, there was my father in the background, which meant do it or else.

RA: So in other words, he was kind of the last word?

LK: Well, he was there as that symbol. But she executed the running of things.

RA: Do you remember which one of them disciplined you? Was it your mother?

LK: No, my father. He was the one that disciplined. My brother took a strong role in that direction.

RA: He was a good deal older than you.

LK: Oh, yes. He's the oldest member of the family, almost the oldest. One sister older than he and then he. But because he learned English immediately, which my father didn't, you see, he certainly took on the father role. Like, I'm in school, for instance, and the immediate contact is my big brother, whereas my father, you know, is off on another tangent. But it gets to him, you know, it's relayed. And then I have to watch my brother, because he's the one that's [reporting].

RA: What is your brother's name?

LK: Irving Lewis Krasner.

Despite feeling constrained under the watchful eye of her brother, Krasner felt her relationship with him was a positive influence, expanding her world artistically.

RA: Now, I'm curious about this: you mentioned a few things that were around the house, a painting over the fireplace—

LK: Yes. Well, that was my brother. You see, that was my brother's artistic—

RA: He brought that in?

LK: Bringing that and the records.

RA: Caruso records?

LK: These touches, you see, of art and the Russian novels came into the house by my brother, which became part of my reading. So anything in that direction was via my brother into the house.

RA: Did you enjoy reading those, and do you remember—

LK: What? The Russian classics?

RA: The Russian novels, yes.

LK: Mad for them. Just totally mad, but you see, it was very confusing to me, because by then, I'm in high school, and I have to be, I'm supposed to be reading Sir Walter Raleigh, you know, my book review is going to be about what color were Lady Rowena's draperies in her bedroom, and current with it I was reading the Russian classics . . . I was doing a double thing there.

RA: You mention Maeterlinck, too, and he's one of my favorite poets, and I was wondering if you had read *Pelléas and Mélisande*.

LK: Had I ever! Oh, my dear. Now, my reading was very strange, because it went from fairy tales, which I ripped through everything the library near our house in Brooklyn contained. In Maeterlinck, it was like a natural for me, and then came the split of the Russian classics, plus what I had to read in high school, which is, you know, the regular, so that that's the way it moved.

RA: Do you remember a particular Russian classic that strikes you?

LK: Dostoevsky was my god. But then I was mad for Chekhov and Gogol. I read them all avidly. This was the big thing in my life, you know.

Her responses prompted me to ask about her grades. I was surprised when she denied what my research repeatedly revealed: she had poor grades throughout her schooling, possibly as a result of her difficulty in reading.

RA: Do you think maybe this is what made your grades in school so poor that you were so much more attracted to these Russian novels?

LK: Well, my grades were not that poor. I always passed. . . . You know, I wasn't, I didn't flunk. The only place I ever flunked was that one term at Girls' High, 'cause I couldn't get into Washington Irving [High School for Girls] to major in art. And I flunked everything left to right.

RA: Now, I have this story . . . that you wouldn't sing "Jesus Christ Is My Lord"?

LK: That's when I'm in Girls' High.

RA: It seems to me that Jesus Christ was never your Lord, because you were a Jew.

LK: That's right. But it was Christmas, and the teacher was [laughs] teaching the class Christmas carols! And part of it was I never sensed their Jesus Christ was my Lord, and I found, since the image of myself is being very shy, lost in the mass, not an outstanding student, not up front, much to my astonishment, I got up and said loud, "I will not say Jesus Christ is my Lord, because he is not my Lord," and sat down. Well! . . . Simultaneously I declared to the family that I don't believe in religion anymore.

RA: OK, that's what I want to get at.

LK: See, so there's rebellion on every level. I won't accept Jesus Christ as my Lord, that's for sure. He never was, and he wasn't going to be at this point. But then I remember walking on Saturday afternoon. My mother and father were there [at home], and a distant relative—they were having Saturday-afternoon tea. And I charged in, and I can't remember, but it was like they all sat and looked at me. I don't know what my outburst was about, but it was against religion.

RA: And you think that was around age twelve or thirteen?

LK: Thirteen to fourteen. Somewhere in there.

RA: Yes. Which I do think happens to a lot of young people, but maybe not at that early an age. Have you ever felt a need for any sort of power above and beyond yourself since then?

LK: I've never ceased to believe for a second that there's a power above and beyond me [laughs]. I couldn't take organized religion. That's what it amounted to.

RA: I see.

LK: And I had a lot of arguments with the Judeo-Christian concept, because of the role of the female in there. So I have tons of arguments that go on indefinitely, but I have certainly never relinquished the thought that there is an energy or a force—and I'm not up to describing it verbally—that has to do with a higher order of things. You know, it's as abstract as that. Well, the minute you zero in and begin confining it for me, I get very irritable. And I don't care whether it's Judeo-Christian or whether it's Eastern. I feel uncomfortable when things begin getting boxed in. And I do, too, today. So this other source I have, since you used the term *higher*—I don't know that it's higher—but there is something that creates an order in the universe. And that source—whatever it is, or energy—is something I have never relinquished believing in for a second. Seems to me blatantly obvious every day of my life in one form or another. In some form it comes through always.

RA: I'm glad we had that cleared up, too, then, because I think the Christmas carol story really denies that you . . .

LK: You mean, it implies that I was through with religion.

RA: Yes, that you had no faith—

LK: Well, you see the world in that sense. Yes, right, yes.

RA: Yes. OK, Girls' High in Brooklyn?

LK: I was only there for six months.

RA: Yes, but you weren't interested.

LK: Flunked everything, and then Washington Irving could admit me [in 1923], which is what I wanted.

RA: And it was the only free school for girls.

LK: The only free school where you could study art, where you could major in art in the boroughs of Manhattan and Brooklyn.

RA: You describe that it was like taking a long trip, and it was very exciting for you to be in Manhattan.

LK: Well, yes. It was about three-quarters of an hour on the subway to get to Washington Irving. It's actually Washington Irving that acquaints me with Manhattan, because that's a daily trip, and that's very different than an occasional trip to Manhattan.

RA: You decide to be an artist, but somehow you don't do well in the art courses. What were they trying to teach you there?

LK: Well, they increased the periods that you majored in art as you moved along from freshman to sophomore. And in the last year you were there, just before you graduated, you were working from a model.

RA: Was it a nude model or clothed? Do you remember?

LK: We must have had some nude, because I can remember the teacher very carefully pulling down that little shade that has a window in the door—I mean, she never forgot that, so if the model had had clothes on, she might have forgotten that sometime. It was never forgotten. I remember it like a religious ceremony. So it must have been because there was a nude there. I think, eventually, you graduated to that point where there was a nude model there, but I can remember, in the beginning, we did these charts with hard pencil.

RA: Value studies?

LK: No. Beetles, bugs of all kinds, butterflies, floral things. I wish I had some of them. Oh, I wish I had some of these things. That you started that way and then evolved and then, she would call on different people to pose in the classroom, so then we went into that. And then eventually, you were given the nude, which is close to graduation.

RA: And probably in between there, you did still life and perspective and all that stuff.

LK: Yes, yes, oh, yes.

RA: Were you encouraged at that point to develop a style of your own, or was it a fairly traditional curriculum?

LK: I had no value judgment. I had no resentment. I thought, "Hallelujah, I'm awfully glad I'm not being left back." I had no point of agreeing or disagreeing or arguing. I was just awfully glad; I would have hated to come back and tell the family.

RA: Yes.

LK: You know, not graduated.

RA: Is the drawing upstairs in the room I am in, of the nude female torso— was that perhaps done in high school?

LK: That's about forty years later. I have nothing of high school work or very little of the Academy [National Academy of Design], which is many years later. There was a fire in the house that my family lived in. I wasn't home at that time, but all the work I had done, an awful lot of the work I had done in Cooper Union and the Academy, was in that house that burned down, so I lost whatever I had had up till that point. Very little survives from way back then.

RA: Now, you were at Washington Irving, you studied there and graduated, and then you went to Women's Art School at Cooper Union in 1926.

LK: Mm-hm.

RA: You worked under Victor Perard.

LK: He was one. [Charles Louis] Hinton and Victor Perard.

RA: And he had you illustrate a book.

LK: He was doing a book on anatomy. And he asked me to do one or two pages in the book of block hands and feet. . . . I remember exactly the drawings I did that were taken and how excited I was. . . . It was drawing from the antique cast. It was block hands and feet. And I had developed a style—this is in Cooper Union, now, where Victor Perard is my teacher—where I extended the line beyond the form . . . and then crossed it this way to show that it ended, the toe ended here, but I left those lines on. Now, apparently, it was this that interested Mr. Perard enough to ask me to do this.

RA: You mentioned that in 1929, you saw paintings by Matisse and Picasso in a show at MoMA.

LK: Yes.

RA: Yes. And I was wondering—

LK: I'm at the Academy at the time. I'm a student at the National Academy.

RA: National Academy of Art and Design.

LK: It wasn't Matisse and Picasso. It was French painting. And Matisse and Picasso were in that show, but there were other painters in that show as well. The show was French painting, and this made such an impact on me, because I guess I couldn't get over there like everyone in the Academy was doing.[19]

RA: And in fact, you saw that in '29. And then in '30, you did the self-portrait, which obviously has influences of both artists.

LK: Right.

RA: All right. I'm really curious about this: when you worked at Sam Johnson's [nightclub] in 1932 . . .

LK: As a waitress.

RA: Wearing your silk pajamas.

LK: Had to, hostess, for example.

RA: Right. How did you feel about yourself?

LK: How do you mean?

RA: Well, the obvious thing today would be to ask you if you felt like a sex object.

LK: Oh, because I had to wear silk—

RA: And wait on tables.

LK: Well, I thought it was a dirty job, and I disliked it, but there was no, you know. But that was the only job I could get working at night. And I was around, a lot of intellectuals came into the place. In some way, it made up for some of the [negatives]. On the other hand, they didn't tip, so, you know [laughs]. It was full of pros and cons. It had advantages and very strong disadvantages. Nevertheless, it fitted to what I needed at the time to leave my days free, because I was taking courses at CCNY [City College of New York] to get my pedagogy certification to teach, so I wouldn't have to be a waitress, you see. And that seemed the only kind of job I could land . . . but I didn't feel like a sex object, no. I was too full of irritations, annoyances, to feel like any kind of an object. Why can't they tip a little bit, these intellectuals? You know?

RA: [laughs] So, in fact, you liked the atmosphere there.

LK: The atmosphere was very comfortable—it was sort of nice.

RA: Then, as a bohemian, your bone to pick about intellectuals was simply that they didn't tip?

LK: Naturally, you waited on them, and they wouldn't drop a quarter for you at the end of the evening. And you counted on your tips as your salary, you see. I got my meals there, or at least I got my dinner there, so that was something. Yes, they had food, you see, they served dinner, and then it became an after-dinner night.

After her schooling, Krasner qualified for Works Progress Administration (WPA) employment during the Depression. She made it clear there was no romanticism in being a young artist. Her single-minded drive for survival was put to good use when she became a member of the executive committee of the Artists Union in 1939 at the age of thirty-one.

RA: All right. Well, let's get on to the WPA. I was wondering, in '39, when you were on the executive committee of the Artists Union, do you remember any events? Do you remember any discussions? And what was your function as a member of the executive committee?

LK: Just what any executive board member's function is—you plan the meetings, you discuss the agenda. It did not deviate from the normal executive board functions. . . . It was a loaded affair. We were constantly fighting to maintain our jobs on WPA.

RA: And weren't there also very heated discussions about art and politics at that time?

LK: No, not in the union. The union was formed and preoccupied with an economic position in the role. The economic position was your job on WPA, and the purpose of the union was to see that we could stay on it. So that you could see there was very little artistic discussion. Occasionally, we planned an exhibition, but it got minimal attention from the union rather than maximum attention. . . . We were artists, but there wasn't any big aesthetic thing going on, if that's what you're asking about. Because our energies went towards the economic maintenance of the job and grievances, anyone getting fired or whatever. We were constantly dealing with this sort of thing.

The tenacity to survive financially as an artist clearly stayed with Krasner her entire life. She wasn't simply determined, she was more than successful because of her intense focus.

Our discussion of the WPA led us to other artists who qualified for the program, including Arshile Gorky, William Baziotes, and Pollock. Krasner was quite the networker at that time, and I enjoyed hearing her describe the social scene.

RA: Now, did you also find that the people that you worked with during that time were at the center of the art world after that? They came out as the first-generation Abstractionist Expressionists?

LK: Well, only some. Some people were on WPA, like Gorky was on WPA. [Mark] Rothko was. I think he denied it, but he was on WPA. Pollock was on WPA. Baziotes was on WPA.

RA: De Kooning.

LK: De Kooning was on WPA. There were others. A lot of others, like Burgoyne Diller.

RA: Rosenberg.

LK: Rosenberg was not a painter, but close enough. Most people I know were on WPA. There were a handful that weren't. But people like—Newman wasn't, never heard the name Newman, don't know where he was at all. Certain names were not there, but by and large, the nitty-gritty, lots of them were there.

RA: Did you get together with each other?

LK: Not as a whole solid group, as such.

RA: But you did socialize individually then?

LK: Well, when I met Pollock, I knew Gorky. I knew de Kooning. I introduced Pollock to de Kooning. And then introduced Pollock to Gorky. But I knew them for years before I knew Pollock. So it isn't at all like a lump that we all knew each other and sat around together. I know I knew de Kooning before the WPA murals. I knew him for a long time. I knew Rosenberg many, many years. I knew Gorky many, many years. I'm living in the Village, and you see people that have a common interest—like French painting is already for me the thing. Well, so you find Gorky and sit in the Jumble Shop [a hangout on Waverly Place] and drink beer and talk about Picasso.

RA: Was de Kooning—can you remember at that time—was he the top man?

LK: No, not at all. It was Gorky, who was far more with it than de Kooning at that point. It was like de Kooning is watching what Gorky is doing. John Graham is aware of what Gorky is doing. And rejecting or accepting. And Gorky is very, very aware of what Picasso is doing.

Before discussing Krasner's education at the Hofmann School, I wanted to talk about her views on influences that might not have been thoroughly researched by art historians, such as Surrealism.

RA: OK. Now, in 1936, which is the year before you joined the Hofmann School, there was a show in New York called "Fantastic Art: Dada and Surrealism." It was at MoMA. And this was kind of the springboard for artists getting involved with Surrealism or getting even any sort of awareness of it.

LK: Now, what are you asking me? Whether I saw this show? I did see this show. Now, what's your further question in regard to that?

RA: I want to know when Surrealism really became part of your artistic awareness.

LK: It wasn't connected with that exhibition. Don't forget we were getting periodicals from Paris. There was a certain amount of work being done here by magazines. I was aware, and one knew there was [something going on] such as Surrealism. One knew of Surrealist painters.

RA: Did you happen to read John Graham's book *System and Dialectics of Art* which was published in 1937?

LK: Very much so. I got a copy from John Graham of that book. Very much I read that book.

RA: Because that had a great deal of Surrealist philosophy in it.

LK: No, it's a composite of many aspects. So that you're not going to be able to pin it down to a show or a book or a person. You don't just collide with something, and zing-o, your life changes. It's a composite. It's in the air. The artists I was seeing were quite aware of Surrealism. If you have your timing, I had mentioned that I had seen artists like Gorky, Graham, de Kooning—now, they all knew what Surrealism was about, and we would argue about it till we were purple in the face. We knew of [André] Breton. We attributed all that to a literary concept so that we favored other artists who had to do with what we considered the visual image. So then to say, did you see that show and did it affect you? Well, yes. Every breath of air I take affects me. I don't know about the Surrealist thing. It had its effect. It did not have the impact of Matisse. You've never heard that I was bowled over by Surrealism, but certainly I knew of it. I was aware of it.

RA: Well, no, I have never heard that, but what I'm trying to do is explore questions that I have never seen mentioned before. Were you as familiar with Wassily Kandinsky as you were with Matisse and Picasso? Did he fall into your realm of interesting artists?

LK: I was familiar with the works of Kandinsky. I admired enormously his early works, that is, the 1913, '14, '15 period. No, he was not the influence on me that Picasso, Matisse, and [Piet] Mondrian were.

RA: Well, on to Hofmann. Do you remember what led you to the Hofmann School? Did other people talk about it? What was so intriguing about it?

LK: What led me to the Hofmann School? There was nothing intriguing about it whatsoever. It was simply that I had reached a point of boredom and wanted to start to work. I was kind of tired of what I was working from. I wanted to start to work from the model, and someone said, "The Hofmann School, over on Ninth Street, there's a model there tonight. It's a good place to be." And I knew a few people that were working there, so I just went over there and joined. So there was no particular, you know, thing that drove me there. It was a combination of many factors. I'd gotten very fed up with the energies that had gone into the Artists Union political scene. Their executive board and the rest of it took a hell of a lot of my energy and time. And I wanted to get back to my work, to painting. Well, I wasn't very excited about what I was doing, which was these street scenes. And I thought, well, start to work from a model again. You must get yourself moving. . . . I went up, and I saw, you know, cased the place and was very impressed.

RA: I understand it was rather a huge atelier.

LK: It was a good-size class, and there was a model up there. It looked serious. There were an awful lot of abstractions around from the model, which I thought was fascinating. And so there I was. And I spoke to Mr. Hofmann and said I would like to join his class. . . . He said he'd like to see my work. And I said I could bring it in, but all I could show him was academic work. And he said, "In that case, you don't have to bother. Come in on Monday and start." And that's how it all started.

RA: You mentioned a quote the other day, a comment he made to you about doing such nice work.

LK: Oh, the thing about Hofmann was that as far as I can remember, he was one of the few instructors I ever had that spoke favorably of my work, except it was said in a peculiar way. He did like what I was doing. This is, of course, after I've been at the school for a while. And in one instance, he came in and said, "This is so good you wouldn't know this is done by a woman." Well, of course, that was a dubious compliment, a confusing compliment, let me put it that way. I had to go home and sit with that one for quite a while.

RA: He had a backlash to him, didn't he?

LK: Uh-huh.

Krasner insisted that although Hofmann's teachings were influenced by his appreciation of Matisse and Picasso, her own appreciation of these painters came directly from the works by those French artists themselves. She studied their works independently.

RA: Hofmann himself had actually assimilated two very strong aspects of European art—Cubism, and Expressionism. And I'm more than aware that the color that he professed to favor was the color of Matisse. I was wondering if perhaps you could make a few comments on that.

LK: Well, I can only speak in hindsight now, . . . but in this case, I would say, on the basis of what he was saying in the classroom, that he himself must have, at that point, been swinging very heavily between Picasso and Matisse. Now that I look back, I can see that. Because at one point he'd scream nothing but color, and there'd be a couple of running weeks of this. And then it would go into form, so that you felt—now that I look back, he himself must have been "swinging the pendulum" between Matisse, let's say, representing color, and form, and that would be, let's say, Picasso at the time.

RA: With Matisse's color, Matisse himself says that it should be intuitive, that one should have it be a spontaneous selection of colors. Now, you've also made a few statements about how your greens turn red.

LK: Mm-hm.

RA: Your intuitive color seems to spring forth in your paintings. Do you think that Hofmann's words about—

LK: Not at all. Not in the slightest. I got nothing about Matisse from Hofmann. Absolutely nothing. . . . I was looking at a Matisse, whenever a Matisse was available, I looked at it. And if it wasn't available, I saw a reproduction. See, I was getting something very different from Hofmann.

RA: OK. Then Hofmann gets into space, positive and negative.

LK: That's right, which is Cubism. This is what he was teaching, and this is mainly what I was receiving, not Matisse. Or Picasso. Because I had

Matisse and Picasso as direct experiences of my own. In other words, I was too influenced by Picasso or Matisse or Mondrian myself to have to get it via Hofmann. Because, remember, I don't see any work of Hofmann's. All he does is come up to my canvas and criticize it. All his criticism was based on the object in front of you. If you didn't get the right volume of weight or light in relation to the object in front of you, that was what he was saying. "This is too light." "This is too heavy." He rigidly stayed to the object. . . . What I got from Hofmann was Cubism, which was very valuable to me. Positive, negative. His enthusiasm and seriousness in approach to art [are] what I got from Hofmann.

RA: Well, you must have been friends later for you to invite him up to Pollock's studio.

LK: Yes, because I think he'd possibly be interested in seeing the work. Oh, of course. Of course, we continue seeing each other.

RA: In 1940, Mondrian comes to New York, and I know, eventually, you do speak to him. He, too, is working from nature, as was Hofmann. The idea of his pure abstractions grew from nature. In reading about Mondrian, he says that his abstractions are derivative of natural objects, and I'm sure you're familiar with the apple tree series that he did.

LK: I know that Mondrian worked from nature and eventually abstracted it into what he did. There were a great many artists in that group that were influenced by Mondrian. I was a Hofmann student and a member of the American Abstract Artists. And Mondrian was one of my very favorite, special artists. And consequently, in the Hofmann School, I got into a strong Mondrian period, as a lot of artists around me did. Not in the Hofmann School but in the American Abstract Artists. And again, working rigidly from the model, one broke it down to a vertical and horizontal measurement of space and adopted Mondrian's color palette so that you came out with the Mondrian, except it had to, in order to get criticism from Hofmann. Remember that I'm at the Hofmann School. He comes in and looks at what I'm doing and criticizes. It had to adhere rigidly to the object in front of me. I'm talking of weight and measurements. Negative and positive space. A violation of the two dimensions, introducing the three, and bringing it back to the two again. I'm talking of that kind of thing in relation to the model, and the fact that it is a vertical and horizontal measurement of space. It still had to adhere rigidly to the object in front of me.

The last topic I ventured to pursue was the all-important Rimbaud poem, *Une saison en enfer* (*A Season in Hell*),[20] lines of which were inscribed on her studio wall as a kind of mantra. It has also been suggested that Rosenberg may have discussed this and other aesthetic theories with Krasner during their WPA conversations.[21]

RA: Lastly, I just was wondering if possibly you wouldn't mind looking at that Rimbaud poem again.

LK: I don't need to look at it again. What is it that you want me to do with it?

RA: Would you perhaps comment on it, having written it on your studio wall so many years ago?

LK: I feel today it is as potent a piece of poetry, as meaningful now as it was then.

I am very happy to have had the privilege of interviewing Krasner, but by the end of our last interview, I was well aware that her patience had run out. She wasn't going to give me much more information than what I already knew. No doubt, the process of interviewing her was made more difficult because she didn't see me as her equal. Still, I hope readers will find it worthwhile to read these excerpts and enjoy the answers she gave that ring true and sincere and those that don't. Certainly, the complete dismissal of Hofmann as an influence must be questioned, as should her denial of the influence of Surrealism and Kandinsky. While she was not as forthcoming as I had wished, the interview itself stands as only one piece among the many that help illuminate this story.

The above excerpts from my 1974 visit with Krasner were organized in order to lend a clearer voice to Krasner's thinking. The unedited Krasner-Appelhof recordings are now in the archives of the Arents Research Library at Syracuse University and have not been published in full. Their use is restricted until 2021.

CHAPTER THREE

The Plan

Lee Krasner was already a fixture on the downtown art scene when she first encountered Jackson Pollock in 1936.[22] She was so well regarded that she was one of the American artists, including Stuart Davis, de Kooning, Pollock, and Walt Kuhn, to be included in the 1942 McMillen Inc. Gallery exhibition of American and French artists that had been organized by the Russian-born artist and writer John Graham.[23] She was ambitious and so totally devoted to life as an artist that William Lieberman—a prominent curator at the Museum of Modern Art from 1949 to 1979 and chair of the department of twentieth-century art at the Metropolitan Museum from 1979 to 2004—said she was "like a Carmelite nun."[24] She struggled in her early years at art school but persevered despite criticism from her teachers. At one point, while at the National Academy of Design, she was told that the women in the class were not allowed in the basement to paint from a still life with fish (a cooler climate was needed to preserve the fish), a rule she ignored.[25] She stated that this was the first time she experienced discrimination, but then, later on, she recalled, "I had absolutely no consciousness of being discriminated against until Abstract Expressionism came into blossom."[26] Finally, after she began attending the Hofmann School in 1937, she won the support of Hofmann himself as both teacher and mentor. He recognized her artistic abilities but criticized her for being a woman.[27]

In 1945, Krasner and Pollock spent the summer at Louse Point in Springs, and in the fall, they rented, then bought, a farmhouse and moved permanently to East Hampton. After they married that year, there began what for Krasner would be more than a decade-long struggle as the wife of a genius and an alcoholic. She determined early on to assume control of both her own and her husband's life and career.[28] After Pollock's death in 1956, she came to fully understand the importance of managing not only her public persona but also his. Most important, she began to craft the myth of Pollock, hoping the public might forget such distasteful stories as his urinating in Peggy Guggenheim's fireplace and engaging in drunken brawls.[29] She was determined to focus attention on Pollock's intellect and talent. In the late 1950s and early '60s, Krasner's career became intimately entangled with the Pollock estate and the tension attendant upon it, which continued, more or less, until her own death in 1984.

Ted Dragon, the longtime companion of Alfonso Ossorio—a wealthy artist, collector, and philanthropist whose family fortune was founded on the Victorias Milling Company, a sugar refinery in the Philippines—was a patron of both Pollock and Krasner.[30] His home, the Creeks, on the water in East Hampton, attracted many art-world celebrities. Dragon, known to be a close friend of Krasner's, observed, "Lee knew how to manipulate. From the moment I met that woman, her mind had one channel: Art, the making of Pollock, and the making of herself."[31] He went on to tell of how Krasner would spread out small pieces of paper containing names of people in the art world for her to study. "It was stepping stone after stepping stone. And if they didn't come through [with an exhibition or a purchase] the relationship ended—like opening a trap door."[32]

Beginning in 1959, Krasner's clever strategies and those of her lover, David Gibbs, in close association with Marlborough Gallery, were the defining steps toward her own fame and fortune.

Me, Lee, and Marlborough Gallery

Marlborough Gallery, which began representing Krasner officially in 1966, had two storage locations in New York, one occupying an entire floor on 135th Street in Harlem and one in Queens near Vernon Boulevard and 21st Street on the south side of the 59th Street Bridge.[33] Both were jammed with Krasner's art in all sizes and shapes. The Harlem space held the Pollock estate as well as Krasner's works on paper, many of the pieces framed, while the Queens location stored Krasner's large paintings and collages. I met Kenneth Polinskie, the gallery's registrar, for the first time in the fall of 1974 at the uptown location and was delighted to see some of Krasner's powerful collages, many of which had been chosen by Gene Baro, the guest curator of the upcoming exhibition "Lee Krasner: Collages and Works on Paper, 1933–1974," at the Corcoran Gallery of Art in Washington, D.C., in January and February 1975. In my May 2018 interview with Polinskie, he remembered my accompanying Baro to view some of the works that he was planning to include in the show.[34] My initial impression was one of awe. The works felt huge to me, and the compositions were aesthetically convincing yet brutal. Many artists of the period were using the collage technique but none with such abandon.

Polinskie, who was fond of Krasner, told me:

> There was a beautiful, handsome trucker from Marlborough. His name was Jimmy Osterberg. Jimmy and I would go to Lee's house in Springs, and

whatever she was working on, we would then move to the apartment in New York, and whatever she needed out of the way, we put back in the Queens warehouse. She knew Donald [McKinney, director of Marlborough Gallery] and I were close, and she loved me. She always had a chicken stew ready. We moved everything out and had chicken stew with vegetables, spring stew, and then [the next spring] we moved the paintings [back] into Pollock's old studio. I had lost my mother very early, and Donald and I had come together. Lee was maternal. She treated me with great warmth, . . . the intimacy was there.[35]

Most clearly, I remember researching the paintings at Marlborough's Queens storage space. That location was presided over by art handler Edward J. Brown, affectionately known as Barney. Polinskie spoke of him with amusement and warmth, recalling, "He was tan-skinned and had black hair, and he was pretty short. Everyone called him the 'itinerant restorer,' because Barney had managed the very difficult process of mounting Rothko's paintings on paper onto huge stabilizing panels."[36]

I met Brown on my first day at the facility. He would pull out the paintings hanging on huge rolling metal racks. On one of my several visits, I viewed some of Krasner's truly monumental paintings. The experience was incomparable—enormous, vibrantly colored canvases fraught with frantic gestures assaulted me on every side.

Brown turned out to have other talents, not least as a stand-up comedian. One day, he asked if I would accompany him to the Greenwich Village Halloween parade that weekend. Although I said no, he continued to insist. After lunch, he returned, dressed only in his handmade costume to seal the deal. It was a beaded jockstrap that jingled when he walked. I did go to the parade but not with him.

The Corcoran Exhibition

Polinskie, thinking back, said he was so happy we had gone there to view the works, telling me how his days were "just boring, because there wasn't a lot of material going in and out. I was doing inventory most of the time." So he was pleased, he said, when he received a call telling him that Baro would be coming up to view the work and make selections.

Baro, whom I found to be easygoing and gracious, had a wide and influential background in the arts, extending from teaching at Williams College and writing for the major art periodicals to organizing more than 150 exhibitions in the United States and abroad. He did a number of important one-person shows, most notably at the Corcoran Gallery and the Brooklyn Museum of Art, including exhibitions devoted to Louise Nevelson, Helen Frankenthaler, Anni Albers, and, of course, Krasner. He was the director of the Corcoran Gallery until November 1972, when, unbeknownst to me

when we met, he had been fired after engaging in a public "fistfight" in the museum's atrium. It was at a black-tie opening with the gallery's chief executive officer, Vincent Melzac. Melzac, who had hired Baro to direct the art rather than the business dealings of the gallery, hit Baro on the side of the head, opening a cut that bled onto his shirtfront, and Baro, in response, threw a drink at Melzac, who claimed Baro had insulted his wife.[37] The two later exchanged apologies.[38] Roy Slade was hired as the interim director after Baro left. In 1974, Baro returned as a curatorial consultant to Slade, who ran the museum from 1972 to 1977.[39] Baro produced several exhibitions following the skirmish, including, of course, the Krasner show in 1975.[40]

Baro chose to include my Krasner bibliography of periodical citations to accompany the essay in the catalog.[41] When we met in D.C. to hang the show, I joined Baro in Slade's massive, dark-paneled office. We had a quick meeting to discuss the installation. Both Slade and Baro had worked in the United States and London. Slade, a native of Wales, was tall and elegant, with a dignified white beard, while Baro was somewhat overweight and slightly balding. It was a brief conversation but one that made me aware that they had known each other previously.

I was then invited to the galleries to discuss the installation of the works. I was too amazed to say much of anything, but the experience was eye-opening. When I entered the gallery, Krasner's works filled the space with a dramatic array of shapes and colors. Her collages at this time, unlike those of a number of other Abstract Expressionists, were rough and crude, with ripped and slashed forms competing for dominance. Discarded sections of works by Pollock were introduced into some of these compositions.

In fact, it turned out that Baro had earlier taken Slade to meet Krasner in order to finalize arrangements. As Slade told me:

> [Baro] was very eager that I go visit Lee Krasner in her apartment in New York. Because he felt that if I did, it would show that the Corcoran and its director were fully behind the exhibition. I always remember going with Gene and ringing the bell, and there was Lee looking up at Gene and then looking up at me, and as dominant as Gene could be, I think he deferred to her and was kind and cautious and respectful and almost servile in his relationship with her. As you know, she was a very tough lady.[42]

Slade remembered being "starstruck" in her presence. He went on to say:

> I asked her if she would agree to my organizing a reception in my director's office. I think you know that room. It's a huge room with a big table. [We planned to] invite a few people [about one hundred] just prior to the opening in order to meet with her, like the Corcoran trustees. It was a very select group. I'm not sure you ever knew this, but Clyfford Still turned up. He was a total Anglophile, drove an English car [a Jaguar] and dressed in English clothes, and he wore a scarf and tweed jacket with a tweed hat, and was very reclusive and of course a very great painter. [He had come] out of respect for Lee, and she was overwhelmed. I remember him saying to her "Let's go," and we went up to see the show together just before the opening. Krasner seemed more than pleased. She was proud to be exhibiting her work in the nation's capital.[43]

These collages, from 1953 to 1955, are among Krasner's strongest works.[44] The scale of the compositions and the handling of the materials showed a courage she had not previously revealed. Unfortunately, the reviews of the Washington show were tepid. Journalists couldn't resist bringing up Krasner's personal relationship with Pollock. The critic for the *Washington Star* was the most positive, saying simply, "Krasner obviously is a talented artist."[45] This cursory assessment did not surprise me. Having grown up in the area, I knew that the D.C. art scene at the time was stodgy and unsophisticated. Nevertheless, this magical initiation into the inner sanctum of the museum world took hold of my imagination and never left.

The complications behind Krasner's decision to show her work at Marlborough became apparent to me only years after my 1974 visit with her. Many have implied that there would have been no Krasner without Pollock, but probably truer still is Barbara Rose's assertion: "There would be no Pollock without Krasner."[46] Krasner introduced him to the artists and intellectuals in the art world and steered his work and career to enormous success. He, in turn, suggested to dealers like Peggy Guggenheim and Betty Parsons that they consider exhibiting her work. Pollock and Krasner, in their own ways, supported each other.

It should be emphasized here that Krasner was not so much under the "shadow" of her husband as art historians and critics have often suggested.[47] From the beginning, she struggled for, and occasionally found, recognition on her own. After a decade of participating in group exhibitions, including the groundbreaking one organized by Graham at the McMillen Gallery, with Europeans such as Picasso and Matisse and Americans, like the then-little-known Jackson Pollock, Krasner was finally being recognized. Critic Ann Pringle of the *New York Herald Tribune* reviewed an exhibition of paintings and decorative arts mounted in 1948 at the Bertha Schaefer Gallery. Although there were a few of Krasner's paintings in the show, it was her

Mosaic Table (1947) that stood out, Pringle observed. She dubbed the huge, intensely colored composition set in a wagon wheel thirty-eight inches in diameter and filled with swirling, multicolored tesserae, "magnificent."[48]

Such recognition apparently made a huge impression on Krasner. Her composition is energized by a freedom, directness, and sense of spontaneity that let her break out of old constraints and burst into a new realm of expression. Some of the pieces of tile she included in the work had been left over from Pollock's WPA mosaic.[49] From the seemingly haphazard placement of these broken tiles and found objects, such as keys, coins, and jewelry, the dynamic contours of intertwined abstract shapes emerge. These forms, soaring through space, continued to pulsate in her work throughout her life.

Unfortunately, this affirmation was followed by disappointment over a lack of sales at the Betty Parsons Gallery in 1951. Sales did pick up for Krasner in 1955, when she received positive notices for her show at Eleanor Ward's Stable Gallery. (Many of these works were exhibited in the

Fig. 15
Krasner in front
of *The Seasons*
(1957) at her
East Hampton
studio, c. 1958.

previously mentioned 1975 Corcoran show.) Stuart Preston, for example, wrote in the *New York Times*: "In Lee Krasner's collages at the Stable Gallery, we find ourselves in the midst of a dense jungle of exotic shapes and color. The eye is fenced in by the myriad scraps of paper, burlap and canvas swabbed with color that she pastes up so energetically. She is a good noisy colorist."[50]

These exhibitions were followed by a show of her "Earth Green" series at the Martha Jackson Gallery in 1958. It was rumored to have gleaned more sympathy for the widow than honest critical response. Perhaps to emphasize Krasner's new beginnings—out of the "shadow" of Pollock, B. H. Friedman, an ardent fan of hers, wrote in the introduction to the accompanying catalog: "In looking at these paintings, listening to them, feeling them, I know this work. Lee Krasner's most mature and personal, as well as most joyous and positive to date, was done entirely during the past year and a half, a period of profound sorrow for the artist. The paintings are a stunning affirmation of life."[51]

Preston stated in the *New York Times*:

> The bravado of Lee Krasner's recent and huge abstract paintings at the Martha Jackson Gallery presents a raw challenge to the eye. . . . What impresses the spectator is the sheer energy that Miss Krasner manages to generate on her picture surfaces. . . . Sensuous, sensual and aggressively decorative, these paintings compel attention to the fact that the artist is directing her compositions, not just submitting to her material, or giving free rein to automatism.[52]

Undoubtedly, the pictures of the 1950s remain some of Krasner's greatest. As Clement Greenberg recalled, they were "a major addition to the American art scene of that era."[53]

Greenberg became an acquaintance of mine in the 1980s, when I was a professor at Syracuse University.[54] While he seemed reluctant to say much, he did occasionally discuss Krasner with me. (In fact, I have letters of his chastising me for "putting words in his mouth" after I asked him questions about her.) Still, he confirmed my assessment: "the work from the '50s was her strongest."[55]

Just a few years after the death of her husband, Krasner was to learn that, as his widow, she had enormous responsibility and, perhaps not surprising to her, considerable power in the art world.

Krasner realized that she had to balance two roles: one as estate manager and widow, the other as a creative, still-struggling artist. To do so, she sought guidance. However, she had closed the door on a number of people, two of them longtime and influential friends of the Pollocks, Harold Rosenberg and Clement Greenberg, who had "insulted" Pollock by turning their backs on him and, additionally, had "ignored" Krasner.[56]

David Gibbs

In my interview with Grace Glueck, a *New York Times* art reporter, she suggested that in order to understand Krasner's career trajectory, I should explore her romantic liaison following Pollock's death with the attractive young art dealer David Gibbs. Glueck, who told me confidentially that she, too, had dated Gibbs, remembered him as being "tall" and "handsome," but she was ultimately not impressed.[57]

Gibbs first met Krasner in the summer of 1959, when, based on his relationship with Betty Parsons (Alfonso Ossorio's New York dealer), he became acquainted with Ossorio and Ted Dragon and spent a weekend at their waterfront home.[58] They bought The Creeks, built for the artists Albert and Adele Herter, because it had been recommended by Krasner as a perfect home for the two companions.[59]

Now, some three years after Pollock's death, Ossorio continued to lend support to Krasner by collecting her work and including her in his social circle. In actual fact, Ossorio may have been the first to purchase a work by Krasner—a "Little Image" painting from the late 1940s.[60] According to the catalogue raisonné, there were two items from the collection of Ossorio, a vertical work dated ca. 1948–1949 and *Untitled* from 1949, and one from the collection of Dragon, Ossorio's life partner, *Black and White Squares No. 1* from 1948.[61] In addition, when I was living with Krasner, I asked her about a fourth work in his collection, the terrifying painting *Prophecy* (1956), wondering if I could contact Ossorio about seeing it. She said it was not possible and went on to say, "He hung it behind a door, and I don't see them anymore." While the painting was completed just before Krasner left for Europe, its figurative motif may have anticipated the arrival of another person in their home: Pollock's lover Ruth Kligman.

A 1959 dinner party at The Creeks was the occasion of the Gibbs-Krasner meeting.[62] Krasner was fifty years old, and Gibbs was only thirty-three, but they seemed to hit it off immediately.[63] Krasner had her own assigned bedroom there, designated by Ossorio so that driving along the pitch-dark winding country roads after an evening of dining and drinking could be avoided.[64] Gibbs also stayed for the weekend, in a room hung with paintings by Krasner and Pollock.[65] On that Sunday, Gibbs went to Krasner's studio and selected a painting to purchase, titled *Cool White* (1959)—this was obviously the way to her heart.

A few months later, just before Christmas, Gibbs wrote to Krasner from London, mentioning a jazz recording they'd been listening to together. It had perhaps been chosen from the record collection in her living room. In the letter, he begs her to come to England, writing that he could pay for the painting when she came to visit. It would save her taxes, and he could pay for it in "sterling."[66]

Krasner always stood by her two main influences: Pablo Picasso for line and composition and Henri Matisse for color.[67] An early work from Krasner's "Umber" series, *Cool White*, more than nine feet wide, was one of her largest to date, with its slashing brushstrokes, radiating from the top center, contained within an exterior orb. Compositionally, it relates to the light bulb or sun radiating in Picasso's *Guernica* (1937), a painting that so shocked Krasner when she saw it in New York in 1939 that she had to leave the Valentine Gallery where it was on view. She recalled first seeing it and then walking around the block and going back for a second look.[68] Even today, the Picasso mural, measuring almost twelve by twenty-six feet, is one of the most stirring artworks of all time. Recalling the bombing of a Basque village in the Spanish Civil War, it depicts the extremities of human cruelty.[69]

In the wings of Krasner's *Cool White* composition, agitated gestural lines are raked across the canvas. Broken strokes seem to allude to humans in battle, while the total composition is embraced by a central sun (the source of light). In a text about Picasso's masterpiece, a similar form is described as "a radiant eye of the dark night . . . [and the] all seeing God's-eye-witness."[70] Krasner told her friend poet Richard Howard that her series of dark, introspective paintings in brown, white, and gray was a response to the death of her mother: "[T]here was so much taking place. My mother dies at this time. A lot happens aside from grief for Jackson. There are many elements. I cancel my show with Greenberg—a show scheduled at French & Co."[71] In contrast to the glorious color of her "Earth Green" paintings of the mid-1950s, these psychoanalytic "mourning" pictures, a group of paintings she personally labeled "night journeys," refer to her mental anguish with a directness that speaks of uncensored depression.[72] This same anguish is seen in many other paintings in the "Umber" series, and again, as in the collages, because of their unbridled passion, they are some of her best.[73]

With the death of her mother in 1959, Krasner was at her most vulnerable. Experiencing what must have been psychic self-doubt, she became close to Gibbs, who was married at the time.[74] The suave Englishman had been a soldier as well as an art dealer, and he was still seeking his fortune. The details of their romance and business relationship are not at all clear, but Gibbs seems to have been at the center of the Pollock-Krasner-Marlborough agreement. I discussed this four-pronged relationship in my interview with Glueck. She had briefly been a guest of Krasner's, needing a place to stay while she was finishing up a piece on Claes Oldenburg. Glueck, who was an art-world insider, thought my theory of artist-gallery collusion had credibility and encouraged me to explore the possibility. Certainly, Gibbs's purchase of Krasner's painting on the Sunday after their dinner at Ossorio's was a calculated next step toward their union.[75] On April 6, 1960, following a transatlantic phone call Gibbs had made to Krasner, he wrote to her from London that it was wonderful to hear her voice, "so clear and so like you—gave me such a kick, I really was knocked over." Gibbs then remarked to her about her possible relationship with the Howard Wise Gallery, calling the dealer "your Mr. Wise" and saying that if he was the man that Gibbs knew, he always had "pleasant dealings" with him when he was at Arthur Tooth & Sons (the gallery where Gibbs worked in London). In fact, Wise showed *Cool White* in Krasner's 1960 exhibition, the checklist recognizing Gibbs's ownership. Further, in the same letter, Gibbs implied that Krasner should not choose Greenberg as a potential dealer for Pollock, that she should "cut away from past associations" and make a new life, "uncluttered with old memories."[76] The last paragraph in the letter sealed the deal. Gibbs said that he was willing to accept the responsibility of helping her handle the problems of Pollock's estate and pledged his "entire energy." He also let her know he would return before the end of the month. Gibbs signed the letter expressing his love and saying that he would write soon. He must have made it back to the States early that spring, because his next letter to Krasner is dated May 7, 1960, from London, saying that he couldn't begin to write about the "last two weeks," which were "wonderful and remarkable," and that he continued to bless her and wish her well. He also, very sweetly, drew a picture of a rather whimsical flower, with a center heavily circled by his pen, and a little bird under his signature. Donald McKinney, the director of Marlborough Gallery from 1968 to 1986, told me recently, in hushed tones, that Krasner had asked his advice about the letter and Gibbs's intentions. When I asked if they were having an affair, McKinney responded, "They were doing their thing, yes, for a while." But there was a time, he added, when Krasner asked him to comment on the letter and on her relationship with Gibbs. "She wouldn't show me the letter," McKinney said, "but she had gotten the letter from David. David had gone back to England, and David was writing to her."[77]

Fig. 16
David Gibbs'
photograph,
accompanying
the article
"Atticus among
The Art Dealers"
in the *Sunday
Times* [London],
May 15, 1960.

In my interview with Glueck, she called Gibbs "the charming charlatan" and confirmed his liaison with Krasner: "She [Krasner] lived at the Adams Hotel. He [Gibbs] had an apartment there to be close to her. They were more or less—what can I say?—as much a pair as they could be. I just think that he filled a number of her needs. I think he told me that she, at one point, was engaged to him. I know she had a studio there. I think at the time she was there, it wasn't exactly fashionable."[78]

Clearly, Krasner was in a quandary.

While Marlborough Gallery represented the Pollock estate in London, there was not yet any public mention of Marlborough coming to the United States and certainly nothing implying that the Pollock estate would be part of the gallery in America. On May 15, 1960, one year after Krasner's first meeting with Gibbs, the London *Sunday Times* identified him as the representative of the Pollock estate abroad.[79]

The article began by introducing the upcoming art events of the spring season: "During the next few weeks one of Britain's least publicized and most luxurious industries moves into top gear." It then described several leaders in the field. One of them was Marlborough, which had opened in 1947: "Just about to cross Bond Street into its new and expensive gallery on the other side, the Marlborough Fine Art is a good example of what can still be done in the art world with knowledge of painting and business flair."

Unrelated to the feature on Marlborough, the article highlighted Gibbs and his operation, David Gibbs & Co., under the heading "Urbane Consultant":

> One of the most interesting of the new men among the West End dealers is thirty-six-year-old David Gibbs. Tall, grey-haired and urbane even for this most urbane of professions, he shares an office with a Bond Street wine merchant and believes that a good dealer should be a cross between a psychoanalyst and a stockbroker.
> He has been soldier, biscuit manufacturer and stockbroker but prefers selling pictures to anything else. He believes that most galleries are far too forbidding to the new potential picture-buying public and does most of his business from his commodious flat in Chesham Place. His chief task is acting as consultant to anyone who wishes to buy a modern painting but does not know how to go about it. His own taste is for modern American abstracts.

Gibbs hadn't wasted any time letting the press know of his new plan. The article went on to state: "He has just been appointed art advisor to the new foundation formed to promote the work of the late Jackson Pollock, the greatest of American action painters."

A July 1960 photograph[80] of Krasner and Gibbs together strolling on the beach in East Hampton appears to confirm that their relationship continued that summer.

McKinney described to me how a written agreement between Krasner and Frank Lloyd, the owner of the Marlborough Gallery, unfolded:

> Lloyd was nervous because he wanted this to happen, and so we finally had a date when she was going to come in and sign the papers. Lee came in with this enormous, floppy sun hat flopped in front of her face.... He wanted her to sign, here's the contract and sign it. She kept saying, "I can't see where to sign." And this hat. She said, "Frank, can't you take a joke?" She did it on purpose, with a sense of humor. She went there with the idea that she was going to do it, but she also wanted to have fun doing it.[81]

As further evidence of this romantic and artistic collaboration, Gibbs's painting by Krasner, *Cool White*, was exhibited in New York at the Howard Wise Gallery in 1960 and then in London, first in Gibbs's "New, New York Scene" organized at Marlborough in the fall of 1961 and then at the Krasner Whitechapel retrospective in 1965.[82]

Gibbs wrote to Wise on December 22, 1960: "I would like you to be one of the first people to know that before I left New York, I concluded an arrangement between Lee and Mr. Lloyd of the Marlborough Fine Art Gallery, whereby I shall make an exhibition of some 65 paintings, drawings and watercolours from her estate, in his new premises in Bond Street, sometime in March next year."[83]

As mentioned above, records testify that Gibbs and Krasner took an extended trip together throughout Europe in June 1961, going from London to Paris, Zurich, Bern, Turin, and Milan and back to London. Among Gibbs's papers is a bill in his name from the Excelsior Hotel Gallia in Milan, signed in his hand as "Mrs. Pollock," indicating that she was underwriting the venture. It is for the night of June 10 and lists only one room, "Appart," for 10,000 lire. They were to travel through Europe for a total of twenty-five nights. This was also at the time of the first Pollock exhibition at the Marlborough Gallery in London, which they had, no doubt, attended together.[84]

It appears that the Marlborough originally seduced Krasner by virtue of the relationship between herself and Gibbs, who was connected with the gallery. Most obvious today, however, is that as a result of these and other efforts to spotlight Krasner the artist, Gibbs achieved his goal of delivering the Pollock estate to Marlborough in London by 1961. The evidence is the exhibition held there in June and an advertisement for the Marlborough Gallery in London, listing the "Pollock Estate" among other artists in its stable.[85]

The next step was to bring it to New York.

A February 12, 1962, letter to Gibbs from Krasner's lawyer, Gerald Dickler, stated that Dickler was representing Krasner, who had asked that the business relationship between Gibbs, Marlborough, and herself cease and desist. It appears that Krasner had expected Gibbs to be her sole agent for the Pollock material and that he would work for her in London. Her objective was to distance herself from the "widow's" burden of responsibility. She had not understood that Gibbs would be working for both her and Marlborough in the United States, an obvious conflict of interest. The letter ended with some kind words about how Dickler and Krasner both had a fondness for Gibbs and hoped to continue their friendly relationship. Given Krasner's erratic personality, it is not surprising that her lawyer wrote to Gibbs that she wanted to clarify the relationship and part company with him, that she was "severely troubled with second thoughts about the triangular relationship between her, you and Marlborough."[86] On August 11, 1962, Gibbs wrote to Krasner about Frank Lloyd and the Marlborough-Gerson Gallery, saying he understood her reluctance to sell Pollock paintings (for "sentimental" reasons) yet recommending that the gallery continue representing her with the estate: "My dear Lee, . . . You are generously trying to handle your paintings with an aesthetic idea behind the plan. I hope to continue to help you in my present role as Consultant. . . . Yours ever, David."[87]

Unfortunately, Krasner's health was threatened on Christmas in 1962, when she experienced a cerebral aneurysm while at dinner with her nephew, Ronald Stein, and his wife, Frances (Patiky). On January 22, 1963, following the incident, Sanford Friedman, brother of B. H. Friedman and intimate companion of Richard Howard, wrote to Gibbs, updating him on Krasner's health, an indication of their continuing relationship. Friedman described Krasner's mental state as very positive: "For the first time since I've known her, she is filled with tolerance, sympathy, even tenderness for her fellow artists and the art world in general."[88]

However, by the next month, Krasner's disposition had changed, and Sanford Friedman wrote to Gibbs in Krasner's "own words": "Once my fury against ART relented it began to waver between Elizabeth Hubbard [her homeopathic doctor] and David Gibbs—though at the moment it seems to favor Elizabeth—No telling how I'll come out with you David."[89]

Confirming this relationship, James Valliere, Krasner's assistant from 1963 to 1965, recalled, "I met David Gibbs; he stayed at the East Hampton house for a few days during the early part of Lee's negotiations with Marlborough."[90] Gibbs had become an influential companion and lover. Despite some possibly questionable maneuverings, he set her on the path that would eventually enable her to accomplish her goals.

In addition to cataloging Krasner and Pollock's library and starting the work on the Pollock catalogue raisonné, Valliere's employment as a research assistant with Krasner focused primarily on redefining Pollock's contribution to the arts.[91] Distancing Pollock from his friend and teacher the out-of-style regionalist Thomas Hart Benton and Pollock's own image as the drunken cowboy from Cody, Wyoming, Valliere spoke to visitors of Pollock having an interest in Renaissance masters, in particular El Greco, and in classic American literature, including Herman Melville's *Billy Budd*.[92] My own experience, while staying at the house on Springs Fireplace Road and surreptitiously perusing the small library in the living room, was to have found a book about El Greco with drawings in the margins. Unfortunately, while the two books listed by Valliere remain, this particular book does not.[93]

No doubt spearheaded by Krasner, the duo, Krasner as priestess and Valliere as her acolyte, unfolded a master plan. It began with a revisionist history, a re-creation of the Pollock story, a story about an artist who would become one of the greatest of our time. It appears also that Krasner did some paintings dating from this period, either in East Hampton or perhaps at the Adams Hotel on 86th Street and Fifth Avenue.[94]

Valliere told me, "I always believed that her goal, while I worked with her from 1963 to 1965, was strictly to build 'Pollock's legacy.' That was her single-minded focus. Her goal was to get Marlborough-Gerson Gallery in New York City to handle Pollock's artworks [his estate] and to have them commit to publishing a catalogue raisonné of his art."[95]

In the 1950s and '60s, Marlborough was among the most successful galleries in London. Krasner's hope was that the gallery would promote the Pollock estate in Europe and then in the United States, followed by attending to her own artistic legacy, as well as that of her nephew, Ronald Stein. Krasner had spent tremendous time and energy promoting Pollock while he was alive, and certainly she felt this investment should not be wasted. It was a plan hatched in stages.[96]

Stein, the son of Krasner's younger sister Ruth, moved to Springs in 1963, into the building that Pollock was hoping to renovate for Krasner as a studio. He came to help her and to "find" himself as an artist. He also wanted to be part of the plan and get in on the Marlborough bandwagon. A letter he wrote to Gibbs, dated April 19, 1963, asked if Gibbs would reach out to Lloyd to also give him a show at Marlborough, something that he implied would make Krasner happy.[97]

Pollock's first exhibition at Marlborough-Gerson Gallery in New York was in January–February 1964.

Although fraught with conflict, negotiations continued. On March 4, 1964, Dickler wrote to Gibbs saying that he was "deeply perturbed about the relationship between Lee and the Gallery." He was looking for payments that hadn't been made to Krasner and expected a complete inventory, noting that a painting had been sold without Krasner's knowledge. He wrote: "I think I am being conservative, however, in attributing them [the difficulties] to a chaotic state of affairs of the Gallery which is hardly calculated to instill confidence in Lee with regard to the future relationship, if any, with Marlborough."[98]

Donald McKinney recalled:

Gibbs was kind of the conduit between her and Marlborough. He was a private dealer. . . . In my personal opinion, he wasn't that effective. He didn't have the strengths that I would think he should have had, but she liked people who were proper Englishmen, and he knew this person and that person, she sort of liked that. She gave him the opportunity to see what he could do. From day one, that was what he really wanted [the Pollock estate]. . . . Then he flattered her about her work, and I think most of that was just [insincere].[99]

The plan was unfolding. Cultivating Krasner was another step toward obtaining the Pollock materials for Marlborough in the United States, finally arriving in 1964.

The Whitechapel Retrospective

From my point of view, Krasner never relinquished her desire to be known and appreciated for her own work. That part of the plan became obvious when, in the fall of 1965, Krasner had her first major one-person exhibition. The venue was the Whitechapel Gallery in London, and the catalog was written by B. H. Friedman. It ran from September 22 to October 31, 1965, and was organized by Whitechapel director Bryan Robertson.

Robertson had been a good friend of Krasner's since the International Council's Pollock show, which had traveled there in 1958, following which he authored the Pollock monograph published by Thames & Hudson in 1960.[100] He was known internationally for showcasing avant-garde American artists.

Hence, the Whitechapel Gallery became an unknowing pawn in guaranteeing the relationship between Krasner and Marlborough to obtain the Pollock estate as part of Marlborough's stable. It is important to note that the acknowledgments in the catalog of Krasner's Whitechapel retrospective include Edward F. (Ted) Dragon, Mr. and Mrs. B. H. Friedman, David Gibbs and Co., Donald McKinney, Hans Namuth, Alfonso Ossorio, Dr. Leonard Siegel (Krasner's psychoanalyst), and the Marlborough-Gerson Gallery.

Confirming his "gold digger" reputation, by some strange twist of fate, or by a lack of scruples, in 1965, Gibbs married Geraldine Stutz. Since 1957, this celebrated businesswoman had been the president of Henri Bendel Inc. and a prominent socialite on the New York scene. The couple married in Newtown, Connecticut, on September 11. The following day, the *New York Times* reported the wedding of Stutz to Gibbs, "of New York, formerly of London." The announcement, noting that his "previous marriage ended in divorce," stated that the couple would reside "at 46 East 56th Street and their farm in Connecticut." This must have come as a surprise to Krasner, since it was just ten days before the opening of the retrospective that she and Gibbs had no doubt initiated during their romantic tour of Europe in 1961. Stein recalled that Krasner was shocked to have read about Gibbs's marriage.[101] Gibbs, who was rumored to be bisexual, and fashion executive Stutz lived in Connecticut until their divorce more than a decade later in 1976.[102] According to Stein, "[Gibbs] literally left [Krasner] at the altar. She was devastated but never made him an enemy."[103]

While Gail Levin stated that Robertson chose to do the show without following the usual procedure (perhaps for funding), the plot turns out to have been a little thicker.[104] Clearly, this exhibition had the full backing—no doubt financial—of Marlborough-Gerson Gallery. Gibbs and McKinney, as well as the gallery itself, are mentioned in the acknowledgments.[105]

Shortly after the London show, as promised by Gibbs, Krasner began to glean even more attention, becoming the only woman invited by William Rubin to show in MoMA's exhibition "The New American Painting and Sculpture: The First Generation." Obviously, Gibbs was right; being represented by the prestigious Marlborough Gallery would be a game changer for her.

Ronald Stein Makes a Play

Molly Barnes, a young art devotee, who dated Willem de Kooning for a few years, spent summers in the Hamptons in the 1970s. She recalled her routine of driving Krasner to garage sales in the area on Saturday mornings and described Krasner as "witty and fun."[106] Molly and her friend Gaby Rodgers interviewed Ronald Stein for a local East Hampton television station (LTV) in 2000. Stein described the intensity of the relationship between his aunt and David Gibbs: "Lee fell for him like a ton of bricks. David was working for the Marlborough Gallery, and Frank Lloyd, the owner of Marlborough, wanted Lee to surrender the Pollock estate to them. She fell in love, but David didn't fall for her. He was the conduit between her and Marlborough."

While there has been no other corroboration of this final piece of the story, Stein went on to say, "Lee and David got engaged and went to Bermuda for an assignation, which must have been very disappointing for both. Lee was very wealthy at that time."

Stein said that he suspected that Gibbs's attraction to Krasner was only for financial gain, and given their age difference, he speculated that they weren't sexually compatible. Her paintings suggest otherwise. She was a woman who knew and took pleasure in her body, and there had to be a compelling motivation, other than a financial one, for her to relinquish the Pollock estate. In the video, Stein, who depended on his aunt for financial support from time to time, talked specifically about his and Krasner's relationship with Marlborough. According to him, the plan was to have works by Krasner, Pollock, and Stein all be part of the gallery. In the interview, Barnes asked Stein if Pollock was supportive of him, and he said, "Yes, he bought the first two paintings I did—for fifty dollars and seventy-five dollars."[107]

Fig. 17
Molly Barnes and Lee Krasner in Springs, East Hampton, 1970s.

As mentioned above, Stein's April 14, 1963, letter to Gibbs, asking him to speak to Lloyd about having his own work exhibited at the New York gallery, seemed to ensure his inclusion.[108] Later, Stein sadly admitted that his show at Marlborough in London in January and February 1967, titled "Ronald Stein: 16½ Portrait-Tableaux," was a disappointment.[109] Donald McKinney hardly remembered this show of Stein's work at all and said that Stein was certainly not one of Marlborough's designated artists.[110] In addition, the Marlborough Gallery has no existing records of the show. In fact, Stein refused to go to his own black-tie opening, claiming that because of the popularity of Pop Art, he had "lost faith" in the art world. It seemed to him that art had become entertainment. In the interview, he went on to say, "I was a man who believed in the God of art. I was seduced by the gallery but finally gave up art."[111]

This statement contradicts the fact that Stein actually continued exhibiting at the Arlene Bujese Gallery in East Hampton from 1986 until his death in 2000.[112] While he recalled that Krasner was disappointed in his loss of interest in art at age forty, he went on to become a successful pilot and "flew every kind of airplane for eighteen years." Stein was at once supportive and brutally critical of Krasner. Finally, in the video interview, he stated, "Lee was never wrong about art, but she was dead wrong about everything else."[113]

Fig. 18
Krasner and her nephew, Ronald Stein,
at the Guild Hall Exhibition, 1964.

The neighbors in Springs remembered Stein with justified concern. It was said that his drinking and raucous behavior were often accompanied by emergency calls reporting domestic violence and requiring police intervention.[114] He ultimately died of alcoholism, leaving behind a cache of guns, which had been hidden in his house. Arlene Bujese told me he kept a gun "in a pot hanging over his kitchen counter."[115]

What Stein didn't say in the interview was that, after Krasner left the hospital following treatment for her aneurysm in 1963, she moved to the Adams Hotel in New York City, where Gibbs also had an apartment.[116] She returned to the Adams again after another serious illness in 1964 and remained there until August 1965. During this period, when the physical act of painting had become a challenge, Krasner, using her left hand, made some remarkable compositions, among them *Eyes in the Weeds* (1963) and *Happy Lady* (1963).[117] While larger in scale, they refer to the "Little Image" paintings of the late 1940s, and they are also precursors to the more figurative paintings to come, in which the calligraphy opens up into a lighter, more joyful expression, such as *Icarus* (1964) and *Bird's Parasol* (1964).

While Krasner often said her paintings were autobiographical, she would nevertheless invite others to title them.[118] However, in my opinion, most of the titles have considerable relevance to the paintings, and this connection should not be overlooked. She would usually agree to the suggestions from others, often after discussion, and for that reason, they provide at least one entry point into the work.[119] Further, according to Levin, Krasner's painting *Courtship* (1966) was titled by the artist and is "an allusion to David Gibbs."[120] The swooping organic forms in *Memory of Love* (1966) seem to relate compositionally to *Courtship*, as well as to her earlier painting *Igor* (ca. 1942–1943), referring to her former lover Igor Pantuhoff.[121]

It turns out that Gibbs too—perhaps because of the lavish lifestyle offered him by his affluent new wife, Geraldine Stutz—decided to try his hand at becoming an artist. Ironically, he shared a studio with Stein in New York. Gibbs also continued his profession as a gallerist, opening the Duffy-Gibbs Gallery around 1977 in SoHo. Mark Schlesinger, a prominent artist now living in San Antonio and a "summer sitter" for Krasner in 1972–1973, whom Gibbs later represented in his gallery, recalled that, "in those days, Gibbs and Krasner continued to be friends." Over the years, Schlesinger and Gibbs would meet for drinks on occasion, and Gibbs would often ask how Krasner was doing.[122]

Although Gibbs was considered by many to be an opportunist, I believe he cared for Krasner, lending her guidance, emotional support, and respect. Some may say that this was just another tragic relationship for Krasner, in which her male partner used her to his own benefit in a humiliating dynamic, but it is plain to see that Krasner truly loved him. Their relationship was, of course, dramatically reconfigured when Gibbs married Stutz.

While Stein said his aunt was devastated by Gibbs's rejection of her, Krasner knew she had reached another of her goals and must have taken consolation in that realization.[123] Perhaps as payback to Pollock, she even relished her career recognition as a result of this illicit romantic relationship with a married man.[124]

Her high level of business and artistic aspirations, which she shared with Gibbs, continued, and while they may have been fueled by Gibbs's driving ambition, they were ignited by hers. As judgmental as Krasner seemed to have been, a clean break from Gibbs was never to take place. While no records remain, Marlborough probably cut ties with Gibbs sometime in the early 1960s. Oddly enough, Gibbs was hired by Pace Gallery after leaving Marlborough, a move Krasner was to make as well. An overlap seems doubtful, since Arne Glimcher, the director of Pace, didn't remember him clearly.[125]

Gibbs's clever collusion strategies, particularly his gigolo tactics, supported by the story above, in close association with the Marlborough Gallery and Krasner herself, were factors that enhanced Krasner's eventual fame. It wasn't only a physical attraction that bound them. Krasner's feelings for Gibbs and his for her continued, in part, for the rest of her life.[126]

Donald McKinney

Donald McKinney, director of Marlborough Gallery and Krasner's good friend, recalled seeing Geraldine Stutz and Gibbs at Krasner soirées over the years.[127]

Soon after Gibbs's departure from Marlborough, McKinney, a student at the Courtauld with significant contacts among the rich and famous and a passionate lover of the arts, arrived in Krasner's life to save the deal, carrying it to fruition. McKinney told me that neither Frank Lloyd nor his nephew, Pierre Levai, could get along with Krasner, so they discreetly passed her along to him: "We [Marlborough Gallery] came to New York, we signed on Lee [1966], and then after a period of time, with a little pressure from Frank about the Pollocks . . . eventually, she broke down. My job, basically, was to get her [to cooperate and relinquish the Pollocks]."[128]

Good-looking and fun to be around, McKinney was, like many of the men in Krasner's life, a devoted companion, but, unlike Gibbs, he was far from a romantic interest.[129] Most important, Krasner and McKinney had a long-lasting, very strong bond of true friendship. He had an unbending loyalty to her, and she, in turn, had found someone she could trust to keep her safe and, using Pollock's paintings as the bait, ensure that he would continue to promote her work. The following is a brief excerpt from my interview with McKinney. His experience echoes that of many of the "summer sitters."

RA: Did your relationship with Lee require you to come out and stay in the Hamptons?
DM: All the time.
RA: Did you stay in the back bedroom?
DM: I stayed upstairs. I went there very often. It was hard. She really wanted me to come out every weekend. She would meet me at the station for the train. Sometimes it was standing-room only—all the way out here. Then, when I was in New York, we would do all these things, and I lived four blocks south. I lived on 74th Street, at one point, on Fifth Avenue. She would do everything to make me stay overnight, because she didn't want to be alone. She would say, "Donald, come and have drinks." There was the point when she stopped drinking. . . . It was late, she still didn't want to go to bed. She'd say, "Donald, you don't want to go home." Then I'd stay in the back room.

Quilts and the Civil Rights Movement

Dedicated to Krasner, McKinney continued to work on building the artist's reputation, and her dependency on him increased. With the Whitechapel exhibition, he had established a significant position for her abroad, and now he was focusing on the United States. For maximum exposure, like many artists of the period, she agreed to speaking engagements, exhibitions, and artist-in-resident gigs at U.S. colleges and universities. Among them was a 1974 show, which started at Miami-Dade Community College before traveling to Beaver College in Glenside, Pennsylvania (arranged by Judith Brodsky), then to the Gibbes Museum of Art in Charleston, South Carolina, and the 1975 Corcoran show that originated in D.C. and traveled to Pennsylvania State University and then to the Rose Art Museum at Brandeis

University. Ironically, of greater importance to Krasner personally was an earlier exhibition in the Garland Hall Gallery at the University of Alabama in Tuscaloosa that ran from February 14 to March 14, 1967. Krasner recalled how this first contact with the women of the South was life-changing.[130]

Rachel Dobson, communications specialist and visual resources curator at the University of Alabama, told me recently that this exhibition was one of the university's most ambitious and that it probably arose from an inaugural celebration of a new gallery, which included contemporary twentieth-century artists like Krasner, prior to her solo show.[131] Dobson confirmed that the university would not have been able to mount such an ambitious show without the financial assistance of Marlborough Gallery. Printed in the gold and black exhibition brochure is the following statement: "The Department of Art of Alabama acknowledges the kindness and assistance of Mr. Donald McKinney and the Marlborough-Gerson Gallery, New York, in making this exhibition possible."

There were twenty-four paintings, including some of Krasner's most important works, all from the 1960s, such as *Primal Resurgence* (1961), *Happy Lady* (1963), *Bird's Parasol* (1964), and *Gaea* (1966), ranging from 43 by 65 inches to 93½ by 161⅜ inches. The effect was spectacular.[132]

McKinney remembered a side trip to visit the Freedom Quilting Bee:

> We had the show at Tuscaloosa, and then the curator [Ted Klitzke, the director] said they wanted to do something to entertain us, and they put us in a car and they took us and said we'd like to show you something. They took us out. I promise you; it was just dirt roads, and there were shacks. There were chickens underneath them, and they were on stilts, and the sunlight was coming through the floor. It was [a] very large [room], maybe seven or eight [women]. It was a group. And [Krasner] bought several quilts. I ordered three, and she ordered three. [They were] ninety dollars or something. We were very, very pleased. I used mine. Unfortunately, they got tired and old. Mine still had flour sacks and things in it. They were beautiful. Black and white. We loved them. Gee's Bend was quite an experience in itself, and I shall long, long remember it. The roof was leaking, and that was the problem. We got back, and we thought we have to do something [to help]. We called Henry Geldzahler, then curator of twentieth-century art at the Metropolitan Museum, to get some sort of financial support for their roof, and he found someone who would pay to repair it.[133]

This scenario had been orchestrated by a few courageous white integrationists who had the vision to entice the sympathetic thinkers from the North to relocate to the South in order to ensure the economic survival of the quilters and, thus, their communities. Ted Klitzke, the director of the University of Alabama Gallery from 1959 to 1968, Reverend Francis Walter, and his wife, Elizabeth (Betty) Walter, were leading this effort. These were the dangerous days when the South was in upheaval. A few years earlier, in 1963, there was the bombing of the 16th Street Baptist Church in Birmingham, a tragedy that killed four young black girls.[134] And just two years later, the Civil Rights Amendment was passed.

During the time that Krasner was the artist-in-residence at Alabama, these three—Klitzke with Francis and Betty Walter—escorted McKinney and Krasner to the tiny town of Alberta in Wilcox County to visit the newly formed Freedom Quilting Bee. The Bee was a cooperative, originally organized through the efforts of the Walters. Eventually to become an exemplary figure in the civil rights movement, Betty at the time was a graduate student in studio art who worked as gallery coordinator, helping Klitzke and McKinney hang the show. Betty Walter would go on to earn her Ph.D. from the University of Georgia in art and architectural history, eventually becoming chair of the art department of the University of Northern Alabama for twelve years before her retirement. She was the first of my interviewees to discuss the significance of Krasner and McKinney's visit to Alabama and specifically to Alberta in 1967.

Records show that Klitzke was well known for bringing notable artists to the South in an effort to initiate cultural change. He also took real risks to support equal rights for African Americans, participating in marches from Selma to Montgomery, which led to the passing of the Voting Rights Act of 1965. Because he was a threat to the sociopolitical old guard, the Ku Klux Klan burned crosses on three separate occasions on the front lawn of his home in Pinehurst, Alabama.[135]

It should be noted that most of the historical information related to this geographical area uses "Gee's Bend" as a generic name for the small settlements of these great African American quilters, descendants of slaves, who established an all-black population, a rare racial distinction even in Alabama. Under the heading of Gee's Bend, the Freedom Quilting Bee communities included Possum Bend, Coy, Beatrice, Alberta, Boykin, Selma, Gastbury, and Lower Peach Tree townships. The co-op headquarters was in Alberta, in an old, weathered wooden house until a new facility was built in 1989.[136] However, and most important, according to Dr. Betty Walter, Krasner and McKinney went to Alberta, not to the Gee's Bend chapter located in Boykin in the bend of the Alabama River.[137]

In her book *The Freedom Quilting Bee*, Nancy Callahan explains that, in fact, Alberta was the gateway to this area located along the river on Route 22, about twenty miles from Selma.[138] It is more than forty miles from Alberta to the hamlet of Boykin, in the heart of Gee's Bend. Travel between the two locations for the poverty-stricken residents was not easy. In the early 1900s, a makeshift and not so safe ferry between the two villages was available during good weather.[139]

Callahan quotes Krasner as saying that "the place really became frightening because [it was pointed out that] that house we passed was the last telephone in relation to the Gee's Bend. . . . We went into this room where there was a stretcher (quilt frame) the full space of the room. Women were seated against the walls of the room, working on a quilt. It was quite a sight to behold." Krasner reiterated what McKinney had said: "I was very taken with what I had seen. I asked about this and that and ordered three quilts. While I was in the house, I saw on the mantelpiece a shell. I collect shells, so after everyone relaxed, I asked where the shell came from." Then they offered to take Krasner to a house where they had a lot of them. She mentioned that the poverty "was beyond description" and that she wanted to help a little girl there, sending her a book about a little girl of color, which she was told "caused a good deal of happy commotion" among her classmates at school.[140]

Walter recalled:

Dr. Theodore Klitzke was department chair at the time. Very forward-looking, liberal-leaning, wonderfully educated, kind, sweet man who made Alabama bearable for some of us. He and his wife, Margaret, entertained Miss Krasner for about, as well as I can remember, about five days at their home. The impetus of her visit was this very large exhibition. Marlborough must have paid a substantial amount, because I don't remember the university having that kind of money at the time. May I say from the outset, she was one of the most gracious, delightful, at the time, older women I'd ever met. As the gallery coordinator, I was quite taken with her. In addition to having a gallery exhibit and a grand opening in Tuscaloosa, she wanted to visit the Black Belt, which at the time had figured so prominently in political news. The Civil Rights Act had just been passed, but nobody down there quite had gotten the results of it.[141]

When Krasner and McKinney were there in 1967, the racial hostility in the South was a frightening element of everyday life, and Krasner certainly wasn't oblivious to this. Contrary to her reputation for not reading books or newspapers in her later years, she was remembered in Tuscaloosa as having "bought and read local newspapers to keep up with area news."[142]

Walter continued:

As well as I remember, there were five of us in the car that day to take Krasner to visit our friends who were running the Freedom Quilting Bee—[me and] my husband Reverend Francis Walter, McKinney, Krasner, and Klitzke. Alberta is up the road. Gee's Bend is actually on the river, and the communities are quite separate in terms of social interaction. It's about an hour and a half drive south of Tuscaloosa, and we left early in the morning. Had just a marvelous trip. I mean, they had never seen any of this part of the country, and we were very gregarious, so we had a lot of tales to tell them. But anyway, when we got down to Alberta, the Witherspoons [Eugene and Estelle, African Americans from the community] entertained us. Well, it so happened that Estelle and Eugene just were natural-born leaders and well respected in their communities. So they were a godsend. If it hadn't been for them, this [community renovation] would never have happened. They were still, at that time, living in a slave cabin that had a red clay mud chimney and two rooms and the little kitchen and a porch on the back with an outhouse. It was quite primitive. When we went to visit, we ate what they offered us. Eugene had had an unfortunate accident as a child, and his leg was broken and never set, so he could only make a living as a hunter and a gatherer. So he hunted for a living, and more often than not, we ate chicken hawk or possum or turtle, which was pretty standard diet, along with their patch of collard greens and eggs.

Dr. Walter confirmed McKinney's recollection of Krasner and him buying quilts: "Miss Krasner and McKinney were able to buy the very earliest examples of the original Freedom Quilting Bee."

While McKinney talked about a "shell" that Krasner was given at the Freedom Quilting Bee, Walter made it clear that the shell Krasner received as a gift was actually a fossil, in the shape of a nautilus or cretaceous ammonite, much larger than most seashells. She explained that along the Alabama River, when the water was low, there was an area in the embankment where you could dig for these fossils. While Krasner inquired about paying for the fossil, Reverend Walter advised her not to offer money for it, so as not to offend her hosts.[143]

Dr. Walter explained how Krasner's visit influenced their efforts toward financial self-sufficiency for Southern blacks:

When Miss Krasner was there, it was only the beginning, before we had any real funds. It took a while to ramp up. All we had was a salary and a car. And it took a while to meet all the right people. The women in Alberta came up with the Freedom Quilting Bee name. It was all their idea. After Miss Krasner came down, there were several people that either she got in touch with or she knew. Aline Saarinen, who was with NBC News at that time, she was down there two times making reports. Diana Vreeland was editor of *Vogue* magazine at the time, and in one of the issues of *Vogue*, she had her squib about it right after my husband was there. . . . So then, it wasn't too long after that, the craze hit the fan, and we did another enormous quilt for Lord & Taylor, and they hung it on the facade of the Fifth Avenue store.[144]

Twenty years after Krasner's trip to Alberta, I was the chief curator of painting, sculpture, and graphic arts at the Birmingham Museum (from 1984 to 1989). My own impression paralleled the enormous respect McKinney and Krasner felt for this enclave of talented women. I recall that the staff members of the museum (many sympathetic "carpetbaggers" from other parts of the country) were filled with respect and admiration for this isolated community, which we, too, called Gee's Bend, and their extraordinary works of art. We also took visiting artists and collectors to this Alabama art destination.

When we consider the work of these female artists in comparison with Krasner's, it's easy to see why Krasner would be supportive of their community for reasons beyond the simple beauty of the quilts they produced. She had much in common with these women. They had learned to survive economically while still making their art and following their passion. As she did with her tables and collages, they used what materials were at hand, letting the process guide the end result. Regardless of race or cultural and geographical background, Krasner was able to find artistic kindred spirits among the African American women of Alberta, Alabama. It was an unexpected outcome of Krasner's ambitious strategy—her plan—for fame.

In June 1976, Krasner took both her work and Pollock's estate away from Marlborough Gallery, possibly because of a scandal involving Mark Rothko and Marlborough, though she denied this was the case.[145] Krasner explained by saying, "All good things come to an end."[146] McKinney continued to be her good friend. He told me he respected her decision to leave, that it was "because of the unpleasant public outcry over the Mark Rothko lawsuit," which proved, after Rothko's death, that the gallery was fixing prices and taking unfair financial advantage of his children, thus incriminating Frank Lloyd.[147] Certainly, it does seem very plausible that her decision to detach both herself and Pollock's estate from Marlborough was in some way connected to the Rothko scandal.[148] A *New York Times Index* dated December 18, 1975, lists Krasner, Donald Blinken (president of the Rothko Foundation and collector of Rothko paintings), and Grace Borgenicht (gallerist) as "commenters" in the suit, which lasted more than four years and involved seven sets of attorneys. It was stated that the case "would set standard(s) for future conduct of dealers and others connected with art transactions."[149] It should be noted that Krasner's discretion in not declaring the gallery's illicit activities publicly was uncharacteristically politic. Her positive relationship served her well.

CHAPTER FOUR

Beauty and the Beast

"I think my painting is so biographical if anyone can take the trouble to read it."[150]

When I was living with Lee Krasner in East Hampton, our conversations would focus mostly on our day-to-day activities—shopping for food, helping with dinner, washing the lawn furniture, and finding time for our interview sessions. We'd often just take walks. Except for our formal recorded interviews, we did not tend to discuss the work she was doing in the studio, a situation that became increasingly frustrating for me. My primary intention was to write about the art and how it related to her unconscious. In fact, for weeks, I was not allowed into this private space, her protected domain, situated only a few feet from the back porch. Although I was certainly intrigued, I was careful not to be caught lingering outside the door. I recall taking a furtive photograph

Fig. 19
Krasner in her studio, East Hampton, 1974.

of a man's handprint on a large sheet of paper, thinking it reminded me of the hand of the fallen soldier in Picasso's *Guernica*, one of Krasner's favorite paintings, and hoping it was the hand of Pollock. Helen Harrison told me that they were probably left by artists Herbert and Mercedes Matter:

> There were several things of Herbert Matter's in the studio flat file, including photos of Mercedes, graphic-art layouts, and the handprint. Also a couple of Duchamp collotypes. They all date from when Jackson was alive, and the flat file was in the studio when it was his, so maybe they date from when Herbert and Mercedes were visiting in the 1940s. Lee just left them in the drawer. But at this point, there's no way to know for sure whose hand it is.[151]

Knowing Krasner, I understood that I would have to wait patiently for an invitation. Magically, the moment finally arrived. This was a historic occasion for me. It was a clear, sunny day when I entered the huge, somewhat empty studio, and there was Krasner sitting in a chair I had seen only in photographs, with her large paintings either leaning against or hanging on the walls. The sun was streaming through the windows. The smell was delicious—turpentine and oil paint floating in the air. She was willing to let me take some photographs of the work and of her. She had her hair carefully combed and wore some lipstick on her large lips. In fact, while we were looking at the paintings, she propped up some of the smaller ones so I could get a better shot. This was a breakthrough. While she didn't talk about the work directly during our recorded interviews, she did drop some clues when the tape recorder was turned off.[152]

As for the paintings, there were four of her monumental works set out for her and my consideration. According to the Krasner catalogue raisonné, the titles of the larger canvases were *Thaw* (1957), *Rose Red* (1958), *Gothic Landscape* (1961), and *Crisis Moment* (ca. 1972–1980).[153] Of the smaller works, there were *Igor* (ca. 1942–1943)[154] and *Untitled (Still Life)* (ca. 1942). Upon close examination, most of these canvases appeared exactly as they are represented in the catalogue raisonné. However, in its early stages, *Crisis Moment* was a much more minimalist concept—blue background and two red organic shapes juxtaposed with white forms that recall many of the nature-inspired paintings from her "Earth Green" series. In 1980, Krasner reworked the painting (as she was known to do), adding collage pieces from an earlier lithograph titled *Pink Stone* (also referred to as *Rose Stone*) (1969)[155] and stronger blue pigment to reinforce the central composition of four orbs bursting from the center.

In this chapter, I discuss key issues in Krasner's life as they affected her personality as well as her physical and mental health and, most important, her work. She always said that if you wanted to understand her, all you had to do was look at the paintings. What follow are some of those casual but revealing observations she made to me back then, some observations regarding her life story, and an examination of the paintings and the nature of their power.

Too Independent-Minded

Krasner told me that her mother said that she would always have problems because she was "too independent-minded. At the time she said it, it didn't mean anything to me. I didn't even know what she was talking about. But it's only later in life that I can remember back, that she used to say this to me." She went on to explain how this affected her much later on in life. "I must have shown an awful lot of signs of this kind of thing for her to have said that, because today I'd say it absolutely is so. I am like that. The image I had of myself [was of being] quiet, in the background. Except that in high school, there's open rebellion."

Around the time of her graduation from high school, in 1922, Krasner had rejected the strict mores of her Orthodox Jewish mother and father. In fact, in my interview with her, she admitted that she had always been something of an outsider—even on the home front, where she felt distanced from her parents, much in the manner of the Jungian archetype, the "powerless and needy . . . orphan."[156] Krasner's mother and father, who at that time had a local grocery stand selling fish and vegetables, toiled from dawn to dusk. While her older siblings worked in the shop, she was left mostly to her own devices. Her mother had another daughter, Ruth, born nine months after Krasner's birth, and then she took over the fish and vegetable store so her husband could spend his time at temple. Krasner's father was everything to her. He was the intellectual. He was the one with the ideas. And to make things worse, her younger sister was always considered "the pretty one."

Because her parents spoke little or no English, her older brother, Irving, began to take charge. He encouraged Krasner to take refuge in books. They would read the Russian classics, fairy tales, and the work of Maurice Maeterlinck.[157] Krasner also found delight in the writings of Edgar Allan Poe.[158] Thus, sometime around her graduation from P.S. 72, in pursuit of her true identity, Krasner declared herself an artist and changed her name from Lena to the more romantic-sounding Lenore. She was, no doubt, inspired by the tragic heroine in her favorite poet Poe's famous poem *The Raven* (1845) and was moved by the suffering wife of a self-serving artist in his poem *Lenore* (1831).[159] These psychologically wounded women could have stimulated in Krasner a certain empathy, an element of fear, and a premonition of a threatening future.

While she was growing up, her father, too, would read fairy tales to her: "I'd sit close to him, and he'd tell the stories. Oh, I was terribly scared at night, scared of the dark, still am."[160]

Fairy tales have played an important part in the theoretical framework of many psychological studies, including those of psychoanalyst Carl Jung and his follower Joseph Campbell, a professor of comparative mythology. Thanks to her father, their importance was certainly not lost on Krasner.

John Graham, her close friend and author of the early book on art and the unconscious, *System and Dialectics of Art*[161] (1937), gave her a book of fairy tales, titled *Silver Voices*.[162] It has, according to the publisher, "hand coloured, comical illustrations," depicting the adventures of a young boy named Harry, his mother, and his sweetheart in a series of adventures focused on helping those who are less fortunate. This dramatic portrait of Harry takes the reader on a fantasy journey through various archetypal stages—from the Orphan leaving his home seeking food for himself and his mother, to the Martyr who loses everything, the Wanderer who suffers loneliness, the Warrior who experiences fear, and finally, to the Magician, exonerated by faith, love, and joy. In one illustration, Harry is depicted with a beautiful fairy, wand in hand. Clearly, the fairy—as the symbol of the Magician—is in charge of Harry's fate, one that has a happy ending.

The book by Marie Louise von Franz, *The Interpretation of Fairy Tales*, follows Jung's theory of archetypes, those originally inspired by fairy tales, which von Franz refers to as "the purest and simplest expression of collective unconscious." Offering us "the best clues to the understanding of the processes going on in the collective psyche," fairy tales are the answer, the path to what seemed lacking in official Christian teaching. They offer a "more vital, earthy and instinctual wisdom."[163] This need for a basic meaning in life "induced the famous brothers Jacob and Wilhelm Grimm to collect folktales."[164] The power of the fairy tales Krasner's father read to her as a child carried over to her psychic explorations on canvas as an adult and can be perceived in the hideous figures in her paintings, those painted just before and immediately after Pollock's death. Their subjects, such as in *Prophecy* (1956), *Three in Two* (1956), *Birth* (1956) and *Embrace* (1956), are deeply violent examples of the Grimms' genre. Even though Krasner had help naming her works, she ultimately agreed to the titles from others because they seemed to fit.[165]

Krasner's life evolved in dramatic ways. While she was enrolled in the National Academy of Design in 1928, she fell into a romantic relationship with a fellow student that would last for more than a decade. The handsome and debonair White Russian Igor Pantuhoff, an award-winning student, and Krasner, a Russian Jew, became lovers. While students would often room together, Krasner and Pantuhoff were known as a couple—in fact, some observers thought they were married.[166] However, Pantuhoff was penniless, and their religious and social differences may have led to his hasty retreat from New York in 1939 to his parents' home in Florida.[167] Upon his departure, he sent a somewhat whimsical note and a drawing of himself on an island, leaning against a palm tree in the shape of a penis. In the letter, he was asking Krasner to return his clothes and paintings. But there is no evidence that she did so.[168] While he became known for his traditional portrait paintings of society matrons, he would also occasionally show up in Krasner's life, sometimes asking for money.[169] Theirs was a painful rift that took years to mend.

I found it sad that her painting *Igor*, no doubt dedicated to him, was still in her studio when I arrived in 1974, so many years later. However, just as the door was closing on her relationship with Pantuhoff, a new one opened. Her reputation as a respected member of the downtown cultural community and an artists' rights advocate guaranteed Krasner a place in the WPA (Works Progress Administration), a significant step forward in her career.

The WPA

Certainly, the WPA under Franklin D. Roosevelt (from 1935 to 1943) had made a huge difference in the way artists thought of themselves and of one another. They were legitimized, able to support their meager lifestyle, while participating in a community of like-minded talents.[170]

Because of the Depression and government efforts to keep artists working, Krasner chose to become employed by the WPA.[171]

RA: Do you remember your salary during that period?

LK: Dear, I didn't think I'd ever forget that salary as long as I lived, but I've forgotten it. I believe it was $23.86. And it wasn't me. It was everybody. Except supervisors got a little more. I think the salary was $23.86 a week

RA: Is that all the money you had to live on at that time?

Fig. 20
Letter from
Igor Pantuhoff
to Krassner.
October 24, 1939.

LK: Oh, yes, because you weren't eligible for a job if you had any source of income. You had to go through relief in order to get on WPA. You had to qualify first for relief, and to qualify for relief, you were investigated into whether you had any sources of support for yourself. And if you did, you didn't qualify for relief. And if you weren't on relief, you could not get on WPA. Except if you were invited, like if you were [Fernand] Léger, they invited him to do a mural. But you'd have to be Léger at that point, and I don't think he got paid anyway. I think he did it as a gesture. . . . It was during the Depression, created for the purpose of helping the poor.

RA: Now, with the WPA, you worked with [Harold] Rosenberg and Max Spivak.

LK: Rosenberg and I are there as assistants to Spivak. He's painting fishes, I think. Whatever it is, he doesn't want us to touch his work of art, that's for sure. But we do have to report to his studio every single day. We have to stay there, because timekeepers come in to check you. This is on WPA. You know, they want to make sure you're there doing your work. We talked, Rosenberg and I. What else are you going to do, you know? [laughs] We talked a lot of political stuff. But because of the size of his mural, he was automatically assigned two assistants. Now, the fact that he was neurotic enough not to want to use us, they couldn't tie into that. But we had to report and be there every day, anyhow. Because the timekeeper would come and check. Well, we did the best we could.

RA: So, in fact, during the mural project, you never really did a mural?

LK: Me specifically? Well, with me specifically, it went like this: I wandered from one [to another]. At one point, de Kooning, who had been on the project, had to leave, and they gave me his mural to execute. And so, he unofficially came in, even though he was no longer on the job, you see, because he was off the WPA. [De Kooning was rejected because he was not a U.S. citizen.] They gave me his sketch to make it into mural size. So, unofficially, even though he wasn't getting paid, he'd come in to take a look to see if I was doing it all right. It was abstract, very abstract. It was sort of hard-edge abstract, the way he worked at that time. And now another thing I remember. Oh, I've forgotten some of these things, but then, at one point, I began getting irritated 'cause they kept giving me so many leftovers for me to execute and carry out that I finally told my supervisor, who was Burgoyne Diller, may his soul rest in peace. He saved an awful lot of artists, because he was a painter himself and he was able to adjust a lot. In any event, . . . I said that I wanted to use the Hofmann School, that I started working there, and I wanted to use that as my studio address and would do whatever was required of me and that was going to be my studio. That was OK with him, so the timekeeper would check me in there, and I'd be working whatever I had been assigned to there, but at the same time, I could also be working from the model if I wanted to. Oh, and they finally gave me this massive, I don't remember what the artist's name was, *History of Navigation*. It was like 180 feet of it, and [they] asked me to do it, because, you see, by this time, so much money had been invested in the cost of that job, all the research. The idea was to get this thing finished. So they asked me to take that job over and get it done. And then I said [to] Diller, I'd only do it on one condition, because by then I had done an awful lot of finishing off of other people's jobs, I said, provided I get my own mural, abstract mural to do. There was only one place that was doing abstract murals, and that was one of the radio stations. And he said, OK, it's a deal. You get this *History of Navigation* cleaned up and you get your own abstract mural to do. So they sent me out on a pier and gave me about ten people. And we stretched hundreds of [feet of] canvas. As a matter of fact, Eleanor Roosevelt visited the pier while we were working on this thing. It was marvelous, because we had these big coal stoves to keep warm with. And we got *History of Navigation* done. And pasted up on some library in Brooklyn on the walls. It was narrow, a very narrow thing. Anyway, we got it finished, and they gave me my [mural]. He held true. He gave me a very small but abstract panel of my own. And I had to do a sketch for it and submit it. And I did the sketch. I submitted it. He kept saying, "Oh, don't worry, there'll be no problem about it." [At that point,] the fine arts were curtailed, and we became a War Services Project. So I never did get to [do it]. Isn't that awful? But that's the way it went. Come to think of it, I got fantastic practical experience out of these endless tons of [canvas]. Talk about big painting! We handled canvas in no uncertain terms, you know. So in a sense, [there was] a very practical aspect in doing all this.[172]

A shift in the WPA program to the War Services Project denied Krasner her mural but did allow her the opportunity to supervise some large collage installations executed in 1942. She was assigned twenty displays, placed in storefront windows in Manhattan and Brooklyn, advertising the war training courses offered at municipal colleges.[173]

Krasner said, "I was given a group of artists, 'misfits,' they called them, to work with, Baziotes, de Kooning, Pollock, among others."[174] Doing her research on the project, Krasner traveled to some local colleges to learn more about what they were doing, including attending courses on "the chemistry of explosives and ballistics, spherical trigonometry, cryptography and decoding, the uses of mathematics in the war, mapmaking," and more.[175] Her approach was to photograph scenes in the classroom, have her assistants enlarge the images, and then cut and paste to create the final compositions. While the actual installations no longer exist, in reviewing the remaining archival images, we can discern a strong Cubist design element.[176] Diagonal forms crisscross in the compositions, creating a depth of field similar to that taught by her former teacher George Brant Bridgman at the Art Students League, where she learned about "wedging," a Cubist design element that implied both three-dimensional structure and movement.[177] (This brief exposure to Bridgman seems to have been indelible. Krasner began at the Art Students League in July 1928,[178] and then she began attending the National Academy of Design in September 1928. We also know she spent time in Greenlawn, New York, with her parents in the summer of 1928, so presumably she was at the Art Students League for roughly a month.[179]) Krasner, seen as an equal despite her gender and ethnic background, was in charge of the other artists assigned to this project. In fact, Pollock was one of her assistants, giving credence to her strong leadership abilities.[180] Propaganda or not, she and her team delivered powerful visual images in what must have been a less than creative environment.

Following World War II and the crisis of identity that befell the Western psyche, many artists and intellectuals were seeking psychological answers to their innermost questions. The world had changed, becoming more introspective, challenging "traditional" values and assumptions. At the same time, the art world was experiencing a pervasive sense of renewal, with New York emerging as its new geographical center, thanks in large part to the Abstract Expressionists. Considered a game changer in refocusing the heart of the art world on New York, "The New American Painting," an exhibition organized by the International Program of the Museum of Modern Art in New York, under the International Council at the Museum of Modern Art, traveled to European countries in 1958–1959 before being displayed at MoMA May 28–September 8, 1959.[181] It was a time for self-reflection, independent thinking, and psychological examination. Artists of Krasner's generation were striking out on their own, seeking more relevant ways to express themselves as individuals in a complex society.

Rimbaud and the Beast

In 1939, shortly after Arthur Rimbaud's *A Season in Hell* had been translated into English by Delmore Schwartz, lines from the poem, which would later inspire the Surrealists, were scrawled on Krasner's studio wall.[182] Krasner, now in her early thirties, might have been influenced by talks she'd had with Rosenberg about poetry while working with the WPA.[183] She had asked her friend, the artist Byron Browne, who had nice handwriting, to paint the words in bold black letters, highlighting one line, "What lie must I maintain?" by painting it in blue.[184]

To whom shall I hire myself out? What beast must one adore? What holy image attack? What hearts shall I break? What lie must I maintain? In what blood must I walk?[185]

Rimbaud was a major figure in the Symbolist movement in the second half of the nineteenth century, and with the Schwartz translation, he became popular with many of the Downtown artists and intellectuals. In addition to Krasner's psychological challenges, what others told her about her appearance was often extremely hurtful. Her own unflinching self-evaluation may have been the most destructive assessment. While many think Pantuhoff, or possibly Pollock, was for her the mythical "beast" in Rimbaud's *A Season in Hell*, I believe that the beast may have been Krasner herself, as represented in her art. There is no doubt that she was generally rebellious throughout her life, a tendency that was extreme enough to suggest some sort of personality disorder. She struggled to give physical form to her psychological vision, portraying it vividly in her creative crusade as she marched, canvas by canvas, through the art world. Even before the death of her husband, Krasner was in the throes of examining and trying to reconfigure her own life through analysis.

Like Rimbaud, Krasner was known for reinventing herself and revising the direction and form of her work. In addition, both revolted against socially prescribed conventions. Rimbaud and Krasner were both conscious of their own "otherness," characterized by polarities in their personalities. Rimbaud has been described as "a blend of compassion and cruelty, innocence and malice, and ideological power and near insanity."[186] It was around this time, in 1936, that Krasner first met Pollock, briefly, and a bit later, in 1941, got to know him. However, I doubt that in their early years together she thought of him in relation to the Rimbaud poem. Given what I knew of her, of her chaotic psyche, I believe that the seduction that drew her to art and to Pollock also made her fearful. Considering Krasner through the mythic lens of the Jungian Warrior archetype, standing up against a world she imagined from childhood to be hostile and dangerous, I realized she was always on guard, physically and mentally, ready to protect herself against any possible violation. Yet ultimately, I doubt she was ever as frightened of Pollock as she was of herself. It was the reflection of herself embedded in her paintings that she feared the most.

As a result, she closely attended my comings and goings. There was no leaving the house, especially after dark, unless she was with me. Thus, I became an unlikely prisoner as well as a protector against dangerous intruders and apparitions. In chapter 5, "The Summer Sitters," there are stories from many others, corroborating this behavior and attesting to this "house rule."

The Monster

While her experiences in the WPA turned out to be less significant than she might have wished, Krasner's time there provided her with a valuable lesson in leading others and in trusting her own exceptional talents. At the same time, she was a woman with a conflicted personality, and her demons became part of her story. In relation to the fear she felt as a child listening to Russian fairy tales, she told me how traumatized she had been during her youth by a recurring dream she'd had about a "monster" coming up out of the basement and crawling over the banister. This dream haunted her throughout her life. Her close friend, the poet Richard Howard, must have known about the monster dream and made the link to myth, because, when asked by the Marlborough Gallery to write an introductory essay for a portfolio of Krasner's prints in 1969, he wrote:

> We sleep, we dream: a constant allusion, a kind
> Of perilous appeal, by the persistence of
> What cannot end, to whatever bulks and bulges
>   Behind the beginning.
> We sleep, we dream we summon up the person—no,
> The Being—of that first time, not the child only
> But beyond the child, further, some vague myth: we dream
>   The void that came before.[187]

In a 1984 unpublished interview with Deborah Solomon, the artist Paul Jenkins recalled a conversation he had with Krasner while she was visiting in Paris during the summer of 1956. Unofficially estranged from Pollock, Krasner was traveling through Europe, staying with Paul and his wife, Esther. Jenkins recalled Krasner telling him about an "extraordinary dream":

> [She said that] Pollock . . . was crucified on a cross and his hands were green mould. A terrifying dream. She talked to me a lot about her unconscious monster. And about a dream she had had that she took to her psychiatrist. When she came back, Jackson saw her and said, "Something's happened to you." [Pollock] made her sit down on the bed and describe it to him. She described this dream, as if there were an actual monster that was in this house where she lived when she was a child, or at some point in her life, and about the cellar, and it was, shall we say, psychologically monumental coming to terms with something in her and her being.[188]

Jenkins said that the day that Krasner had shared these dreams with him was also to be "the day she knew that Jackson died."

The art critic Eleanor Munro recalled a similar conversation in which Krasner told her that once, when she was about five, she was standing in a dark hall, and she thought she saw something jump over the banister and land on the floor beside her. She was so frightened she could only say, "Half man half beast."[189]

Munro pointed out how Krasner's painting *Prophecy* (1956) is a clear reflection of the same "fear of darkness and instinct for prophecy" that she experienced her entire life.[190] Two, maybe three, figures commingle in what could be identified as a sexual struggle to the death, with the all-present "eye" in the upper right corner passing judgment on the unfolding scene. It is well known that Krasner showed the painting to Pollock before she left for Europe in the summer of 1956. He advised her to remove the eye (advice she didn't take) but to leave the rest until her return.

Munro wrote, "At a bad time, she would paint a very strange work titled *Prophecy*, and only then, when events drove her into analysis and she began to question the meaning of the painting, would she remember the vision [of the monster] and the words she had used to describe it ["half-man half-beast"]."[191] While she didn't title the work until then, she recognized that the subject itself, the commingling of human and animal forms, was a product of her psychic power—a harbinger, a warning, of imminent danger.[192]

That August, her fears came to fruition when Krasner, in Paris, was sleeping on the Jenkinses' couch beside the telephone. Jenkins remembered, "She could tell from the way we [Jenkins and Greenberg] were talking. . . . All of a sudden, she screamed, 'Jackson is dead!' . . . And then Lee was . . . for a period of about a half an hour, she had uncontrollable grief. I just kept an armlock on her. I didn't let her go. We lived on the top floor, and there was a balcony outside. We were in a very strange place."[193]

Another, even more revealing incident was recalled by Clement Greenberg's young wife, Janice van Horne. In 1955, soon after she married Greenberg (twenty-five years her senior), the four of them—van Horne, Greenberg, Pollock, and Krasner—were sitting around the kitchen table in Springs. According to van Horne, Krasner and Greenberg were having an "often addressed conversation" about their dreams, a study encouraged by their Sullivanian analysts Ralph Klein and Leonard Siegel.

As van Horne recalled, in this conversation:

> Lee wants to talk about a dream she had the previous week, although she said she had it before, but never so vividly. She was in an old house reminiscent of a childhood house. She was looking for something and went downstairs to the cellar. In the gloomy shadows she saw something move. She was terrified but moved closer. And then she saw it: a faceless, formless monster, not human, not animal. She couldn't move or scream. Then she woke up, panicked and so fearful she couldn't return to sleep. Clem then observes that the "monster" no doubt represents the concealed part of her—concealed not just from others but from herself—that finally revealed itself. [194]

Van Horne went on to say that her husband saw it as a "breakthrough dream," and Krasner agreed. Like a cautionary tale, it was a "warning dream alerting her to the danger around her." The monster and Rimbaud's beast have a great deal in common. Although Krasner's psychological state may always have been fragile, it clearly declined in the later years of her marriage and those immediately following. Her fascination with and dread of the monster in her dreams and the "beast" written on her wall were the most obvious manifestations of her fears. As Greenberg observed, the monster was the hidden, fearful part of Krasner as finally revealed in her paintings.[195] If we follow this line of thought, referring to the Jungian archetype of the Magician, Krasner is the monster/beast that she must recognize, understand, and, finally, "adore."

John Graham

Well before Krasner met Pollock, she had become a close friend of the Russian John Graham (born Ivan Gratianovitch Dombrowsky). Graham studied law, served on the staff of the tsar, and was in a cavalry unit during World War I. He was very familiar with the prominent Ivan Morosov and Sergei Shchukin collections from Russia, and was thus aware the most advanced French and Russian avant-garde artists of the time.[196]

Of particular interest, Graham was an employee of the Russian mystic Nicholas Roerich, teaching painting and drawing for five years (1930–1935). He worked at the Master Apartments, 310 Riverside Drive.[197] Built in 1929 for Roerich, the Master Apartments, or Master Building, was the tallest building on Riverside Drive, in which the first three floors originally held a museum, a school of fine and performing arts, and an international arts center. As a teacher at the Master Institute, Graham would have been exposed to Roerich's theosophical vision, well acquainted with his theories, "opening the gates to spiritual enlightenment through culture."[198] His interest in primitive cultures must have been awakened by Roerich's view of "the wisdom of ancient gurus as related to modern man."[199]

As a close friend of both Pollock and Krasner for many years, Graham could have inspired her fascination with mysticism. His understanding of French art, theosophy, Freud, and Jung and his influence on Krasner as well as other Abstract Expressionist artists cannot be denied. It was Graham who organized the exhibition "American and French Paintings" at the McMillen Gallery in New York, which opened on January 20, 1942. "He brought the excitement of the French art world to us," showing them [Pollock and Krasner] copies of *Cahiers d'art* and other French publications.[200] His book *System and Dialectics of Art* (1937), which states that "Abstract painting is the highest and most difficult form of painting because it requires of the artist the ability to take full stock of reality and the ability to make a departure from it," is in the Pollock-Krasner House and Study Center Library.[201] Graham examined the meaning of abstract art and raised for Krasner the psychological issues she went on to pursue. Graham also mentioned in his writings Helena Blavatsky's book *The Key to Theosophy*, which, like Graham's, is written in the form of a Socratic dialogue with questions and answers (his interest in Blavatsky could have come directly from Roerich).[202] In his questions, he investigates the role of the unconscious as it relates to the creative process. Graham's studies of Jung and Freud were integral to his theories about the unconscious, and perhaps, even more so, was his devotion to theosophy as described by Blavatsky in her quest for "inner knowledge, . . . insisting that mysticism fed art."[203]

Organized by Barbara Rose in 1983 and held first at the Museum of Fine Arts, Houston and then at the Cooper Union, to accompany the Krasner retrospective, was the exhibition "Lee Krasner: The Education of an American

Artist" which included books, school records, and other Krasner memorabilia.[204] A beautiful African beaded necklace (now missing) and a book of fairy tales, *Silver Voices*, were identified as gifts from Graham to her.

Krasner was intrigued by Graham and his theories, which opened a window into her own unconscious. He also may have introduced her to the Surrealists—their writings and their art. She explained to me that the Surrealists' automatic writing was more interesting than their art,[205] offering deeper entry into the psychic realm, which she longed to probe. Despite this statement, her early work on paper *Untitled (Surrealist Drawing)* (ca. 1935–1938) reveals her testing the power of the Surrealist image. Floating eyes, a skeletal hand reaching out of a classic Greek column, and a ghost in a white robe add up to an enigmatic composition that needs to be considered when looking at her later work.[206] The eye symbol, a powerful image throughout her life, appeared in Krasner's work long before she met Pollock and may have derived from their artist colleague Arshile Gorky and his interest in primitivism and Jung.

Theosophy, Archetypes, and Mysticism

While it is known that Pollock had undergone Jungian analysis for years, it is unclear what Krasner's own relation was to Jung. According to art historian and Krasner scholar Robert Hobbs, she embraced and subsequently seemed to deny Jungian theories. Hobbs, a 1975 Helena Rubinstein Fellow in the Whitney Museum's Independent Study Program, organized a show that included Krasner and was titled "Subjects of the Artist: New York Painting, 1941–1947." It was mounted in the Whitney's Downtown branch (then at 55 Water Street) and was expanded in 1978, with the help of curator Gail Levin, into "Abstract Expressionism: The Formative Years," on view at the Herbert F. Johnson Museum of Art at Cornell University, the Seibu Museum of Art in Tokyo, and the Whitney in New York. These two exhibitions lent new credence to Krasner's importance as a key figure in the Abstract Expressionist movement and helped ensure her place in the Abstract Expressionist hierarchy. Hobbs later organized a solo exhibition of Krasner's work, which traveled to four locations between 1999 and 2001, ending at the Brooklyn Museum from October 6, 2000 to January 7, 2001. In the catalog accompanying the exhibition, his writing on Krasner is both compassionate and inspiring.[207] Despite Hobbs having written in 1985 that "their [the Abstract Expressionists'] interest in Jung's archetypes was a working premise," he told me, "I think she was very anti-Jung," and then modified that position, reflecting that the differences between the Jungian aspects of Pollock's beliefs and those of Krasner were complex and "deserve further exploration."[208] I would like to assume that there was a move from Freudian-based Surrealism to Jungian-based Abstract Expressionism; however, history shows that the various developments in psychotherapy were not definitive but rather over-lapped and remain in constant flux.

In my view, given the tenor of the times, together with Pollock's associ-ation with Jung and the fact that Krasner was undergoing Sullivanian anal-ysis, it seems likely that Krasner was exposed to the basic assumptions of Jungian psychology and the premises (those originally from Jung) that Har-ry Stack Sullivan had incorporated into his own theories.[209] Most significant in this regard was Jung's concept of the archetype, which Sullivan linked to the interactions that take place in human relationships.[210] The Sullivanians, who co-opted Jungian psychology and put it in more interpersonal terms, are best known for their belief in the importance of identifying and remov-ing difficult relationships that might lead to psychological disintegration.[211] The Sullivanians provided "a new lens for a Jungian theory of psychological complexes," moving from a conceptual approach to an interpersonal one.[212]

The house in Springs had a bookcase with works by and about Jung, in-cluding one by Joseph Campbell, who described in his book *The Hero with a Thousand Faces* what could easily be the psychological path taken by Krasner: "to retreat to those zones of the psyche where the difficulties really reside . . . and break through to the undistorted, direct experience and assimilation of what C. G. Jung called 'archetypal images.'"[213] Campbell pointed out that Jung was not the only one interested in the archetypal image. In his book, he listed Friedrich Nietzsche, Adolf Bastian, Franz Boas, James Frazer, and Sigmund Freud as having recognized this spiritual assimilation, the "symbolism related to the unconscious . . . found in folklore, myths, legends, linguistic idioms."[214]

Among the many other connections Krasner had with Jungian theory were those linked to the Dutch artist Piet Mondrian. Krasner reveled in her stories of going dancing with Mondrian in 1941 when he joined the Ameri-can Abstract Artists (AAA) group.[215] A theosophist and an ardent follower of Jung, he befriended her when she was at the Hofmann School and took se-riously her painting in the fifth annual AAA show at the Riverside Museum in February 9–23, 1941. He, Krasner, and thirty-two other AAA members participated in it.[216] Krasner walked through the exhibition with Mondrian, who told her, "You have a very strong inner rhythm. Never lose it."[217] Em-bracing the basic theosophist cycle of death and rebirth, Mondrian believed deeply in the role of spirituality in his artwork: "All the time I'm driven to the spiritual. Through Theosophy I became aware that art could provide a transition to the finer regions, which I will call the spiritual realm."[218] Kras-ner discussed with me Mondrian's powerful influence on her.

Turning Over the Table

The oft-told story of Pollock turning over the dining-room table during a dinner with friends marks the end of his sobriety. It was a week after

Thanksgiving in 1950; he had been on the wagon for two years. According to Krasner, Namuth, who had been photographing Pollock since July, was, in November, filming him painting on glass behind the house in the bitter cold.[219] Barbara Rose's book *Pollock Painting*, published in 1980, quoted Krasner as saying, "I don't know why Pollock agreed to permit Namuth to film him working. It was entirely contrary to his nature. However, we are very fortunate that he did and that we have such a document."[220] Krasner here showed concern for Pollock's state of mind but also understood the importance of his legacy. She felt fortunate to have the film for posterity.

In *Jackson Pollock: An American Saga*, authors Steven Naifeh and Gregory White Smith describe anger that Pollock supposedly felt toward Namuth for expecting him to brave the elements, which they stated had pushed Jackson to fall off the wagon, ultimately leading to his death.[221]

However, this could be wrongly ascribed to the photographer who helped build the careers of both Pollock and Krasner. Certainly, as a recovering alcoholic, any number of factors could have contributed to Pollock's relapse.[222] Finances continued to haunt him, but a more important factor was likely the 1950 death in a car accident of his doctor Edwin H. Heller. Heller was the only doctor who managed to keep Pollock sober.[223] Additionally, Pollock had recently received what he considered negative criticism for his exhibitions in Venice and Milan, with the press calling his work "chaotic."[224] The daughter of Namuth, Tessa, said that Namuth, Krasner, and Pollock remained good friends after the table-turning incident. In fact, they attended Namuth's annual Labor Day parties in the following years. In addition, Namuth photographed Krasner in her studio in 1962.[225] Of course, the 1949 *Life* magazine article titled "Jackson Pollock: Is He the Greatest Living Painter in the United States?" is often mentioned as having been too much public exposure for this anxiety-ridden artist.[226] In his essay for the book that accompanied the Pollock retrospective exhibition in 1998, the late MoMA curator Kirk Varnedoe states: "From this moment until his death, six years later, alcohol will play an increasingly disruptive role in Pollock's life."[227]

As Krasner mentioned to Hermine Freed in a video interview in 1973, "It was a heavy load to bear."[228]

It's never easy to live with an alcoholic, as I know from my own experience. One is left with a terrible feeling of helplessness and guilt. I suspect my father, whom I adored, had a "drinking problem." Although I was ten when he died, I remember him as always holding a Manhattan in one hand and a Camel in the other. While I never saw him strike my mother, I do remember a fancy dinner with my aunts and uncles around the table. It might have been Christmas, and after many courses, my mother, a very thoughtful and kind woman, said she wished that someone, anyone, would come and "do the dishes." In response, my father furiously pulled the lace tablecloth off the table, sending dishes, glassware, and food into the air. While everyone was shocked, it made an even more indelible impression on me as a child. Lesson learned. It was a cautionary tale about men and power. Abuse comes in many forms, and long after my parents passed away, my aunt Helen, during a family dinner party at Normandy Farms outside of D.C., told me that my father had had an affair with a woman I had considered a close family friend. Thinking back, since my father was never mentioned by my mother after his death, I have to assume my mother tucked him away in one of her imaginary "pockets," where women were expected to hide their grievances—advice she often gave me during my first marriage. In fact, when I was too young to understand, she told me she "might consider remarrying if the new husband were in a wheelchair."

Pollock, in the last years of their marriage, would speak of Krasner's "ugly" appearance and continually make advances to other women.[229] In an interview with Jeffrey Potter in 1982, the artist and CalArts dean Paul Brach said that when they would see each other in the local restaurant Jungle Pete's, Pollock would "come on to all the girls." In fact, he remembered his wife, Miriam Schapiro, one of the leaders of the feminist art movement, telling Pollock when he approached her, "Cut it out, or I'll kick you in the balls." Brach went on to tell Potter, "Jack was fucked up by sexuality." Brach also remembered Krasner calling the couple to come over in the evenings when Pollock was out, to sit with her until "one or two o'clock," ostensibly to help Pollock struggle up to bed but also assuring Krasner that she wouldn't be alone. "Lee was suffering, Jackson was bad, but something very strong was holding them together."[230] In July 1955, Greenberg visited the couple in Springs. In addition to his having written a negative review of Pollock's show at Sidney Janis Gallery the previous year, the lack of hospitality must have been palpable as Krasner and Pollock were fighting—he was drunk, she was enraged. Years later, Greenberg remarked, "He had a sharp sense of how to find someone's soft spot and he was out to wreck her . . . calling her a 'Jewish cunt' and shouting that he had never loved her."[231]

In an infamous conversation between Audrey Flack and Ruth Kligman, Pollock's last "girlfriend," Kligman asked Flack for a list of the most important artists in New York—she reportedly wanted to have relationships with all of them. Pollock was at the top of the list, followed by Willem de Kooning, Franz Kline, Jasper Johns, and others, not to mention Carlos Sansegundo, who would be Kligman's husband from 1964 to 1971.[232] Perhaps most humiliating for Krasner were Kligman's other lovers, those who were to follow Pollock, thus ensuring Kligman's continued high-profile participation in the Hamptons art colony.

Athos Zacharias, artist and de Kooning's studio assistant, recalled Kligman this way: "So Bill told me, he said, 'Go over to Ruth [Kligman's] apartment, because she has some of those [drawings] in frames.' He asked if I could help her sell them. I found an intermediary. Anyway, she hit on me."[233]

Krasner endured many other humiliations—not least those during her years with Marlborough, from 1966 to 1976, when the gallery had to use Pollock's paintings as bait to sell her work. McKinney said, "To me, the only way I could get Lee to release a [Pollock] painting . . . [although] she gave us the paintings to sell, was to offer her work as well. The point is, I didn't dare call her and tell her I just sold a Pollock, because [she would say], 'That's nice. Did they look at Krasner? Did they even look at Krasner?' It was very hard on me. So I'd make sure I showed Krasner. Which I did."[234] As her friend, McKinney tried to protect her, but because she was a woman and the wife and then widow of Pollock, Krasner was continually marginalized and treated with disrespect.

The Artists Club

Crucial to a study of Krasner's art are the inspirations that she incorporated in her work both consciously and unconsciously. While she readily admitted to seeing and directly assimilating works by Matisse, Picasso, and Mondrian, there were other influences to be considered. An assortment of loosely organized artists had begun meeting at the Waldorf Cafeteria (a late-night hangout on Sixth Avenue off 8th Street). Organized by Ibram Lassaw in his studio in 1949, the group was called the Artists Club, and members later gathered in a rented loft at 39 East 8th Street. While the formal 1951 list of charter members did not include Pollock or Krasner, who were then based in East Hampton, guests were always welcome to attend meetings.[235] In 1950 we know Krasner and Pollock were often coming to New York on business. Krasner told Barbara Novak that she and Pollock were "in the Springs" when the Artists Club started, so they wouldn't have attended any lectures.[236] However, both Audrey Flack and Philip Pavia recalled Pollock attending the meetings on 8th Street.[237] Pavia said Pollock was standing in the back during the meetings, "sometimes drunk." Most important, Pavia said that the "women's movement was born" there. "They would get up there and tell us off—aggressive," he said, "and the joke was that we'd make monsters out of these women and got even the wives to talk. They did, too—like Lee, wanting to compete against Jackson."[238] Krasner recalled, "About the club, we used to go and talk about painting, but it got so boring when Motherwell and Rothko discovered how much they loved to talk. They were *always* talking, regular professors. But even though you might not see each other socially as often, you were always seeing each other in some other context, and there was always something that brought you together. You see, it had become a *society* of artists."[239]

Pollock's third solo show at the Betty Parsons Gallery opened in November 1949. During the early winter months of 1950, Pollock and Krasner stayed in Ossorio's home at 9 MacDougal Alley in Manhattan. Further,

Krasner was included in a group show at Betty Parsons in 1950, a year before her solo show there. She recalled that Pollock went to some of the Artists Club meetings, then held at the Cedar Bar, where there was "heavy drinking."[240] They both participated in the "9th Street Show" organized by Leo Castelli in May 1951.[241] Additionally, Lassaw, eventually a neighbor of Krasner's in East Hampton, was reading Jung and was a friend of Campbell's, spending time with him discussing the psychologist's theories.[242] So it seems the couple were often in the city at the time, and as they knew many of the Artists Club members, they must have been aware of Campbell's inspirational teachings. He is listed as one of the early lecturers, a guest speaker at the Artists Club.[243] Thus, it may be fair to suggest that the couple knew about Campbell and that Krasner was familiar with the copy of Campbell's *The Hero with a Thousand Faces* in their Springs living-room library.

In a 1979 interview with Krasner conducted by Novak, we learn that Krasner was moved by Jung's theories after reading *Integration of Personality* in the summer of 1940: "It was fabulous, and I thought how marvelous, you know, that he speaks in my language, even though it has nothing to do with art."[244] In a conflicting statement, she goes on to renounce Jung, in particular, when he starts discussing art and analyzing some of his patients' drawings. However, her thoughts about this form of analysis must have eventually changed, as she and Siegel did a painting together that was to be a tool for her own analysis.[245] Further confirming her interest in Jung, Krasner said she was upset when she attended a conference in Virginia in 1978 and art historians were discussing the Jung book she owned "as if it had been Pollock's."[246] As for Pollock's interest in Jung, it is undeniable. Joseph L. Henderson, a coauthor of *Carl G. Jung: Man and His Symbols*, worked with Pollock for eighteen months, from 1939 to September 1940, and he claimed a breakthrough in Pollock's mental health while using Jung's theories.[247] Henderson is also well known for his ethically questionable public sharing of the artist's drawings.[248]

Leonard Siegel and the Sullivanians

Krasner's introduction to psychiatry may have resulted from Greenberg's suggestion that she seek treatment. He recommended his own analyst, Dr. Jane Pearce, who then directed her to Leonard Israel Siegel.[249]

Krasner seems to have rejected the theoretical Jungian premises to which Pollock subscribed. While he was undergoing treatment with Dr. Joseph L. Henderson between 1939 and September 1940, Pollock created psychologically inspired sketches that related closely to Picasso's *Guernica* and Jungian archetypes.[250] Violet Staub de Laszlo, also a follower of Jung, treated Pollock from April 1941 to 1943.[251] Early on in their relationship, it was Krasner who persuaded Pollock to leave Jungian analysis in favor of homeopathy. However, beginning in the mid-1950s, both were seeing

Sullivanian psychologists, with Pollock under the care of Ralph Klein and Krasner being treated by Siegel.[252]

One should not underestimate the prevalence of the Sullivanian/Jungian movement in the New York art world, especially during the 1950s and '60s. Saul B. Newton officially founded the Sullivan Institute in 1957 with his wife, Jane Pearce, in an attempt to create a viable alternative to the traditional nuclear family, which he viewed as the root of all social anxiety. Located in three buildings on the Upper West Side of Manhattan, the Sullivan Institute operated as both a therapy center and a polyamorous commune, despite the fact that Newton, the leader, had no formal training as a therapist. Unlike other practicing therapists, who were bound by a strict code of ethics, the Sullivanians, as the members of the institute were known, adhered to no such limitations; therapists and other members of the community regularly slept with one another. All members were encouraged to cut ties with their presumably dysfunctional friends and family members. In the 1970s, the group had some five hundred members. After seeing a decline in membership in the 1980s, the Sullivan Institute terminated with the death of Newton in 1991.

Siegel's daughter, Celia, wrote from Australia to Helen Harrison, asking about a painting the doctor had created together with Krasner.[253] She attached a reproduction of the painting, titled *White Clean* (1956), and an image of the back of what appears to be a plywood surface of about 20 by 30 inches, for further examination. The composition itself is a simple white swirl in the center with a figure on the left and calligraphic lines in the lower right, relating to the hieroglyphic gestures in lower right-hand corners of *Rose Red* (1958), *Sun Woman I* (1957), and *Sun Woman II* (1957–ca.1973). It underscores Krasner's compulsion to use her signature in large, looping gestures as a compositional element, working backward from right to left. As Krasner explained, it's "a kind of crazy writing that isn't real," with origins in Hebrew script, which she learned as a child.[254] Perhaps most interesting is the relationship of this no doubt unfinished painting to her eventual gouache series from 1968 to 1969, in which drawing (more a technique of Pollock's) takes command. Given that Krasner, in psychoanalytic discussions with Siegel, was working out her anxieties, the painting could refer to her lifelong difficulty in relationships, especially with straight men (including her father, Pantuhoff, Pollock, and possibly Gibbs). Siegel may have been encouraging Krasner to break with Pollock before she left for Europe in 1956. Written on the reverse side, in Siegel's handwriting, are the title *White Clean* and "Lee Pollock Krasner, 1956."

Celia Siegel, in her August 5, 2008, email, told Harrison:

As I mentioned to you on the phone, my father was Dr. Leonard Israel Siegel, a psychiatrist Lee Krasner saw. From my father's stories it also sounds like they were good friends—my dad used to attend social gatherings at the

Pollock home and describes one party, in particular, that was gatecrashed by Jack Kerouac, leaving Lee rather upset. In 1956, in a therapy session, my father and Lee did this work together. I cannot tell you the exact date of the work unfortunately, nor who did what part of the painting.[255]

In light of the Sullivanian emphasis on avoiding anxiety in relationships, it is not surprising that Klein told Jeffrey Potter in a 1982 interview that he had advised Pollock that his relationship with Krasner "was not useful anymore."[256] Even before Pollock's death, Krasner was working with Siegel, and she, in turn, may have been similarly advised that her relationship with Pollock was no longer useful.

Krasner, a "difficult" woman, steeled by fate, ambition, and talent, had a life that was at once heartbreaking and inspiring. A woman in love, she willingly enabled the physical and psychological needs of Pollock throughout their relationship. In fact, his trusted Jungian psychoanalyst Staub de Laszlo stated that once Pollock married Krasner, he had no need for her analytical services.[257] It is important to note that the psychoanalyst wrote a definitive book on Jung, three years after Pollock was killed.[258]

Dr. Jane Pearce, immediately after seeing Krasner, told her to start therapy. Pollock, at first balking, also went. Greenberg said, "Jackson couldn't stand the idea of Lee and me in therapy without him." That fall, Pollock started sessions with Klein (three times a week), and Krasner began with Siegel.[259] It is possible that she was with him until the early 1960s.[260] As a psychiatrist, with offices in New York City and East Hampton, he was affiliated with the Sullivanians. McKinney remembered that Krasner would go to see Siegel every other day while living in New York City.[261]

Although he was well trained, having earned his M.D. from Johns Hopkins University and been at Bellevue Hospital in New York, Siegel, who had an affiliation with the Sullivanians, was known by East End locals as a psychiatrist of questionable repute.[262] The Sullivanians advocated breaking off with other people to relieve the anxieties of "interpersonal problems." They also advocated freedom among sexual partners.

Zacharias, also a friend of Siegel's, recalled how much the doctor enjoyed an active social life in New York City as well as in East Hampton and how he became a close friend of Krasner's. Siegel finally gave up treating her professionally in favor of squiring her to events. Gail Levin hints that there could have been more to the relationship, especially as he professed open sexual relationships. Levin alluded to Krasner's friend Cile Downs's comment that Siegel "believed that therapists slept with their patients."[263]

Zacharias recalled Siegel as being out of control. My interview with Zacharias, who is still painting Abstract Expressionist canvases in his home in Springs, follows:

AZ: [In the summer, Siegel lived in East Hampton] down by the water. On Three Mile Harbor Road in that house that he lost to his wife. In the winter he had this apartment [in New York City]. He was once, I think, in Ireland or Scotland, he was arrested. He was incoherent. He was painting paintings on his bedsheets. Once he came to my studio, after I got divorced. I had a studio on West 48th Street. He came in and he started painting on one of my canvases.

RA: He was a psychologist?

AZ: Yeah, but he was going off the deep end at that time. He had rented a house; he owned a house out by the water there, he lost it in the divorce. He'd be playing loud music there and smoke his cigars, and God knows what drugs he was taking. He employed me. I was kind of his assistant also. I was taking care of people like him and my wife and Bill [de Kooning]. All alcoholics. That was my role. When someone in the family died, Len sent my son somewhere to grab up some diamonds, a safe deposit box or something, and deliver them to Len. I wasn't part of that. I was teaching, I think. Len was a good friend, and around that time, I was divorced, so he and I would double-date sometimes. He had a place on the West Side, a very nice apartment, and then he was toning down. He wasn't taking drugs, and he wasn't drinking too much. Then he moved to Australia, I think, to escape [alimony] payments. He had one or two children. Two boys, I think.

RA: He had a daughter, because the daughter wrote a letter to the Pollock-Krasner House. The daughter's name is Celia. . . . So you think Len went to Australia to escape?

AZ: Payments. Payments for custody. Family court. Divorce. I mean, she was going to take him for all that she could, right? She was mean, too.

RA: I actually heard that his wife was in Australia.

AZ: Oh, I think he married again. He married again, then he made a trip to New York with his new wife, and he was arranging to meet me and another good friend of his, but the meeting never happened. I guess he was afraid we would say too much to the new wife.

RA: So did you ever go to him as a doctor?

AZ: No.

RA: Do you know anyone else besides Lee who used him as a psychoanalyst?

AZ: Well, he once had me do some carpentry in his office [on the] Upper West Side. Before he married the woman, who was my model, and he said something which I thought was very inappropriate. He said that the young lady waiting outside in the office there, she's got a sexual problem. I guess he was trying to enlist me in [taking care of her sexual needs] . . . you know. That's not for me. . . . I never got involved in any of it, but I think he was with a group of psychologists called the Sullivanians. I put up with it because I figured he was a little off.[264]

In the late 1960s and '70s, I, too, was undergoing psychiatric treatment. With an abusive husband, I found the violence in my marriage had become intolerable, but I was torn by guilt because of my children. I couldn't deal with their not having a father present, a situation I had experienced in my own life thirty years earlier. My father, Edward Charles Stevens, educated in Washington, D.C., as a lawyer, had reluctantly stayed in the family business at the request of his father until Pearl Harbor, when he enlisted in the Marine Corps and was assigned to the Intelligence Division at Fort DeRussy in Hawaii. He died as a young man of forty-two, having incurred a war-related disability—rheumatic fever, or "cat" fever in Marine Corps jargon, which resulted in his suffering a lethal heart attack in 1950 when I was ten years old.

My mother and I moved to a tiny two-bedroom house in Kensington, Maryland, across the street from the home of a pedophile. The years that followed were confusing and full of guilt. In high school, I began seeing a psychiatrist who had a home office in the neighborhood, a Dr. Katzenellenbogen; and again, toward the end of my marriage in 1968, I sought care from the head of psychiatry at Upstate Medical Center in Syracuse, New York. Dr. Frank Reed guided me, ever so painfully, into a new way of seeing myself and others. I continued seeing various analysts over the course of the next thirty years.

I was certainly not unique. Many in the art world, including artists working mid-century in East Hampton, were also focusing on their internal dilemmas, studying the theories of Jung and Freud, in order to come to terms with their doubts and fears.

Psychic Powers

In my 1974 interview with Krasner, she said she didn't believe in God, but she did acknowledge a higher power. I particularly enjoyed the conversation we had about her paternal grandmother, who was said to have had psychic powers—mystical powers to tell fortunes and prophesy the future.[265] I suspect these were talents that Krasner recognized in herself as well.

When asked if she thought Krasner believed in mystical elements, Barbara Rose said, "My impression was that she thought Jackson's ghost was there [in the house] right after he died. He was guiding her hand" when she was painting. She also recalled Krasner "believing in spirits," saying that, like her grandmother, she was "definitely psychic."[266]

In the course of our interactions, I told Krasner about my own family. Growing up, I was often reminded of the Salem witch to whom I was related via my maternal grandfather, Henry Spaulding Parsons, who was a member of the Parsons clan from Northampton, Massachusetts.[267] According to the records of the Church of Latter-Day Saints, there are several witches to whom I am related. The most recent was Martha Ingalls Allen Carrier, who was born in Andover, Massachusetts between 1643 and 1650 and who was convicted and hanged in Salem on August 19, 1692. Martha was the first to be accused of witchcraft in Andover. She went to prison with two of her children, who were hung by their feet until they testified to her wrongdoing.[268] Martha never confessed. The Massachusetts government apologized to Thomas Carrier for the hanging of his wife and then reversed the conviction. She was exonerated in 1711, and her family received a small sum as recompense for her conviction: seven pounds, six shillings. While the court documents do not specifically mention her psychic powers, they do reveal that her crime was "an independence of mind and an unsubmissive character."[269] Of course, Krasner, recalling her mother's words about her being "too independent-minded," would have related to these witchlike traits.

In Search of Beauty

Krasner showed an interest in fashion design even in her youth, when she would draw pictures based on style-magazine layouts.[270] Pantuhoff, her first serious relationship, was known to have dressed her and even applied her makeup, something the Surrealists did for their wives. In Provincetown, Pantuhoff took sensuous nude photographs of Krasner on the beach. Clearly, in her early years as a young single woman on the Greenwich Village art scene, she exuded an aura of sensuality. Her large lips and breasts defined her appearance. She had been a model for the photographer Herbert Matter and seemed to be quite comfortable in silk pajamas as a waitress serving drinks to art-world figures such as Harold Rosenberg at Sam Johnson's in 1932.[271] When she arrived at the Hofmann School to enroll in classes, wearing black net stockings, high-heeled shoes, and a tight skirt, Lillian Olinsky (later married to Frederick Kiesler) checked her in and was so impressed that she arranged with Hofmann for Krasner to receive a scholarship to take the classes.[272]

Donald McKinney remembered: "When Lee walked across the room, you noticed it. Her movement was beautiful. She had that narrow waist, and the rest was all there. She was sexually exciting to certain men, I would say. In a way, she was attractive."[273]

Fig. 21
Lee Krasner at the beach in Provincetown, MA c. 1935-38.

Fig. 22
Krasner on the
beach in East
Hampton, NY,
1954.

Her interest in fashion would later extend to the Charles James wardrobe she acquired for her visit to London in May 1961. The occasion was the Pollock exhibition (of Krasner's collection) at the Marlborough Gallery. She was meeting Gibbs, her lover, for the event. Also, her nephew Ron Stein had married Frances Patiky, a fashion editor and artistic director for Chanel.[274] Beginning in 1963, Stein and Patiky spent time in their house (originally the "small barn") on Krasner's adjacent property and were very closely involved with Krasner's social life.

R. Couri Hay, a writer for *Interview* magazine and a New York marketing director, told me about Charles James in a 2017 interview:

I believe she [sculptor Elizabeth Strong-Cuevas, granddaughter of John D. Rockefeller] was the conduit. Because there was a conduit between Lee and Charles [James], and what they told Lee was, you cannot go to Europe, to London [for the Pollock exhibition in 1961], with the clothes you have—you need a wardrobe. You need to look fabulous. You need to represent, you know, all that is America. All that is the great historical role you played in Pollock's life, and your own role. You gotta dress up, you gotta look good, you gotta be sharp, you gotta be edgy. Because in those days no one could do edgy and classic. Who kept the line between sex and vulgarity and complete properness? Charles knew what that line [was] between oh my god, isn't that over the top and isn't it completely a proper dress. So he drew that line.

Hay, a protégé of James and the lover of the celebrated designer Halston, said:

Charles told her himself, "You must have a wardrobe." So he set about making her a nine-piece wardrobe, which was called a travel wardrobe, for this show at the Marlborough Gallery. And during this process, they became friendly, because you couldn't help it. You can be a client without being a friend but not with Charles. Because you had to care about Charles. Charles screamed, Charles always wanted to be appreciated, but there was this little "take care of me" part, there was always this little boy part of Charles that wanted to be taken care of. And so he set about making quite an ambitious nine pieces. Lee gave all the pieces to the Metropolitan Museum of Art, where they are today.[275]

Elizabeth Strong-Cuevas told me she had given a dinner party for James to which Krasner had been invited. It turned out to be a hilarious evening; at one point, Strong-Cuevas was carrying a tray of food in the air while James was pinning a halter around her breasts.[276]

The designer Harry Striebel created the wardrobe for Krasner's opening at the Whitechapel Gallery in London in 1965, and her fur coats were from Ritter Brothers, including a sable, as well as a leopard coat which she wore to her exhibition in Tuscaloosa, Alabama.[277]

In my interview with McKinney, he remembered: "If we were staying at the Ritz, she would dress for the Ritz. But she would do it with confidence. She wouldn't be a little nobody. I always liked the way she was with everything."[278]

The Western artist husband of artist Grace Hartigan, Harry Jackson, for whom Krasner had great disdain, told Helen Harrison, "Her ass was God."[279]

Fig. 23
Travel suit by
Charles James,
designed for
Krasner.

Yet clearly never a slave to fashion, Krasner, when I knew her, wore a tentlike dress that effectively hid her body. Having had a surprise "in the buff" encounter with her in the upstairs hallway, I recall she looked rather like the *Venus of Willendorf*. But even then, as I can't help noting in the photographs I took of her in 1974 in her loose yellow housedress, she came off as comfortable and almost friendly-looking, well groomed, with a neat hairdo and a hint of a smile.

The Women's Movement in East Hampton

In a 2011 article in the *East Hampton Star*, Krasner's biographer Gail Levin wrote: "Ashawagh Hall in Springs often hosts art, but one show, in 1975, made art history. For the United Nations' International Women's Year, two artists, Joyce Kozloff and Joan Semmel, organized *Women Here and Now*."[280]

On view were major paintings by the two organizers and by Audrey Flack, Miriam Schapiro, Perle Fine, Li-lan, Jane Wilson, Hedda Sterne, Jane Freilicher, Betty Parsons, Leatrice Rose, Alice Baber, Lynda Benglis, Buffie Johnson, Fay Lansner, and Elaine de Kooning, as well as work by three photographers: Anne Schwartz (Sager), Dorothy Beskind, and Tracy Boyd, all of whom were affiliated with the East End of Long Island. Semmel and Kozloff, who started organizing the show that summer, found themselves living in East Hampton among the legendary figures of Abstract Expressionism and felt overwhelmed by the male patriarchy that dominated both art and criticism. Propelled by their feminist beliefs, they succeeded in raising the money to rent Ashawagh Hall.

Not all of the women invited agreed to participate. Even though Krasner had designed a poster for the annual Springs exhibition the previous year, it was no surprise that she curtly refused to exhibit with the other women.[281] She feared being marginalized as a woman painter, particularly in a community where she had long been exhibiting side by side with her husband

and others, including de Kooning and Motherwell at Guild Hall and at the artist-run Signa Gallery.[282]

Semmel told of how she was assigned "the unpleasant chore of calling her" about being in the show: "I had to screw up all my courage for that. . . . I can recall her answer when I phoned about Ashawagh Hall, in her inimitable raspy voice, 'I don't want Women's Lib in East Hampton!'"[283]

It was 1975, and Semmel, who was staying in Elaine de Kooning's studio, recalled:

> [Elaine and I] shared it for a little while. Then I was there the rest of the summer by myself. While Joyce [Kozloff] was there, we curated the show called "Women Artists Here and Now." We called Lee to invite her. I got an earful. First Joyce tried talking to her, and then I tried talking to her. She was adamant. She was an artist, and she wasn't at this time going to be classified as a woman artist. There was no way she was going to show in a women's [exhibition]. She was very particular about it, in no uncertain terms. There was no way I could convince her. There was no way Joyce could convince her. P.S., she was never in the show. I, of course, was disappointed that she wouldn't do that, and a little bit pissed. That's the word. She wasn't interested in being in anything, even political, but I understood, and she made it clear that she had worked very hard all her life to be seen as a professional, and she was an artist before she was anything else, and that she didn't want that undermined.[284]

Looking back on it, "feminism" was a dirty word. The women who said they were "feminists paid a heavy price for it in a lot of different ways. Some of the best known of the women artists [Semmel, Kozloff, Frankenthaler, Joan Mitchell, de Kooning] benefited by virtue of the men they were with. They adopted the attitudes and ideas of these men. They had entrée into their circles but were always viewed condescendingly. In the end, Lee promoted Pollock far more than herself. He needed a mother. He needed a secretary. He needed somebody who managed his work, and she did all that for him . . . [and yet] was humiliated publicly. It was really very bad. One understands why she might've been somewhat grumpy at being asked, especially out here, to be in a women's show.[285]

Since I was invited to Springs as a card-carrying feminist to interview Krasner the year prior to the Ashawagh Hall exhibition, I know she had accepted, in part, the practical importance of the women's movement. Her effort was to separate herself from those claiming a specific feminist aesthetic. Semmel and Kozloff explained the importance of the show: "We needed to be seen as separate to establish identity." They realized that to achieve that goal, radical action would be necessary.

This was the moment when there was considerable discussion about what constituted feminist art. Consciousness-raising groups and those of us who worked, albeit unsuccessfully, to pass the Equal Rights Amendment stood up for equality of opportunity with red-hot passion. Language changed from *Mrs./Miss* to *Ms*. Women's behavior shifted from humble dependency to responsible independence. We were on our own, calling our own shots, raising our voices, and thus enjoying self-worth and entitlement. In the professional art world, both Krasner and I were involved in organizations such as the Women's Caucus for Art, where she received an award in 1979. I was proud to help make whatever efforts came to fruition that much more successful.[286]

McKinney explained Krasner's position to me:

> When the women's lib started, Lee was going to have nothing to do with it. It annoyed her. . . . She would try to divorce herself from the movement: "They should do it and fight their own battles and that kind of thing," she said. She was very ambiguous with her affections with women. When they picked her up as the banner, she changed her tune. She really did. . . . She's smart. She realized what was happening and, all of a sudden, she was being courted and taken and reviewed.[287]

Describing the moment, Robert Goldwater, art historian and husband of Louise Bourgeois, recalled, "The consciousness of being on the frontier, of being ahead rather than behind, of having absolutely no models . . . of being entirely and completely on one's own—this was a new and heady atmosphere."[288]

Lucy Lippard, one of the important leaders in the feminist art movement, explained that while misogyny was pervasive, it could be easily overlooked even by the most diligent feminist. She said that "after the birth of my feminine consciousness [in 1970], I still have to question every assumption, every reaction I have, in order to examine them for signs of preconditioning."[289]

In 1980, at one of our Sunday evening Women's Caucus meetings at Printed Matter bookstore in New York, Lippard spoke further about her thoughts on the evolution of the movement. She discussed the appropriate path to building a feminist society, a society where men and women were equals, suggesting that the approach would be a combination of action and theory. In addition to discussing practical ways women artists could find support for their work, she also talked about aesthetic theory. One important point that came up during the meeting which I associated with Krasner was Lippard's declaration that the women's art movement was no longer interested in identifying primary forms relating to gender. She was further adamant that she "doesn't want to take women out of nature and put them into culture—there was no need for a dichotomy!"[290] Krasner may have had the soul of a "chauvinist" (competing somewhat unscrupulously with both men and women in the art marketplace) but the heart of a feminist (embracing equality of the sexes). Despite her refutations, the feminist "sensibility," as seen in the paintings, comes from deep within her soul and helps define the message.

Reading

There were many occasions when people read aloud to Krasner, as is revealed in the chapter five. Hobbs and Levin have both posited that dyslexia may have contributed to her difficulty in reading.[291] I would speculate that while Krasner enjoyed being read to by her father and brother when she was young, her real problems with reading comprehension came as an adult.[292] As Hobbs observed, she believed her house had become haunted after Pollock's death, and this triggered in her a need to have someone there, ostensibly to read to her, as Richard Howard and Sanford Friedman did when they slept in the small barn on the adjacent property.[293] In addition, the traumatic brain injury or stroke she suffered in 1963 may have added to her reading disorder as well as to her growing psychological unrest.[294]

James Valliere asked Krasner to mark up the list of books accounting for what was in the Springs home library, indicating which were hers and which had been Pollock's. Because she returned the list to him unmarked, Valliere assumed they were all Pollock's.[295] But another possibility is that she simply couldn't read the list. Of course, B. H. Friedman, was summoned to recite from his Pollock book, and likewise, Eugene Thaw and Francis O'Connor read Krasner contributions to the Pollock catalogue raisonné before publication. I, too, was called into action to read aloud from our interview transcript in 1974. She delighted in editing it by striking out huge passages.[296]

The Paintings as Self-Portraits

Krasner told me once that as a child, after her sister Ruth was born, she came to see herself as the "ugly duckling. Ruth was the pretty one!"[297] Further, Igor Pantuhoff, Krasner's lover in the 1930s, was known to have called her "ugly" to her face. In Jeffrey Potter's biography of Pollock, *To a Violent Grave*, an artist friend and one of the "Irascibles," Fritz Bultman, recalled Krasner's early relationship with Pantuhoff: "Her relationship with Igor was very difficult; she was tormented by him, such as saying in front of her, 'I like being with an ugly woman because it makes me feel more handsome.' . . . There was a large element of masochism in Lee, just as there was a large element of sadism."[298] However, it is not necessarily how others see her but as she saw herself that is one of the keys to the meaning of her explosive work.

Examining more than five decades of Krasner's life together with the work she created during that time offered me the opportunity to view her paintings and her often dramatic artistic transitions. Viewing her through the lens of female archetypes—an approach inspired by Jung and Campbell and outlined by Carol Pearson in her book *The Hero Within: Six Archetypes We Live By*—provides a broad platform for theoretical discussion and offers some new ways to understand the significance of Krasner's contribution in the arts.

Pearson lays out stages in the course of a woman's psychological development represented by commonly held archetypes. She points out six such milestones that I discerned in Krasner's work: the Orphan, in *Self Portrait* (ca. 1928), in bibbed overalls; the Innocent, in *Self Portrait* (ca.1929–1930), with flower; the Martyr, in the dying and rebirth of the 1950s and 1976–1977 collages; the Wanderer, in the "Earth Green" series (1957–1958); the Warrior, in the "Umber" series (1959–1962); and the Magician, in the "Eleven Ways to Use the Words To See" series (1976–1978). Krasner's work spans a universe of complex emotions. While she is both her own worst enemy and her hero within, she gives rise to an entirely unique artistic vocabulary.

Figs. 24-25
Krasner in her studio, 1969, painting *Portrait in Green* with large, sweeping gestures.

The Orphan

My study of Krasner's early self-portraits makes an interesting case for their relationship with Jungian archetypes and allows for insights into Krasner's personality. However, because they are not all signed or dated, their sequence is somewhat in question. Dating the self-portraits is made difficult because Krasner made a series of them at the National Academy of Design over a two- or three-year period around 1930. The 1928 self-portrait is firmly dated because it was used as entry in the life-drawing class starting in January 1929.[299] In my interview with her, Krasner discussed a number of self-portraits, "in the Academy vein." As she continued to paint these, she remembered, "I've got more academic, I'm trying like crazy to get everybody, and I got that far."

The *Self-Portrait* of 1928, done at her parents' home in Greenlawn, New York, introduces a new Krasner to the stage. Campbell observed in *The Hero with a Thousand Faces* how young women, striking out on their own, tend to experience an "awakening of the self."[300] He called it the "mystery of transfiguration—a rite or moment of spiritual passage, which when complete, amounts to a dying and a birth."[301] Krasner was making a stand, taking charge, and showing the fierceness for which she became known. As she said, she continued throughout her life to deal with the "same polarities that are in this portrait."[302] These polarities may also have to do with her other assertion—that her work is like the "swing of a pendulum."[303] In discussing the painting in relation to the Orphan archetype, we can surmise that Krasner was declaring a growing independence from her family. With bib overalls, short cropped hair, and a steely gaze, she was cutting herself loose and charging ahead. On her own, she claimed the polarities of both her male and her female psyche. This duality in her personality suggests a sharp contrast within Krasner, regarded by some as a benevolent friend and by others as an angry adversary. The yin and yang of her personality adds significance to the heart of her story. In the landscape, she finds freedom—assimilating herself into the realm of nature. Of course, the subject of that gaze is herself in the mirror. "I think my painting is so biographical if anyone can take the trouble to read it," she told Cindy Nemser in 1973.[304]

Krasner's teachers questioned her claim that she painted *Self Portrait* (1928) outdoors. Was their concern that she had defied the Academy's protocol by venturing outside? Or was it that they didn't believe she had painted it herself because it was so well done? Krasner was accused of defying the "rules," just as she had done when she ventured into the basement to paint the still life with fish.[305] She was choosing her own path, turning her back on the false distinction between male and female mores.

The Innocent

The Innocent archetype is someone who lives in an unfallen world, a green Eden, where all his or her needs are cared for. The Krasner self-portrait of around 1929–1930, created at her family home in Brooklyn, apparently after the self-portrait with bib overalls, could easily be another of this series she did to please her teachers at the Academy, getting more "academic." It shows the artist holding a single flower, a symbol of nature and innocence. Her hair is thick and brushed back from her face, her white smocked blouse provides a soft drape over her body, a big fern sits on a bare wooden table behind her, and the basement window is open, welcoming in fresh air and sunshine. There is even a trace of a halo around her, perhaps a mere convention Krasner picked up at the Academy but one that is nonetheless effective. The painting was done in the more traditional style of Charles Courtney Curran, her teacher at the Academy, and could relate to a portrait by Gauguin, *The Delightful Land* (1892), of a young woman holding a flower, the fantasy of the innocent girl and the unfallen world. Krasner, who remembered walking through a field of flowers near her home, knew Gauguin's work from one of her favorite exhibitions at MoMA, "Cézanne, Gauguin, Seurat, van Gogh" in 1929. Although this particular painting was not included in the show[306] similar paintings were. Krasner's self-portrait with a flower became a gift to her good friend Eda Mirsky, who witnessed her painting it.[307] Of course, at this time, we know that Krasner was dealing with many challenges of family, religion, and school, but even so, her intention to portray herself as the untainted, the "innocent," was done convincingly.

The Martyr

Although she never wavered from supporting her husband, Krasner also became his prisoner. Driving was a problem for her, and therefore, she only sporadically left the house.[308] On occasion, however, she did drive, according to McKinney on his stay in the early 1960s, but for the most part, she would say she couldn't. In 1954, Patsy Southgate offered to give Krasner driving lessons in return for art classes.[309] However, Pollock's behavior was so erratic that leaving his side was risky. Reflecting the archetype of the Martyr, Krasner worked and took responsibility, made sacrifices, suffered, but also, with her domineering personality, may have deprived others (Pollock) of a sense of self.[310]

Amazingly, during these tumultuous times, despite her sacrifices and constant humiliation, Krasner was able to develop remarkable new avenues for artistic expressions, primarily in the medium of collage.

The Martyr archetype as it relates to Krasner and her work, plays out in the collages of the 1950s. These works represent a recycling of materials that led to life-size canvases of extraordinary color and power. Perhaps Krasner's first encounter with Hans Hofmann in his classes led her to see how effective—in fact, magical—the art of collage could be. She must have been shocked when he took her drawing and tore it in half and then put it back to show her a different compositional path.[311] In my interview with her, contradicting what she and others have said, she didn't give Hofmann much credit for her development, citing instead Matisse and Picasso as her true inspirations. Certainly, the energy she felt in that classroom with Hofmann and his students gave her confidence, and his Friday-night lectures, to which Krasner invited Greenberg, must have been full of the kind of art theory that would have appealed to any young artist.[312] Of course, Picasso and Matisse were famous for their collage compositions, incorporating everything from newspaper headlines to ball fringe. Like paint and canvas, found materials had become a valid medium in the work of many contemporary artists, especially those of the Abstract Expressionist school, including Anne Ryan, de Kooning, Bultman, and Motherwell. But none made their compositions so uniquely to reflect their "own image" as Krasner had.

Following her experience with Hofmann, Krasner's early interest in collage, especially as it relates to her mosaic tables of 1947 and '48, demonstrates her passion for the handmade. The simple task of art making becomes increasingly evident. Both she and Pollock experimented in "crafts"—he, while in the WPA, using small pieces of glass and tile to make mosaic paintings, later throwing clay pots, and finally introducing found objects into his paintings such as *Full Fathom Five* (1947), and she with her wagon-wheel "found object" tables, made as she huddled in front of the stove during their early winters in Springs. The source of her passion for taking materials destined for the trash bin (discarded, torn paper and canvas, sometimes even from Pollock's and her own cast-off drawings) and turning them into art probably derived from her financially strapped years during the WPA but also from the feminist refocus on the value of handmade art, such as weaving, ceramics, and basket making.

While Pollock, who had been sober for two years (1948-1950), again became a serious problem, Krasner was coming into her own. She was upstairs in the tiny spare bedroom expressing her rage in a torrent of tearing and cutting. Many of the resulting fragments had been applied to earlier paintings shown at the 1951 Betty Parsons exhibition. These included collages created between 1953 and 1955, those on view at the Stable Gallery in 1955 and others at the Corcoran in 1975. Scraps from Pollock's drawings and paintings were applied to her compositions, such as *Bald Eagle* (1955) and *Color Totem* (1955), additions he would have certainly known about and agreed to.[313] Also in the Stable and Corcoran exhibitions were *Milkweed* (1955), *Shooting Gold* (1955), and *Stretched Yellow* (1955), exhibiting a process by which Krasner would destroy the old to create the new, an aesthetic filtering of what she thought did or didn't "work."

The Wanderer

The Wanderer archetype allows for a way to view Krasner's work completed soon after Pollock's death. While she was not prepared for this life-changing event, she had somehow reset her psyche, producing unexpectedly jubilant works. Pearson wrote: "Individuals need to address Wanderer issues every time they go through major transitions to answer the question, 'Who am I this time?'"[314]

Wanderers set off alone in pursuit of their identity and desires, often acting in "direct opposition to a conformist norm."[315] In her "Earth Green" series (1957–1958), Krasner turned her paintings into erotic celebrations, sexual romps through nature guided by her libido.[316]

Breasts dangle from the monumental canvases as if wishing to be stroked; vibrant colors scream for attention. Filled with joy, the paintings point to unanticipated discoveries and welcome taboo subjects. Certainly, Krasner's new studio, the barn originally used by Pollock, gave her room to breathe, to explore, to explode—and she did. She freed herself from Hofmann, who advocated nature as subject matter, and Pollock, who claimed he was nature but was often trapped in the formal concerns of art making, the materials and the technique. Yet, as she would be the first to point out, both of them informed her new phase, the "Earth Green" series.

As Pearson explains: "If wanderers choose their own journey, they may feel guilty, for the act of claiming one's own identity and developing an ego is portrayed as an insult to the gods."[317] The "Earth Green" series is among Krasner's most beautiful work.

Exhibited in 1958 at the Martha Jackson Gallery, these paintings signaled a new direction for Krasner. In 1957, she started consistently signing her full name, Lee Krasner, to the paintings, thus taking her rightful place in the art-world hierarchy. And in one of her most glorious paintings of the period, *Listen* (1957), she scrawled her signature as an element of the painting composition itself. This painting became synonymous with the situation in which Krasner found herself—free of the burden of her husband, still anguished and guilty over her loss and her imminent solitary life, yet alert with anticipation for what her future might bring. Many women maintaining the illusion of self-sufficiency are terrified of abandonment.[318] While she was frantically leaping in the air, brush in hand, as she told Richard Howard, she was crying: "[The] tears were literally pouring down."[319]

In *Listen* (1957), a looping tan outline of fecund shapes, in which human forms morph into scented blossoms, is filled with vibrant pinks, fuchsias, and citrus greens.[320] In other paintings from this series—*Sun Woman I* (1957) and *The Seasons* (1957)—she used the same motifs. According to *New York Times* critic John Russell, *The Seasons* is "one of the most remarkable American paintings of its date."[321] The "Earth Green" series culminates in a monumental canvas (69¼ by 127⅞ inches) titled *Rose Red* (1958), in which breasts have been transformed into seed pods, and the scrawled signature from the lower right-hand corner of previous paintings is more of an abstract scribble. Interestingly, *Butterfly Weed* (formerly titled *Orange*, 1957–1981) exemplifies Krasner's ability to reimagine a painting of the '50s into one of the '80s. From a figurative composition with eyes—similar to *Prophecy* (1956)—to an abstract view of nature, she moves comfortably from her earlier imagery of embracing figures to plants entangled in the undergrowth. She has shifted from the Abstract Expressionist idioms of the unconscious and returned to nature as subject matter, reestablishing human connection in these lush odes to rebirth and renewal.

The Warrior

It's worth noting that Krasner met Gibbs in 1959, which is about the same time that she began painting the "Umber" series. In fact, two days after they met, Gibbs bought *Cool White* (1959), one of the earliest of these works. It seems she had already begun using the minimal colors of the "Umber" series before the two met, but the work continued to evolve and expand for the next four years.[322] Many of the paintings feature tightly rendered calligraphy and a muted palette. *Eyes in the Weeds* (1963), which Krasner painted with her left hand about six months after having the aneurysm and just after injuring her right arm by falling on the sidewalk in East Hampton, is an example of her more reflective attitude, as is the classic *Kufic* (1965), one of her most successful compositions using this reductive approach.[323] In this work, the drawing turns to writing, which in turn transforms into hieroglyphs.[324] It is Krasner speaking to us through symbols, like writing on a chalkboard.[325] There are certain significant breakthroughs in the series, works in the style of Arshile Gorky's sensuous *The Liver Is the Cock's Comb* (1944), which relate to Krasner's *Right Bird Left* (1965), *Pollination* (1968), and *The Green Fuse* (1968), which combine her signature green and red along with soft leaf- and breastlike forms, portraying nature at its most verdant. Hundreds of gestures crammed into an enormous space, more than eleven feet in length, *Right Bird Left* invites the viewer to step inside and experience the jarring effect of confrontational vibrations.

"The ritual that underlies the Warrior myth is found, of course, in war" and in Krasner's case, in the battle she fought with herself as well as the one she fought with the art world.[326] The death of her mother, not long after that of her husband, heightened her internal battering.[327] As Campbell states, it is "the hero that guides society," not in the moments of great victories but "in the silences of his personal despair."[328] Krasner emerged from this series having created one of her most powerful bodies of work: the "Umber" paintings (1959–1962).

Perhaps, in addition to the influences related to her personal grief, her visit to Jean Fautrier while she was in Paris inspired her to explore the tragic side of her psyche.[329] The leader of the Tachisme group of artists in France, Fautrier created paintings and sculptures, closely associated with the unsettling war-related guilt of the French public that constituted "a dialogue about the horror of war and torture" in Europe.[330] Krasner knew his work well—his dark, scratchy compositions—as he was included with her and Pollock in the McMillen Inc. Gallery exhibition in 1942. Krasner went out of her way to go to Chatenay-Malabry, a few miles outside Paris, to visit Fautrier.

A complete reversal from the "Earth Green" series, the "Umber" works were composed mainly in black, brown, and ochre pigment. When I saw them at the 1979 Pace Gallery exhibition "Lee Krasner: Paintings 1959–1962," during which Krasner and I had our picture taken in front of *Night Watch* (1960), I was struck by the variety and power of these huge canvases. In the last stage of the paintings, she seems to have gone back into the snarling black coils with some dabs of creamy white, used to open up the composition. In most of the canvases, there is a chorus of eyes watching from every angle.

Of particular importance was *The Guardian* (1960), first exhibited at the Howard Wise Gallery in 1960, again in 1962, and then at the Whitechapel Gallery in 1965, followed by six group exhibitions at the Whitney. It was on the title wall of the 1979 Pace show. It was purchased by B. H. Friedman's Uris Brothers Foundation as a gift to the Whitney the following year.

Krasner's friends, and "summer sitters" Richard Howard and Sanford Friedman have been credited with helping her title her works, many of which bear ominous suggestions of danger and death, such as *The Guardian* (1960), *Night Watch* (1960), and *The Gate* (1959).[331] With her psychically charged brushwork, the tragic moment of loss influenced many of her works, including *Charred Landscape* (1960), *Polar Stampede* (1960), *What Beast Must I Adore?* (1961), *White Rage* (1961), and *Assault on the Solar Plexus* (1961), reflecting the anger and fear Krasner was experiencing. Her bouts of insomnia led her to paint these dark personal battles of the unconscious.[332] The Warrior archetype is often related to the concept of the hero, and in Krasner's case, the hero must go to war and fight the "beast," her own emotions.

David Anfam suggested that Krasner was independent of the ever-present specter of Pollock: "Metaphorically couched, this is not Pollock's ventriloquism, as it were, still less is it the muted 'Lena Krassner'; but the sovereign Lee Krasner at last speaking loud, clear, and often with anger."[333]

Going deep into the unconscious, she searched for some kind of revelation that would give her work clarity, authenticity, meaning. She also took on the Abstract Expressionist "establishment." Her disagreement with Greenberg over the "Umber" series not being what he had wanted for her 1959 one-person French & Co. exhibition, her questioning of Rosenberg's Action Painting theory, her battles with de Kooning, Ossorio, and Friedman—all these conflicts, and more, are documented in the paintings.[334] According to Pearson, "Warriors must be tough-minded and realistic in order to change the world by slaying the dragons [beasts]."[335]

Warriors might also look inward to extract the dragons of the psyche. In a world where females were undervalued, Krasner fought fiercely against the invisibility of the woman artist. She also raged against herself and the beast within.[336]

Describing her travels into the depths of the underworld, Krasner said, "I was going down deep into something which wasn't easy or pleasant."[337] This conflict, as seen in the "Umber" series—those without significant color or harmony, angry dismissals of more acceptable abstract forms—led Krasner to isolation and even eclipse. Fortunately, Gibbs—her consultant, dealer, friend, and lover—gave Howard Wise the "thumbs-up" when she asked him for advice about the possibility of Wise showing her work.[338] Unfortunately, Krasner's relationship with the Howard Wise Gallery ended in 1963, when she asked Wise to fund the shipping of her paintings to London for the Whitechapel exhibition. While Wise declined to underwrite the shipping expenses to England, he also released Krasner from her contract with him.[339] Although the catalog thanks the Marlborough-Gerson Gallery,[340] Jeffrey D. Grove, in his biographical addendum to the Lee Krasner catalogue raisonné, states that she paid for the Whitechapel exhibition herself.[341] With the "Umber" series, she had turned her back on all the earlier elements of her compositions, particularly those deemed attractive or decorative, with vibrant colors and organic shapes; she then dug into a world of despair with an authenticity that cannot be denied. Unlike the late melancholic works of Rothko, Krasner's paintings are far from repetitive in tone or content. She maintained a stand against the Abstract Expressionist painters who continually repeated themselves, stating that they had turned their backs on art as a living statement; they were "dead."[342]

As I walked into the gallery at the Royal Academy exhibition in 2016, curated by David Anfam and Edith Devaney, with Pollock's painting hanging on one side and David Smith's sculpture in the middle of the room, I was overjoyed to see that Krasner took center stage. She held her own. I thought Anfam made an amazing choice. Almost sixteen feet in length, *The Eye Is the First Circle* (1960) has a quiet certitude that others in the "Umber" series do not. It is Krasner without pretensions, at her most vulnerable and, at the same time, her most confident. There is a minimal lacelike tracery of thin brushstrokes outlining soft tan puddles that did not allow for second thoughts. The work is a single bold expression.

Anfam wrote of the "Umber" paintings: "Indeed, the final impact is electric, tonic and thus life-affirming."[343] When I asked him recently about his choice of *The Eye Is the First Circle* (1960) for the Royal Academy of Arts exhibition, "Abstract Expressionism," in 2016, he said it was "so brilliant" that he "had to have it."[344] By installing it in the same room with Smith's and Pollock's work, Anfam announced to the world that Lee Krasner held her own among all these giants in the Abstract Expressionist movement.

The Magician

In her final series of large paintings, Krasner returned to collage, as seen in the series "Eleven Ways to Use the Words To See" (1976–1978). These works exemplify the archetype of the Magician, who teaches about creation, about our capacity to bring into being what never was there before, about claiming our role as co-creators of the universe.[345] Her fascination with time and the verb declensions of *to see* as a way to look back over her life gave Krasner an opportunity to evaluate her creative arch.

While Bryan Robertson is documented reviewing the Hofmann drawings with Krasner and helping her select for the Pace exhibition which to save and which to destroy, McKinney was also called upon for advice. He told me: "[We looked at] all those on paper, because she wanted to do a collage. That was the show. It was a great, beautiful show. She really did something. . . . I told her what to destroy, what not to destroy. That's where material came from. She pretty well listened to me. Then I think the exhibition went well."[346]

The idea of doing this series came from four friends who had long supported her: Saul Steinberg, Bryan Robertson, Donald McKinney, and John Bernard Myers.[347] Steinberg, the *New Yorker* cartoonist and her neighbor in Springs, suggested a series on linguistic forms based on the passage of time, and thus, she was coming to terms with her own history, devouring her past and giving birth to her future.[348] The choice of the number eleven may be serendipitous or a reference to astrology and tarot cards. Knowledgeable about the psychic world and as a "professed" Scorpio, Krasner may have understood the implications of the number eleven. It is the link between the mortal and the immortal, between man and spirit, between darkness and light, ignorance and enlightenment.

In 1972, Robertson, who had organized Krasner's 1965 retrospective at Whitechapel, visited her in Springs and saw her Hofmann charcoal drawings; McKinney ushered her through the Marlborough years and beyond; and Myers discussed with her on the phone the underlying meaning of the work even before seeing it. There was a fifth friend, her new dealer, Arne Glimcher, the director of the Pace Gallery. While both Robertson and McKinney had, at different times, looked with her through the Hofmann School portfolios of charcoal figure drawings, those she made between 1937 and 1940, it was Glimcher who was so taken with the collages she made from them that he invited her to exhibit them at the Pace Gallery.[349]

Judging from the works she decided to leave untouched, it is difficult for me to say why the others were repurposed or sacrificed. By this point, Krasner was not simply tearing but was instead cutting the paper, and the layering was much more integrated with the whole. These eleven (actually twelve) pictures seem to have been very carefully thought out. There is no suggestion of reckless cacophony as in the past. What comes through is a carefully measured design that gives the compositions a balanced clarity, as if Picasso's Cubist figures were integrated into a design of Matisse cutouts.[350]

The materials, as well as the actual title of this series, "Eleven Ways to Use the Words To See," sums up much of the significant work from Krasner's past. It is a much more intellectual look into the unconscious, an investigation into the past, an evaluation of her artistic contribution then and now. This lifelong obsession with the activity of the eye brings my experience with Krasner into the forefront. In my tiny bedroom in Springs, Krasner had a huge vase of peacock feathers standing close to the door. They were out of sync with the rest of the bare interior, but I know that, like the shelves of seashells, they were important to her. She may or may not have known that the peacock feathers were symbols of the "Eye" Goddess or that Campbell observed that the eye "in the middle of the forehead, opens to the vision of eternity" or that the eye of the Cyclops is the one through which Odysseus passed or, as in Hindu iconography, it is the "bird of the eye of danger."[351] Certainly, it is often associated with the Mother Goddess and is considered a window into the soul, and we know from her many paintings of it that Krasner was obsessed with the eye, its formal function as well as its symbolism.

Years later, I interviewed Glimcher at the Pace Gallery regarding Krasner. The following is an excerpt from those discussions.[352]

AG: I'd known Lee for a long time, as I've been in the New York art world since 1963. We've seen each other off and on since then. It was Barbara Rose who was the matchmaker for Lee to join the gallery. Barbara Rose was aware that I knew Lee, we were acquaintances, more than friends. She suggested that we visit Lee's apartment. Lee was working on assembling some collages that she made from her early Cubist charcoal drawings. Reconfiguring them into large complex collages. I thought they were wonderful. A kind of transforming of the drawings that, in their own right, were accomplished, but not highly original, into something more. She put them together as grids, cutting away pieces of the page and collaging them to other sheets. I told Lee that I would love to show them. She was very happy. Ultimately, we presented the exhibition and sold it out. It was a critical success as well, and Lee was visible again. It brought Lee back to the consciousness of the scene. She had really disappeared, and that exhibition [1977] and the subsequent exhibitions we made reestablished Lee's reputation. She had lived so long in Pollock's shadow. Now it was long enough since Pollock's death for her to be seen as her own gifted artist.

RA: What was your relationship with her like?

AG: Nevelson was very much responsible for the beginning of this gallery and the success of the gallery. She was the first artist of note that came with us. With Lee, you were always on your toes trying to keep her happy. She was such a good artist, and she was such a sad character.

RA: In what way? Why was she sad?

AG: She always felt that she was never considered in a way that she should have been. She was Mrs. Pollock—but always played the Mrs. Pollock role very strong. She liked luxuries. . . . It was friendly, but she at times was cantankerous. We always got along, although she complained about everything around her. In truth, she was very jealous of my relationship with Nevelson. It was palpable, although we went on for several years together in harmony. She started the rumor that Nevelson was a lesbian, which was not true, and gave her the nickname of Luigi. "How's your friend Luigi?" She would ask me from time to time when Nevelson would have some big acclaim in the papers or a museum show, and she'd say, "I saw your friend Luigi's show." That wasn't good for her, either, because she lived in Pollock's shadow, and she felt that she was suddenly in Nevelson's shadow. I do think that we made a huge push and effort for her and reestablished her reputation as a major artist in her own right. Finally, our relationship ended because of that jealousy. I never had the relationship with her that I had with Nevelson. My relationship with Nevelson lasted over thirty years. . . . [Lee would go to] Kenneth's to have her hair done. She would come into the gallery after Kenneth's to rest and have a coffee. "I've just come from Kenneth's," she would announce, and tell me stories of her modeling days or her Charles James clothes.

RA: What stands out in your mind that art historians may have missed about Lee?

AG: I think that she's getting her due now. Lee is a really fine artist. She was pitting herself against Pollock, de Kooning, Rothko. There are only a couple of those people in history. Everyone isn't a Picasso and can still be important to the history of art. In addition to her own greatness, one can underestimate the contribution that she made through Pollock. She was very much a part of Pollock's history and of the evolution of his paintings. She was his muse, but that didn't satisfy her, although it certainly satisfied history. Instead of enjoying what she was, she was bitter [about] what she wasn't and the accolades that she was denied.

RA: Where do you think her sense of determination came from?

AG: I think it was genetic, the immigrant's necessity to excel, really, to over-achieve. The first- and second-generation Jews were upwardly mobile people. I think she felt that it was her responsibility to become a star. She did, she was a star.

RA: One of the things I'm looking at is that she had this kind of duality. The duality in her personality, in her work, in her relationships. Did you see that? Can you talk a little bit about that?

AG: I think when she was painting, she was in ecstasy. It was about self-confidence. Then, when she wasn't painting, she always worried about her position in art history. She could be incredibly charming, and she could be incredibly nasty, two sides of the same coin. I always thought that she was bipolar. She had the capacity to be flying and then to be so depressed. There was a cruelty in the relationship with Pollock; as much of a genius that he was, he certainly was not very nice to her. She was living with a firecracker that could explode any second.

RA: I have read that he had other affairs besides that with Kligman.

AG: I have heard the same.

RA: I think that was certainly part of the cross she was bearing. . . . It's interesting that she couldn't be alone at night, and yet she appeared very strong and in charge.

AG: I think that's part of the duality.

RA: Do you know anything about her psychoanalysis?

AG: No. I knew that she talked about being in psychoanalysis. She was proud of it.

RA: How do you think the collages fit in with her whole oeuvre?

AG: It's interesting. I have not thought about it. I think you're right in that she reexamines and manipulates the structure of her work. In the Cubist collages, she cut an arc out of one sheet and then placed it someplace else and created another shape by the void between the two areas.

RA: Gorgeous. As with all artists, their work stands as a kind of self-portrait. Even though occasionally she would name something after nature, I really think that she, like Pollock, thought of herself as nature.

AG: I think that's true. The paintings that are more muscular and fragmented, like leaves and branches in brighter colors, feel like Matisse's cut-outs. I think that she was always aware of what was happening in the art world at the moment, compared it with what happened in art history, and then turned it into her own expression. I think the work is always about how Lee relates to her environment at the time.

Marcia Tucker (curator of painting and sculpture at the Whitney Museum of American Art from 1969 to 1977 and founder of the New Museum in 1977) was the first to organize a significant museum show of Krasner's work in New York. "Lee Krasner: Large Paintings" was on view at the Whitney from November 13, 1973, through January 6, 1974. At that time, Tucker was one of the most important women in the art world and a powerful leader of the feminist art movement in New York. In the catalog, she wrote of the 1950s collages: "They are rough, intense, brilliantly colored and commanding in presence. . . . In their use of color the collages anticipate her most recent paintings where color, no longer subservient to line, reasserts its autonomy and ability to shape and change the nature of forms."[353] While Tucker had fought for a full floor to display the work, the exhibition was mounted in half the space and included only eighteen works. The critic Hilton Kramer asked why it was such a "fragmentary view" of a career that "has remained far too obscure."[354] Still, at this moment in time, Krasner's artistic credentials were beginning to be confirmed, as supported by the portrait of Krasner on the cover of *Art in America* (November–December 1973).

Back in the '70s, I was hanging out with friends on East 74th and attending feminist consciousness-raising sessions downtown. This led to my being offered a Helena Rubenstein Fellowship at the Whitney in 1980, where I participated in the Independent Studies Program. Senior members of the staff, under the director Tom Armstrong, included Lloyd Goodrich working on a book about Thomas Eakins, Gail Levin on Edward Hopper, Barbara Haskell on the American modernists, and Patterson Sims organizing an Ellsworth Kelly exhibition, for which I compiled the bibliography. While I had proposed an all-women exhibition for the Fairfield County Whitney branch in Stamford, Connecticut, the suggestion was flatly declined. Instead, we organized an exhibition of contemporary landscape painting, "American Landscape: Recent Developments," in 1981. The following year, the New York chapter of the Women's Caucus for Art sponsored sixteen independently organized shows, titled "Views by Women Artists," at galleries and alternative spaces throughout New York City. I was ultimately invited to present my women's show, "Nature as Image and Metaphor: Works by Contemporary Women Artists," at the Greene Space, then at 105 Greene Street, on view from February 23 to March 13, 1982. It included Krasner's Indian-red *Nightbloom #2* (1962) alongside Michelle Stuart, Louise Bourgeois, Marisol, and more.[355]

During that time, I was with Krasner at her New York apartment, in the bedroom she had transformed into a studio when she was working on the "Eleven Ways to Use the Words To See" series (1976–1978).

Physically, she didn't have the strength to deal with huge canvases tacked to the wall. Now in her mid-sixties, suffering from arthritis and colitis, she had to approach the work with less vigor. Using the Hofmann

Fig. 26
Lee Krasner.
Behind her is
Rising Green
(1972). Photo
by Arnold
Newman. Art in
America cover,
Nov-Dec, 1973.

drawings and a pair of scissors, she used Revit glue to adhere the collage elements to the canvas. The ensuing work was intellectually commanding and full of mystery. An uncontrollable urge led her to attack her drawings from the Hofmann School, recycling as she was wont to do but also creating something entirely new, something highly structured, minimally colored, and hard-edged. If you compare these with the early collages she did for the WPA department-store windows, it is evident that her approach reflects Hofmann's teaching—including diagonal chevrons piercing the composition. She also returned to this approach in the 1976 Olympics poster and the Ashawagh Hall "Springs Arts Exhibition" (1974) poster, as well as those in these 1976 works.

Female nudes are cut and pasted in ways that almost deny any reference to flesh and blood. Again, as in her earlier collages, the original works were eradicated and then reborn. Many appear to resemble stained-glass windows. Such destruction of her past could be viewed as recognition of the pain she had experienced throughout her life. Krasner finally appeared to understand that to try to deny pain is to hold on to it. Only by going through it, as the Magician does, allowing it, feeling it, visually acknowledging it, was she able to learn from it and go on to feel joy and power in a new way.[356] As Pearson notes, "Magicians move beyond good and bad into seeing life as a process."[357]

Barbara Rose observes, "She was recycling and reclaiming her past. They were strictly hers. No Jackson. She was going to soldier on alone. She refused to be the WIDOW Pollock. She had been Lee before; she would be Lee after."[358]

No longer the victim, Krasner as the Magician discovered that the antidote to violence (as exemplified by her monster and Rimbaud's beast) is not self-control and repression but self-knowledge and the skills of self-expression and assertiveness.[359] The "Eleven Ways" series was Krasner's path to her own personal affirmation. The Magician archetype takes responsibility. She examined her disturbing history and, by embracing it, rendered it helpless. The Magician is not other, we discover, but ourselves.[360] She moved on to accepting herself. She did not slay the beast—within or without—but embraced it, thus affirming the deepest level of truth, that is, that we are all one.[361]

Campbell wrote: "There is no separateness. Thus, just as the way of social participation may lead in the end to a realization of the All in the individual, so that of exile brings the hero to the Self in all."[362]

Plates

1. Lee Krasner, *Self-Portrait*, c. 1929–1930. The Metropolitan Museum of Art, New York.

2. Lee Krasner, *Self-Portrait*, c. 1928. The Jewish Museum, New York.

3. Lee Krasner, *Untitled (Surrealist Composition)*, c. 1935–1936. Pollock-Krasner Foundation, New York.

4. Lee Krasner, *Untitled*, c. 1940. Private collection.

5. Lee Krasner, *Igor*, c. 1943. Private collection.

6. Lee Krasner, *Mosaic Table*, 1947. Private Collection.

7. Lee Krasner, *Shattered Color*, 1947. Guild Hall Museum, East Hampton, NY.

8. Lee Krasner, *Blue and Black*, c. 1953-54. Museum of Fine Arts, Houston, TX.

9. Lee Krasner, *Lame Shadow*, 1955. Private collection.

10. Lee Krasner, *Bald Eagle*, 1955. Audrey and Sidney Irmas, Los Angeles.

11. Lee Krasner, *Milkweed*, 1955. Albright-Knox Art Gallery, Buffalo, NY.

12. Lee Krasner, *Prophecy*, 1956. Private collection.

13. Lee Krasner, *The Seasons*, 1957. Whitney Museum of American Art, New York.

14. Lee Krasner, *Cool White*, 1959. National Gallery of Australia, Canberra.

15. Lee Krasner, *The Eye is the First Circle*, 1960. Glenstone, Potomac, MD.

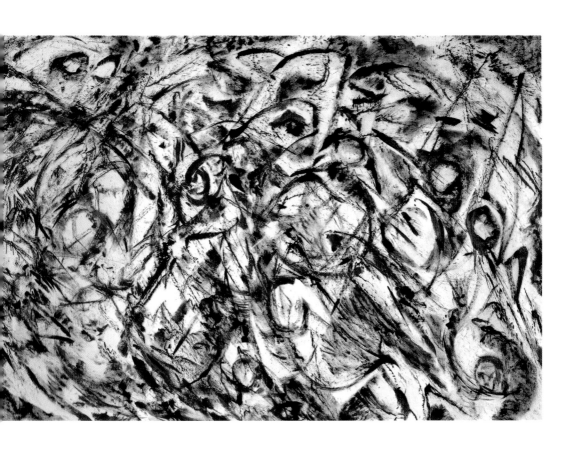

16. Lee Krasner, *Cosmic Fragments*, 1962. Pollock-Krasner Foundation, New York.

17. Lee Krasner, *Happy Lady*, 1963. Flint Institute of Arts, Michigan.

18. Lee Krasner, *Right Bird Left*, 1965. Ball State University Museum of Art, Muncie, IN.

19. Lee Krasner, *Palingenesis*, 1971. Pollock-Krasner Foundation, New York.

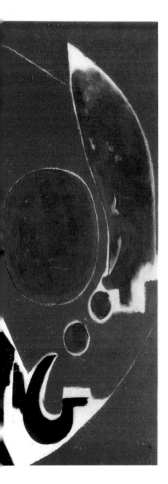

20. Lee Krasner, *Rising Green*, 1972. The Metropolitan Museum of Art, New York.

21. Lee Krasner, *Imperative*, 1976. National Gallery of Art, Washington DC.

22. Lee Krasner, *Butterfly Weed*, 1957-81. Pollock-Krasner Foundation, New York.

23. Lee Krasner, *Untitled*, 1982. Private Collection.

Summer Sitters

Lee Krasner's fear of the dark had begun to manifest itself increasingly toward the end of Jackson Pollock's life. Krasner's "monster" dream and her phobia about being alone, especially at night, were intimately related, to the point where Krasner would call friends to wait with her until Pollock came stumbling home. They'd then help her get him up the stairs and into bed.[363] Some, but not many, were aware of her state of mind, including a few of Krasner's trusted "summer sitters," those whom she had carefully selected to stay with her following Pollock's death. Furthermore, Krasner cleverly concealed her vulnerability—her "weakness"—especially from those she thought could help her career. At the same time as she was protecting Pollock's reputation as an artist, she was pushing forward to ensure that her own reputation would be enhanced as well.

Krasner was affiliated with the Marlborough Gallery in the 1970s. Donald McKinney, the gallery's director, told me she would often persuade him to stay at her Hamptons' house on weekends and to stay over at her apartment in New York City following dinners, sleeping in the maid's room. Even as a widow, when she was invited to Alfonso Ossorio's East Hampton estate, rather than return home after an event or dinner, she would often remain at his place, staying in the "Krasner/Pollock" bedroom, a special room that Ossorio had assigned to the couple.

Krasner's desperate need for companionship led to many difficult, funny, and complicated situations. The *New York Times* critic Grace Glueck remembered Krasner offering to put her up one weekend as Glueck was finishing up a piece on Claes Oldenburg and needed a quiet place to write. Glueck accepted the invitation with gracious appreciation, but she made the mistake of washing her hair. This was a "serious infraction," as her hostess pointed out, ostensibly because the well might run dry. Perhaps the funniest story was one told to me by John Post Lee, then a senior at Vassar College. He came to the house under the guise of writing a paper on Krasner's last series of paintings, "Eleven Ways to Use the Words To See." Knowing that he was not allowed to leave the house for the evening, he still tried to make a clandestine getaway to meet college friends. Krasner caught him hiding under the bed in the guest room, shoes clutched to his chest.

The house on Springs Fireplace Road, with its steady stream of overnight guests, became legendary. Among the twenty or so overnight visitors I interviewed were the gallerist Elizabeth (Betsy) Miller (who shared her birthday with Krasner), the poet and translator Richard Howard (who often suggested titles for Krasner's paintings), director of the Marlborough Gallery Donald McKinney (who traveled with her to Alabama), art curator and critic Barbara Rose (who organized her retrospective exhibition), and art historians Robert Hobbs and Amei Wallach (who wrote about her work with great compassion).

In addition to the summer sitters, so many other people in the art world agreed to these interviews. My good fortune here was certainly a result of the position I held for seventeen years as the executive director of Guild Hall in East Hampton. Many of these interviewees are close friends and neighbors, and all are colleagues for whom I have deep respect. I owe them a huge debt of gratitude for their time and insights.

As I conducted these interviews, I came to realize that each of us had a story to tell. Together we might remember Krasner with fear, humor, and awe, but all of us experienced her formidable personality, which was as present in her inflexible convictions as in her powerful paintings. It was the strength of that personality that elevated her to the high reaches of the Abstract Expressionist movement.

While they have been edited and excerpted here for space concerns, all interviews in their totality are available at the Pollock-Krasner House and Study Center in East Hampton, available for visitors and scholars to review. Unfortunately, so many fascinating people graciously agreed to be interviewed that all their stories could not be included in this book. It is my hope that others interested in Krasner and the Abstract Expressionist period will take advantage of this remarkable archive.

Richard Howard
October 5, 2017

Pulitzer Prize–winning poet, literary critic, essayist, and translator. Professor emeritus of writing at Columbia University in New York.

RA: When did you first meet Lee?

RH: Right after I first came back East. I think I was still in college. I was in my twenties. I knew Lee without her husband, even though I knew all about him. But she was alone.

RA: So, it was after 1956. After he died.

RH: I knew her before then, but we didn't become friends until she was alone. We had lots to talk about, and got along very nicely, and managed to do so for thirty years, forty, whatever. It was wonderful. Lee was a difficult person, and she had many demanding requirements. I think I pleased her by being able to appear to add them up. And so we really got along very nicely.

RA: Like, what were some of the demanding requirements?

RH: Well, she didn't like to be alone. If there was no reason not to, she would call and say, "I'm alone. Please come over." Or "Let's do something together. Let's go out to dinner." And so forth.

RA: So where were you staying then?

RH: I was living right nearby. I lived with Sanford Friedman [B. H. Friedman's brother] in a house very nearby [in Springs].

RA: And he was really your partner.

RH: At that time.

RA: Yes. And you and he stayed in a little house outside of Lee's house, right?

RH: Yes, that's right. And then Sandy left, and David Alexander appeared. And he knew Lee, as well. For almost as many years. We were all very close friends, I believe. Lee was very specific about the fact that she didn't like everybody.

RA: Yes, I know that, yes. Whom did she not like, do you remember?

RH: Yes, but . . . her reasons were not reasons that would be everybody's. I mean, it was so clear that Lee needed certain things, and if she couldn't get them, then she would drop the person. . . . I think one of the reasons we got along so well was that I was really so taken with her work. I talked with her about it a lot. I gave her names for things. I really loved her work. . . . I think she is really one of the most remarkable American artists. I loved being able to make that clear to her. And it made certain things very easy for us . . . and she was curious about mine. I write.

RA: Yes, I know.

RH: And she was curious, interested, and would ask questions, too. I can remember just so many evenings, just the two of us, when we'd go out to dinner and come back, and talk about other people and about our own work. It was easy for her, partly because I appeared on the scene after the life that she had lived with [Pollock]. It was all my relationship to her, unlike many, many people, it only related to her, and there was nothing about the other person. I think that was why my life with her was so easy. But it was delightful. She didn't very much like to do most of the things I do, like reading.

RA: Yes. But you read to her?

RH: Very often.

RA: Do you remember what you read?

RH: It would be things I suggested, either stories or sometimes it would be subjects that would come up, and then I found something interesting, especially out there in East Hampton. We knew a lot of people who were writing. Some of them political, but many of them in the same kind of world of the arts.

RA: Like Edward Albee. Did you know him?

RH: We had been friends for so long. And they got along very well. He was very fond of her. Also, Eddie understood Lee enough so that when either of us would talk about Lee, the other would have something to say exactly to connect it, or even [be] different, but it was something that we understood about this person. It was very nice to be together, all three of us, but each of us had a strong sense of who the other person was, and that was nice. There were other people there. And I could talk to her about Edward's work, as I would my own. She could be comfortable about listening and interested and so forth.

RA: What did she say, or what did you say to her, about her work?

RH: I, from the beginning, in the first place, was startled by different kinds of her work. And I was quite thrilled by some of the more striking things, the big things that she would make . . .

RA: Like the "Umber" paintings that you wrote the catalog for?

RH: She did have remarkable taste. She was quite free to do whatever she wanted. I think there would be many people who ran the institutions who would find Lee very difficult, and also not really get the work. But she had no trouble finding the people who did get the work.

RA: Why was she difficult?

RH: I mean, you're very right to think of it that way. Well, many aspects of her life were involved with not getting along with her family, or with people, and even though I think Lee's appearance was really quite stunning sometimes as a younger woman, as she grew older, she became very clearly someone who had a look that was no longer going to be an attempt to not only attract but to satisfy other people. She made herself look as she did, but I think she was not eager to satisfy or interest people by her appearance. She had already decided what that was and could be. And I think she didn't really come through all that to the point where she no longer cared much if they liked her with some relation to her looks.

RA: But there was a time when she was with David Gibbs, and she had the dresses from Charles James, and you know all about that.

RH: Yes, I remember that very well.

RA: So what happened? Why did she suddenly get interested in beautiful dresses and fur coats?

RH: Well, when she came to a party, or to a reading, or to a situation where she had to give a talk, she was delighted to be able to wear what she thought was attractive and interesting. That was really a big part of her life. Lee certainly influenced me. We would often talk about how people dressed, how people looked, and so forth. Her style was interesting and not conventional.

RA: Yes. Yes. Did you get to know Elizabeth Strong-Cuevas? Bessie Cuevas?

RH: I don't think so.

RA: She was a part of the Rockefeller family.

RH: Yes.

RA: I talked to her. She's a sculptor, and she also has a very real flair for clothes. And she knew Charles James and Lee Krasner. So I was wondering if there was kind of an influence there, as well.

RH: Probably. But the Charles James thing was very important. Yes, he would be there. And as the years went by, life was difficult, and he found it so, and he was so pleased to see Lee. And he would come, and Lee and I happened to be there, I lived very nearby. Eventually, at times, I lived in the little house.

RA: Did you write? Did you write poetry when you were there?

RH: Yes. Of course.

RA: Did you write anything about Lee, or about living there, or Louse Point?

RH: I did, but not as such. I was always writing about things that Lee did and said. I made up characters who were rather like her and so forth. . . . She would come to some of my readings, but I think she realized that . . . I found her interesting and exciting, and also, I was so impressed by the work. She found it easy, therefore, to be with me about other things. . . . I think that the one thing I hoped to be able to say to you was that it was the kind of friendship that made it possible for both of us. I mean, she would be very critical sometimes, and very careful to tell me exactly what she thought.

RA: She didn't soft-soap anything.

RH: No. That's right. But it was very close. It was really like family. I think that's one of the things I certainly felt all those years. And here in New York, during the winter, for instance, when I was teaching at Columbia,

I was free to see her a lot. We saw each other here all the time. But it was not the same, like the times that we lived out—

RA: In East Hampton.

RH: Yes.

RA: You were one of her very best friends. Would you say that certain bodies of work tell you about her? She always said that they were autobiographical.

RH: Yes. I know.

RA: Do you think that's true?

RH: Oh, I'm sure it is true. I saw the work so clearly as this work that this person had made, and that I knew the person so well, and we were so intimate. "I see that you see it—might be a good way to talk about it," she'd say. Or I remember many times when she would say, "Yes, you can call it that." She loved that. She wasn't happy about naming her pictures.

RA: One of the things that I'm hoping to make a case for is how the names of the paintings are an important part of the paintings.

RH: They became that.

RA: Yes. Because she paints the painting, then you have a conversation with her, and she says, that's a wonderful idea. It appears that you named the paintings, but I think in that conversation with her, the titles reflected the feelings she brought into it.

RH: Oh, absolutely. I don't really think it was mine, but I do feel that it was the work, and I would ask her, "Is that right that I feel that way?" I loved the early work that she did. I thought it was remarkable.

RA: The "Little Image" paintings?

RH: Yes.

RA: I thought they were remarkable.

RH: That's what I meant about the entirety of her work. As opposed to knowing that there was a series. Sometimes, toward the end of her life, she really was doing things so different and so strong, and so other, that she was free to do that, I think, surprisingly so. . . . There were some of the men that I think she liked. But some of the women, I think, she often was quite annoyed by some of the women.

RA: I actually think that she didn't like women very much.

RH: Women artists. She liked gay men. And she liked David [Alexander] and me. And we were gay men. I never really had the feeling that she would allow the same kind of feeling about gay women.

RA: What she has said in print is that she didn't even want to be any part of the women's movement. And then finally, when I showed up, the women's movement really was so excited about "discovering" her and putting her on the map, so to speak, that she began to appreciate the movement. And so she didn't want to be in any women's shows. She didn't mind the attention. It was back and forth all the time. But she didn't want to be called a feminist at all. And yet I have a quote from her that she very much appreciated the feminist movement and how it helped her. . . . Now, of course, everyone has picked up on the fact that she was crying while she was painting *Listen* (1957), the beautiful, colorful painting that appears to be so joyful, and that she was afraid of the painting *Prophecy* (1956), which was the painting that she did just before Jackson died. What do you think? Do you think she was really upset after Jackson died, truly, and those paintings just kept coming out of her anyway? She said that her feelings were delayed. But I don't know, I'm not sure I can buy it.

RH: It has to do with the fact that she had feelings for Jackson, but the life between them had gone into many bad moments, which I knew nothing about. It was my good fortune to become a friend of Lee's, not as if I were a friend of Mrs. Pollock.

RA: When she got to the "Umber" paintings, then she was having some sleeping problems. She decided to paint them at night. She was wandering around at night.

RH: I remember it being so unusual. I thought that often she would just spend days and days and days indoors, in there, painting. And at night, she really enjoyed [her] social life. . . . She would call and say, "I'm ready. Let's do something." . . . I must say, when we're talking here, it's fun for me to hear the kind of questions you ask, because it seems to me you are just seeing it exactly the way it seems to me one should.

RA: Oh, thank you.

RH: She worked all the time, after all. She just worked all the time. One of the other things that we had in common was dogs. It was lots of fun to talk about animals together. Lee had a very strong interest in them.

RA: She had that dog Ahab, and I think you said to her, "These are Ahab-colored paintings."

RH: Yes, that's right.

RA: Because they were those "Umber" paintings that were the same color as Ahab.

RH: Yes . . . when you speak of coincidences. It's very strong. . . . There were times when, I remember very well, Lee was not a happy woman.

RA: Tell me about David Gibbs. Did you know him very well?

RH: I remember the way that they became friends, and they would talk a lot about things, their clothes, or going out and eating. That was a kind of fancy life that she enjoyed, and that he managed to put over on her, I think. And that was fine. She was really happy with him.

RA: Do you think it was David Gibbs who persuaded her to do the Pollock show in London?

RH: Yes, of course.

RA: And they had the Pollock exhibition, with Marlborough in New York, so I would assume David Gibbs had a lot to do with that.

RH: I think, yes, probably.

RA: And then the Whitechapel Gallery, the show that she had there, that one-person show. I noticed that in the front of that catalog, it thanks David Gibbs. So he must have had something to do with that show, too.

RH: Sure.

RA: I'm just putting all the pieces together now. How many years did you know her? Thirty?

RH: Well, when did Jackson die?

RA: In 1956. And she died in '84.

RH: Well, certainly, those years, all together. Now, I knew her before that, but not really well. It was very much an unmarried person that I knew, that was alone.

RA: Just one more question. Do you know who Grace Glueck is?

RH: Well, sure.

RA: She said, "Track down David Gibbs, and you'll find something."

RH: Yes. Well, I think that's true.

RA: Do you? What would I find?

RH: I mean, that was a real relationship.

RA: Yes, I think it was, too. She was actually fifty years old, and he was thirty-three.

RH: Yes, that's right.

RA: But I think she cared a lot about him.

RH: She did. He used the fact that she liked and admired him. I can remember a lot about his clothes, and his dressiness, and so forth. But you're right, . . . I would say that was one of the people that you must go after.

RA: Yes. Because actually, one of the things I've learned is that he met Lee, I think, in 1959. And the next day, he bought a painting by her. So it was pretty obvious that he was out to woo her.

RH: Yes, and he was very eager to get to that position with her. And he got to it.

RA: Yes. And I think he knew Bryan Robertson, who did the show at Whitechapel. I think they were all friends.

RH: I knew Bryan, too. I remember that.

RA: Do you think that Gibbs knew Bryan Robertson?

RH: I don't know, but I'm sure he did. Sure.

RA: How about Howard Moss?

RH: Yes, well, that's a dear friend. I just did a class up at Columbia about Howard's work. I love his poetry.

RA: Yes, well, you know, one of the last paintings she did was called *Morning Glory* (1982).

RH: Yes, I know.

RA: And it was Howard Moss's poem . . . about the morning glory. But then Lee learned about it, or saw it, and . . . I guess, she agreed to work with him. And so she then did the painting after he did the poem. So it's kind of wonderful, because it goes back to all her nature influences. . . . She gets to the point where she's not hiding it anymore. She loved nature. Did you go to the funeral?

RH: Oh, sure. We cared for her a lot. And at the end, we spent as much time as we could with her. And then when she died, the funeral, I remember all of those things.

James Valliere
March 14, 2018, email

Krasner's first research assistant; he worked with her from 1963 to 1965. Art historian and author of *Lee Krasner and Jackson Pollock's Legacy* about his time with Krasner.

RA: First, I wonder whom you interviewed for your book and if the interviews are available online at the Archives of American Art? Did you discuss Lee?

JV: Yes, my interviews with Pollock contemporaries are available online from the AAA.[364] Lee introduced me to all of these people, except Clement Greenberg. The Greenberg interview was the last one I did.

RA: Your conclusion on the last page of your book indicates that you believe that her focus was to "build Pollock's legacy." But can you now say what was fact and what was myth?

JV: I always believed that her goal, while I worked with her from 1963 to 1965, was strictly to build "Pollock's legacy." That was her single-minded focus. During these years I never saw her draw or paint or even mention her artworks. . . . By 1965 her goal was to get the Marlborough-Gerson Gallery in NYC to handle Pollock's artworks (his estate) and to have them commit to publishing a catalogue raisonné of his art.

RA: I remember a book in their library on El Greco in which Pollock had drawn in the margins. It doesn't seem to be there anymore. Do you remember this?

JV: I indexed Pollock's library, which is published in his catalogue raisonné. I never saw an El Greco book with drawings in the margins. I paid particular attention to the El Greco books, as they played a key role in my *Art Journal* article on "El Greco's Influence on Jackson Pollock's Early Works."[365]

RA: I suspect that Krasner wanted an academic pedigree for both Jackson and herself. Can you elaborate?

JV: I never felt Lee was "looking for an academic pedigree" to work on

Jackson's "CR [catalogue raisonné]" in 1963–1965. And, of course, she never spoke about any wish she had for herself. It was all "Pollock" and of course she was always referred to as "Mrs. Pollock" in those days. Friends called her "Lee." I also called her "Lee."

RA: Did you meet David Gibbs?

JV: I met David Gibbs, he stayed at the East Hampton house for a few days during the early part of Lee's negotiations with Marlborough. I never heard what [Ronald] Stein [Krasner's nephew] said about them.

RA: Is there any possibility that she found it difficult to read—or did not enjoy reading? This seems to have been common knowledge. Does this mean that when she returned the library list to you unannotated, she may not have even read it?

JV: Her reading habits were definitely unusual. I also gave her transcripts of every interview. She would bring them upstairs to her room and return them to me the next day without any notations. She would generally smile approvingly but make no verbal comment. I assumed she read them, but I have no proof of this. . . . Francis O'Connor mentioned to me in a telephone conversation that Lee had absolutely no respect for historical documents or printed materials.

RA: Did you discuss fashion with her—Charles James, Frances Stein? Despite others' ridicule of her appearance, I believe she had pride in her body and in fashion design. When I was with her, she often wandered the hall naked, devoid of modesty.

JV: I never discussed fashion with her or with others she knew. . . . Lee and I talked more about her goals of getting the "Pollock Papers" to Yale University and having Marlborough handle his estate. I strongly urged her not to encourage Marlborough to establish its gallery in Boston—as I was living there part-time and knew it was not a good location for the work of a major contemporary "abstract" artist like Pollock. . . . My work relationship with Lee ended in the fall of 1965 after I declined an offer from Marlborough to continue my work on Pollock for them in NYC. . . . At that point, Lee and I agreed that I would continue my work with the interviews as my personal project, and I would own the copyright on them. We both hoped that they would eventually be published as a book. . . . I believe that she contacted me in 1971, while I was living in Vermont, and asked me to provide her with the original tape recordings and transcripts of the interviews that she wanted to give to the AAA. I met her in NYC with these documents and that's when I first met Francis O'Connor. He had taken over the work I had begun in 1963–65 on J.P.'s early works (1930s) for the forthcoming full catalogue raisonné of his works.

Grace Glueck
April 10, 2018

Longtime reporter and art critic for the *New York Times*. She often wrote about both Pollock and Krasner. She first met Krasner in 1964.

RA: When and how did you meet Lee Krasner?

GG: I was given all kinds of assignments, and I think I suggested that I should go out [to East Hampton] because the whole scene was beginning to buzz and make waves in Big New York Culture and so forth. [Pollock] had died long since, and she had become a widow. I thought I'd look into that. At any rate, I went to a place in Amagansett for about a month. I got to know the scene, and of course I was introduced to Lee, I think by Alfonso [Ossorio]. I was doing a piece on Claes Oldenburg for the *New York Times Magazine*. I couldn't finish it in time for the lease to be up. She, very graciously, said to me, "Why don't you come and stay with me for a weekend and finish it?" I took her up on it. We got along all right. I found her to be quite grumpy. She is an angry person, basically . . . and she had a reason to be angry, I think. She told me about her life with Jackson, somewhat. [But] she didn't have a bad word to say about him. . . . I stayed there for a weekend in 1965 or 1966, and I did get to finish my piece.

RA: I'd like to establish a context here for Lee's network of associations. First, do you remember David Gibbs?

GG: I know his name . . . a strange character. I think he befriended her. I think he was after her, or [after] something from her. [Lee and I] were friends, more or less. I wrote a couple of pieces on her . . . I think I wrote an interview on her, and, of course, Barbara Rose and other people were busy doing that. As she got sick, she got more fractious and she didn't want to see anybody. I asked if I could come up and see her. She said no. What are you gonna do? . . . I never met Jackson, of course. I knew Ruth Kligman, who asked me if I would write her biography—Ruth's autobiography. I thought about it at the time because I knew all her story. Lee just hated her and went to Europe, I think, to escape her. I mean, to escape the whole situation. It was really a terrible setup for her [Ruth]. She told me later she had brought a friend with her [Edith Metzger], and of course, you know that accident. . . . Her friend was tossed out of the car and flipped. She's told me she could never get over the [accident]. She's not important, but she was a real disturbance. . . . She slept around.

RA: Yes. I heard she went from Jackson to de Kooning . . .

GG: Yes.

RA: What stands out in your mind about Lee that art historians have overlooked?

GG: That she was temperamentally . . . very at odds with herself. Mostly angry. She used to have big arguments with Barney [Barnett] Newman about Judaism. He thought himself the grand rabbi, and of course, like all of those guys, he had no use for women. A lot of them let their wives support them. Lee, I think, was not religious at all.

RA: No, she wasn't, but she was brought up in a very religious family.

GG: Jewish. That's right. I guess she wanted to get away from that. She would argue about all kinds of things, but particularly the Jewish religion. She understood very well her problem, but these guys haggle women. I think that was a big chip on her shoulder.

RA: And why do you think she turned her back on Judaism?

GG: Well, it's an impossible religion. I mean, I come from a Jewish background, but my parents weren't very religious. In fact, I think my father was an atheist. I don't know. I think she might have turned against any religion.

RA: But she had a certain spirituality to her, do you think?

GG: Oh, I do, but I don't know that it was by religion. . . . I think partly she was determined to get away from her family. I think the determination was just born in her. She certainly was very ambitious for herself. And ambitious for him.

RA: Did you notice a duality in her personality?

GG: Well, she could be very nice, as we know, and pleasant, and she could be this angry person.

RA: All I know is that there were a lot of dualities in her work. Remember, she always talked about the swing of the pendulum?

GG: Yes.

RA: Matisse and Picasso?

GG: Yes.

RA: And then, I certainly think in her personality there was that anger, but also a genuine kindness for people. I just felt that maybe even the paintings themselves showed a more depressing theme, and then this joyful bursting.

GG: Yes. Lightness. Very much. She painted very lyrically. In the beginning, she was very much influenced by the French.

RA: Is it correct to say that she finally got Jackson to recognize Matisse?

GG: Yes. I think it's fair to say that. I think she was responsible for a lot of his European influences in his work.

RA: She certainly introduced him to everyone. She was happy to get Hans Hofmann up there and Clement Greenberg. Every person she met, she got them to go over to Jackson's studio. . . . She was always painting. Even when she was taking care of him. Her sense of determination fascinates me and also this duality in her personality, which I think I see in her work as well.

GG: I find her early work not very interesting or appealing.

RA: The early work, we're talking about the "Little Image" paintings that were kind of tight.

GG: I don't know. Maybe this all started after she got rid of Jackson. She didn't want to get rid of him, but she did. . . . What kind of a role did David Gibbs play?

RA: What I read in Gail Levin's book is that he was interested in helping her distribute the Jackson Pollock paintings.

GG: I think he was helping her get a share of her dough.

Donald McKinney
April 11, 2018

President of Marlborough Gallery in New York, 1971–1978; senior director of Hirschl & Adler Modern Galleries in New York, 1981–1993; senior director of the André Emmerich/Sotheby's Gallery in New York, 1993–1997. In 1972, he joined art dealer Eugene V. Thaw, curator William S. Lieberman, and art history professor Francis V. O'Connor in a commission to assess the authenticity of works by Pollock.

RA: I know you were the president of Marlborough Gallery.

DM: Right.

RA: And what were those dates?

DM: Well, I was going to London University, at the Courtauld [Institute of Art]. I ran out of money. A good friend said, "Marlborough's looking for somebody, and you might be of help." I said, "Well, I'm an American. I need a green card. It's not going to be easy." . . . Nevertheless, I went, and immediately they basically hired me. Fortunately, I was very lucky. . . . I was there [at Marlborough Gallery, London] a total of seven years. After two years or so, Marlborough was going to open in New York, and they were having big trouble [figuring out] how to organize it and so forth and so on. I had already made quite a reputation there. Enough that Frank Lloyd said, "I want him to come to New York and help me get started." He was hiring all these people to get the gallery going. . . . I flew in with the idea of being here for a couple [of months]. . . . I loved my life in London, I had very good friends, I had a decent apartment, but it got to be [so exciting] . . . and I loved art so much, so I decided to stay in New York. . . . That was 1963. That was just when they were opening. I stayed there for eighteen years. Then, of course, I met the artists and all these friends over the years. Every single one of them, [Clement] Greenberg and [Harold] Rosenberg and everybody, and Barnett Newman.

RA: You decided, in 1963, to come to New York. I found an article in the *London Times* in 1960 that said that David Gibbs had been put in charge of the Pollock estate. Then I'm realizing in 1962, two years later, Marlborough says that they're representing Pollock.

DM: Lee wanted to get Jackson's work out there, particularly in Europe. She felt he was well known in America but not in Europe. I think she was somewhat infatuated with David.

RA: He was kind of the conduit between her and Marlborough?

DM: He was, yes. He was a private dealer. He wasn't very, in my personal opinion, he . . . didn't have the strengths that I would think he should have had, but she liked people who were proper Englishmen, and he knew this person and that person, she sort of liked that. She gave him the opportunity to see what he could do. From day one, that was what he really wanted. . . . Then he flattered her about her work, and I think most of that was just a way to get the Pollock work, which most people did.

RA: Actually, when I arrived in her life, she didn't want to talk about Pollock at all. It was off the table. There was never a conversation about Pollock.

DM: She would talk to me about Pollock often enough, but her concern was her work. . . . I handled her work, and I handled Jackson's work. I handled both.

RA: How was David?

DM: David Gibbs was long gone. He wasn't there for very long.

RA: Did he go to the Pace Gallery after that?

DM: I don't know. Well, he did go to the Pace eventually, yes.

RA: I talked to Arne Glimcher, and he said he remembered hiring David Gibbs, and you know Lee went to Pace, too, but I don't know if it was at the same time.

DM: No, well, he may have been gone when she went there. [At first] Arne wanted to take Lee, not Pollock's work. Pace was doing that all the time, as you know in the Rothko case, they got right in there, and they were volunteering at the trial and everything else. They got the Rothko [estate].

RA: So Pace would step in, Arne would step in—

DM: They would step in, and their motives were very clear.

RA: Arne has told me that he had no intention of taking the Pollock estate when he took Lee.

DM: Well, when you say, "when he took Lee," I don't know, because what I understood from Lee was she left Pace because Arne started pressing her for the Pollock estate. That is definite.

RA: You remember that?

DM: Yes, and unfortunately, Claire Thaw or Gene Thaw could confirm that, but they're not here.

RA: Lee told me, and she told Arne, that she really was not comfortable at Pace because of Louise Nevelson. Because Louise Nevelson was always the top woman.

DM: Well, that's true, but she went there, so she knew Louise.

RA: "Luigi," she would call her.

DM: She was making her comments. She had her pet peeves, and she [Nevelson] was one of them. . . . She just thought she was artificial. She wasn't real, with the eyelashes and the cloaks. She wasn't the artist. She was a performance more than the artist. She didn't like Judy Chicago.

RA: You met Lee when you came to the U.S.?

DM: Yes. Frank Lloyd was terrified of her. He said, "Donald, I cannot work with her."

RA: And Frank was the head of the gallery with Pierre [Levai] then, in London?

DM: Yes, he had a partnership. . . . Pierre had nothing to do with Lee. He couldn't get along with Lee, either. I did. So he said, "I'm going to give you Lee." . . . Eventually he wanted the Pollock estate, too.

RA: So you took Lee first.

DM: We took Lee first.

RA: Was there some sort of an agreement when you took Lee that she would come with the estate? Or did that come later? I thought there was a deal.

DM: Well . . . they had Pollock in London, with Marlborough. They had that officially. They could sell Pollock in Europe but not in America. That was the deal. . . . Then we came to New York, we signed on Lee, and then after a period of time, with a little pressure from Frank [Lloyd] about the Pollock [estate] . . . "We can do this," and you know, and request things. "No, no, these paintings are not for sale," [she'd say]. Eventually, she broke down, and that was my job, basically, [to get her to agree to a Pollock sale]. . . . She listened, for whatever reason, she listened to me a great deal, and I did the price structure with them. She didn't just pick figures for the paintings. I did that, basically; I did that with her. She would always say, "What is Rothko getting?"

RA: All right, I just want to make this clear, because I thought that there was a package deal, and the deal was that they would—Marlborough, you— would agree to take on Lee if she gave you the Pollock estate.

DM: We took Lee on first [in New York]. . . . She felt comfortable with us, and she had her first exhibition, and she got fond of the gallery, and she liked the other artists who were showing. She would always bring chocolates to the reception, you know, and bring lunches for people. . . . She was very involved in being attentive to [people at the gallery]. . . . I think. . . . Gail [Levin] didn't even get a sandwich from her. But our handyman, who would deliver her paintings and everything else, she would whip up a stew, and she would do everything. It would be all so beautifully done. . . . As you know, I think after Pollock's death and everything else, she was very lonely. She was looking for somebody in her life. She really was. David [Gibbs] came in, and he was glamorous and all that.

RA: Let me get some dates right. David arrived then, after you arrived. He came later?

DM: David had been in touch with her before I was in New York.

RA: That's right, because it was announced that he was going to represent the Pollock estate.

DM: In London but not in America. . . . She wouldn't allow that.

RA: So they had already met in 1959, and then she had this aneurysm in December '62.

DM: That's right. Yes.

RA: And broke her arm after that [summer 1963]. There are some letters from B. H. Friedman saying, "Well, Lee is feeling better," and then, the next day, "Lee isn't feeling better." . . . But evidently, David is in London at the time.

DM: Let me see. I think her arm was still [broken] . . . when she signed the contract for Jackson Pollock. [The date of the signing is in question. Levin said it was 1960.] Lloyd was nervous because he wanted this to happen, and so we finally had a date when she was going to come in and sign the papers. Lee came in with this enormous, floppy sun hat flopped in front of her face, and with her arm still not good. He wanted her to sign, here's the contract and sign it. She kept saying, "I can't see where to sign." And this hat. She said, "Frank, can't you take a joke?" She did it on purpose, with a sense of humor. She went there with the idea that she was going to do it, but she also wanted to have fun doing it. . . . She bought her fur coat, she did these things, that was fun. It didn't mean that much to her. I think when she got very sick, she started giving those things away to the nurses.

RA: Actually, one of the things that I've gotten interested in is Lee and fashion. So many people have said how ugly she is. Jackson said it, even Igor [Pantuhoff], the first boyfriend, said it. She really, at times, became interested in fashion. . . . I have found photographs of her taken by Igor on the beach in Provincetown, and she's naked. She has a beautiful body.

DM: That was attractive to the men, I think.

RA: Then, later on, she went to Charles James and had him design a new wardrobe for her trip to London in 1961 for the opening of Pollock's show at Marlborough. Did you meet him?

DM: No. I never met him.

RA: But you know about her wardrobe.

DM: Oh, yes. She was proud of that. That was one of those little fantasies. She lived it and did it. That was it. I went, when she had her show at the Whitechapel Gallery [in 1965], I went with her. . . . We stayed at the Ritz. She said, "Don't bother getting a room." I slept on the sofa. She had a sitting room. . . . Bryan Robertson did the show, and he was drunk or whatever, and everybody puts their shoes out at the Ritz to be polished, and he switched the shoes around so people got the wrong shoes back. Lee thought that was the funniest thing. It was . . . three days of just fun.

RA: Did David Gibbs somehow organize that?

DM: No.

RA: He's thanked in the catalog.

DM: He may have done that as just a polite procedure, because he was no-where in sight during that time.

RA: Yes, his name is in the catalog, as is Marlborough.

DM: Yes, well, Marlborough had already—

RA: Represented Lee. How did that come about? I know the story about Bryan Robertson, and he did Jackson's show and so she trusted him. Did Marl-borough steer that?

DM: Marlborough . . . equaled what Gagosian is today, here in the world. They had the greatest paintings. They had van Gogh; we had all the current artists. You could go in there, and you could find anything. We're doing the twentieth century, but we would do these "Masters of the Nineteenth Century" shows, and we would have early [Gustave] Courbet, and you name it, we would have it. It was extraordinary. Not one or two but five Cézannes.

RA: So they would have the power to suggest to Bryan at the Whitechapel Gallery. Bryan was the head of Whitechapel Gallery.

DM: They [Whitechapel] obviously didn't have any money, so he would get these grants from the city or the state and—

RA: Well, I know all about that. Having raised a lot of money over seventeen years at Guild Hall, and you often do go to the gallery.

DM: That I don't know. I don't know what transpired. We were already in New York, and whatever arrangements were made from London. The London gallery was still very much there.

RA: So after you left Marlborough, you went to Hirschl & Adler Modern?

DM: Yes.

RA: What date was that?

DM: Oh, in 1980. I think Lee left around 1976 or 1978. It was around 1980. . . . By the way, she left because she was tired of the Rothko case. She was tired of everyone talking about Rothko and not about Pollock or not about Krasner.

RA: I found a court document that she was consulted on the Rothko case.

DM: No, she did not participate.

RA: I found a document that said that she did.

DM: Maybe. Maybe they inquired to see if the Pollock estate was treated badly or something. They may have made an inquiry with her and made it offi-cial. But no, she didn't go to trial. . . . I can't know what they did privately. She had, at that point, really had it with this, because she didn't want that conversation going on all the time. She loved gossip, but it was art gossip. She talked about art all the time.

RA: But it was "Who was it?" "What gallery?" That sort of thing.

DM: Not aesthetics. Could be who was sleeping with whom, that kind of thing. You know, you have Georgia O'Keeffe and her man. That bothered the daylights out of her. That was another one of her dislikes, Georgia O'Keeffe.

RA: Did you come out and stay in the Hamptons?

DM: I went there very often. It was hard. She really wanted me to come out every weekend. She would meet me at the station for the train. Sometimes it was standing room only. . . . Then she would take my bag, dump it into the room, [and say,] "Now we're going to Alfonso's [Ossorio] for dinner."

RA: Was she driving?

DM: She was driving then, initially.

RA: So this was in 1960?

DM: The early '60s, yes . . . I didn't drive at that point, I don't think.

RA: So you would be picked up at the train, and she would dash you off to various places to eat and drink.

DM: Then we'd get back—that's when she was still drinking a little bit—she'd want to talk and talk, until three a.m. I never went to the beach. Finally, we got to go to Louse Point, maybe the third year. It took her a long time to get going in the morning. . . . Then, when I was in New York, we would do all these things, and I lived four blocks south. I lived on 74th Street, at one point, on Fifth Avenue. She would do everything to make me stay overnight, because she didn't want to be alone. She would say, "Donald, come and have drinks." There was the point when she stopped drinking, but you know, we'd done all that. It was late, she still didn't want to go to bed.

RA: So let me ask you about her paintings. I was quite interested in David Gibbs being the center of Lee's interest in Marlborough, but now I realize that maybe it was you.

DM: David was out of the scene fairly soon after . . . she signed on the Pollock estate, then David went back to Europe. David was not on the scene. When she left, he was with Pace for a moment. . . . I think Pace took him on with the idea that he'd get the Pollock. . . . It never happened. That bothered her. She had no intention of letting that happen. That's why she went to Robert Miller [Gallery]. She went to people [she knew and trusted]. . . . When we did the catalogue raisonné, she said, "No, I'm going to ask Gene Thaw. I don't want it to be a dealer's book, because most of these books are influenced by the dealer." So Gene promised not to do that [make it a dealer's book] and then [after taking on the Pollock estate from Pace] said he wants to retire. . . . Then she gave the work [the Pollock estate] to Jason McCoy. . . . That's not normal, but that's the way [it happened]. It benefited Gene, and it worked out.

RA: So you never thought that Lee tried in any way to change the history of Jackson?

DM: No. I always took her as an honest person. Honest to the bone. . . . Whatever she would tell you was the truth. He [Pollock] didn't read a lot of books, but he read certain things.

RA: What about Lee, what did she read?

DM: Well, that's another thing. During the time that I was with her, you would have to read everything to her.

RA: Why was that, do you think?

DM: There was obviously one time that she read on her own. I don't know what it could be. She gave me [a book], which I returned twenty years later, I borrowed a [Joan] Miró book that she said was already written down as part of the collection. There were duplicates. I got it, and then I realized after so many years, and I gave it back to Helen [Harrison]. I said, "This is [Lee's]," . . . and she said, "Well, it's not on the list." I said, "Well, it was early when it came off the shelf."

RA: I remember, when I was there, sneaking downstairs to look at the books, and there was an El Greco book there with drawings in the margins. It's not there anymore and not on the list.

DM: That's interesting.

RA: I think some of those things got away. That was a good one.

DM: That would be a good one. A very important book.

RA: Just to finish up on David Gibbs, it seems that he got engaged to Geraldine Stutz, without Lee knowing. . . . Very famous woman . . . the head of [Henri] Bendel. . . . They were married for about a decade.

DM: Yes, and Lee decided to be friendly with him. To continue the friendship. . . . [I met] Geraldine at Lee's house. . . . We did these [dinners]. . . . Sometimes she would just go on about some people she didn't like, like Barney [Barnett Newman]. She would do these fancy, big dinners. They would be so carefully planned, and the next day she would say, "Did you see what Barney did? It's just what Barney does." He insisted that Annalee [Newman] pull up her skirt so everyone could see. Annalee has the most beautiful legs I've ever seen on anybody. This is a sixty-year-old woman, whatever it was. And Lee was just [angry] . . . because he was obviously bringing the women down. That's what he was doing. Lee saw it right away, and she was furious.

RA: Good for her. I was listening to a tape by a man, it was Harry Jackson, who was a painter of the Western—

DM: He did the cowboys.

RA: Oh, my God, he talked forever. He didn't like Lee at all.

DM: She didn't like him, either.

RA: No. I'm sure not. He sounded absolutely dreadful, but finally, he says, "Well, I shouldn't say this, but Jackson told me that she fucks like a mink."

DM: That's the Cedar Bar conversation.

RA: Once I asked her if we could go to Ossorio's because he had that wonderful painting she did, *Prophecy.*

DM: Yes.

RA: She said no, they weren't talking.

DM: It was true. There were points [when she was arguing with friends, but] two months later, they'd be dining and wining. I've been there quite a few times, and she adored Ted Dragon very much.

RA: At this time, other than the Littles—do you remember John Little?

DM: John Little, of course.

RA: Other than the Littles, there really weren't any other people around. Including [Willem] de Kooning. She wouldn't let me go see him.

DM: I never saw de Kooning [while with Krasner]. I met de Kooning through Lee Eastman [de Kooning's lawyer].

RA: Oh, yes.

DM: Not through her. No, she was not in favor of de Kooning very much.

RA: And B. H. Friedman?

DM: Well, B. H. Friedman I would see because he would always come to her openings. I think I went to his home at one point, but . . . when he wrote that book [on Pollock], that was it. She took strong [positions], and usually you could see her point of view. Right or wrong, but she did have a clear point of view. . . . She was a very honest lady. That's why I think the story of her maneuvering the things that he read and didn't read . . . I think there's something wrong with that story. It's not in the character of Lee. She wasn't trying to create myths.

RA: At a show she was in at the Teaching Gallery of Miami-Dade Community College in 1974, someone in the audience asked her about the Ruth Kligman book, and she said, "Pollock had many affairs that I knew about." Did she ever talk to you about Pollock and his affairs?

DM: She talked to me about Ruth Kligman, and she said that he obviously had other things in his life. Again, that's the honesty that she had. I mean, it annoyed her, and it made her angry—all these issues—but she didn't back away from it. Or she didn't want to create more of a myth about it.

RA: When I was visiting Lee, I think it was after my summer with her, so it was probably '75. Linda Nochlin was there with a bunch of other feminists. . . . I was thrilled because I, too, was a feminist but not in their category. We were all sitting around the living room, and Linda said to Lee, "Have you seen the book that Ruth Kligman wrote?" And Lee just flew into a rage. I didn't know what they were talking about at the time. I had never heard of Ruth Kligman. Lee must have known about it.

DM: Oh, yes, she knew about it. She knew about the book, too. She's very well informed. She knew about it.

RA: I know that that hung over her. It was terrible.

DM: She was the woman that killed her husband. From her point of view.

RA: Yes. Terrible for her to carry that around. I wonder if you think that any of this business with Jackson, with his death, or any of her other personal feelings could be seen in her work? I'm thinking about the '60s, the "Umber" paintings.

DM: I see her aggressiveness. . . . She just pushed forward. It's part of [her] anger. Because they're very masculine, those paintings. . . . You would never think of a woman doing those paintings.

RA: No. It's wonderful. I love them.

DM: Yes. She asked me once, I told her I loved those paintings, the brown paintings. She was kind of surprised, but I do. I mean, they were very authentic. Things have worked out for her. It's the story of all artists. Your time does come, and particularly [as] she never gave up. No matter how . . . they walked [all] over her over the years. People, the closest people, I mean, Greenberg and [others] ignored her. They basically called her names. [The] Newmans were there for her when Jackson died, and all those issues. But they also treated her [badly]. She couldn't stand Barnett Newman, the idea that he compared his paintings to religion, you know? She would just go insane.

RA: She was very upset about that. When he said to her that he was going to make sure the women were not up in the balcony but in the choir of the synagogue. She wanted to be seated with the men in the congregation.

DM: I don't know why, my mind just flipped, but I think one of the cruelest things that happened was putting her gravestone at the foot of Jackson's. . . . It should have been next to him, it could have been a smaller stone, but to put it at the foot. [Krasner had been] displeased with [her nephew] Ronnie [and he retaliated with a smaller stone]. [See chapter 6 for clarification.]

RA: Well, Ron Stein wouldn't go to the MoMA opening. . . . I found a letter that he wrote, "Can't come to the MoMA opening," because he was having a problem with Gerald Dickler, Krasner's lawyer. So I think there was a lot of animosity there.

DM: He died, didn't he?

RA: Yes.

DM: Yes, I thought he died. Didn't Lee give him the house next door?

RA: Yes.

DM: His house. I knew that. So Lee treated him well.

RA: Oh, very well.

DM: Always pushing. When she got up to here, and he and Frances [Ron and his wife] were fighting . . . the scenes you wouldn't believe. Starting with me, he wanted very much to be part of the gallery, and so we would [get together on the] weekends. They would go into a rage, and his wife would take a broom, and they would smash windows from the outside. . . . I locked myself in my bedroom.

RA: Later on, he had guns in the house.

DM: Yes. For Lee to deal with [him]. He made her nervous, and she really saw what was happening about him.

RA: You know, he married Frances Patiky. . . . Her brother, Mark Patiky, took photographs of Lee painting. Unfortunately, it's not a film clip, but it's fast-frame photographs, so you can see Lee jumping around, and he took all these pictures, and I said to him, "Well, can I talk to your sister?" And he said, "Well, I'll see." And the word back was no, she won't talk to me.

DM: I know that Gail [Levin, Krasner's biographer] had a terrible time trying to [deal] with David Gibbs's family, and no one would talk to her. . . . They had just washed their hands of David Gibbs.

RA: Let's talk about Lee's opinion of some of these people. That really interests me. Like, with Greenberg, what did she tell you about Greenberg? He was going to do a show of her work, and then he didn't like the work and all this.

DM: Well, everything with Lee was either hate or love, you know? . . . Bill Rubin she couldn't abide. Bill Rubin and I worked very closely with the Pollock retrospective at the Museum of Modern Art in 1967, and Bill Rubin wanted to be the curator. . . . Oh, because [the poet] Frank O'Hara had died, and he was chosen as the one to do the show. It was all settled. Then the army of Philip Johnson, everybody came over to convince me, and convince us that Bill should do the [Pollock] retrospective. Lee would have nothing to do with it.

RA: Bernice Rose?

DM: No, well, Bernice Rose was always to do the drawings. No, she said, it's got to be Bill Lieberman. So Bill had that. They worked along very beautifully together, but he wouldn't tell Lee anything, and she accepted it. . . . [He] said, "Wait till the show is open." And wouldn't let her see the hanging.

RA: Well, that kind of makes sense, doesn't it?

DM: Yes. He wanted to do his thing. . . . Lee came up and visited me upstate. . . . I had bought my first home in northern Dutchess County. It was a long story. . . . I came back from England, and I had a few friends in this town called Berrytown [New York]. I decided to go, and there was this one woman, Mary Lee Settle, who was a Southern writer. . . . She went broke, and she said, "I've got to sell my house in two weeks; will you buy it?" I said, "I don't have any money." This is when I started. She said, "You've got to buy it." Those days, like Lee's house, everything was [more affordable]. It was very similar to Lee's house. It was a Victorian house. But the location was unique and wonderful. I decided to go ahead. . . . The woman invites me to dinner, to lunch, and says I'll drive you back to New York, and she gave me some brownies. We had some brownies. Well, the brownies had hashish in them. I had no idea. I don't take any of that stuff. I had no idea. Obviously, I bought the house, and

I had to come up with the money. I had a little bit of money but nothing of significance. I approached Lee, and Lee gave me a check for five thousand dollars right away.

RA: What year was that?

DM: Oh, 1968. Then, one day, I wrote her a check and paid it off. She had no idea. She'd forgotten totally about loaning me the money. She never talked about it. I never talked about it. But the day I had the money, I wrote her a check, and she was [saying], "Oh, you don't have to do that." She took it. That was the deal. So then I invited her [to stay]. She came up once, and it was a hot summer. She loved the house because it was so similar to her home. It was unique. It was on a little finger, a little peninsula, the house was just on top of this little peninsula, and the Hudson was down there. . . . We decided to go to see the Hudson. I said there was a place called Cruger Island where this family, the Crugers, lived and built an old mansion, and the daughter died there, and it was all ruins. It was part land owned by Bard College. Bard College then was a little tiny place. It was poverty. They had no money at all. They graduated ninety students. It was called the whorehouse of the Hudson. We parked our car, and it was a little dirt road going down like that, and there were those old horrible rosebushes, and things were all coming down. It had rained, and the ground was all muddy, and the road was just not as wide as this room [ten feet]. Lee came, and she was wearing her floppy dress or something like that. She was picking up things, little rocks, flowers, and we were talking. Well, it was horrendous, and then the mosquitoes. It was so dense, and it was going darker, and darker. The tunnel of overgrown [bushes], no one went down there; it was just for the hunters. When you got down there, you'd have to go through a swamp to get to the island. But we kept walking, and walking, and walking, and finally . . . we were in a mess. We didn't know what to do with ourselves. So all of a sudden, a Jeep comes by, a hunter. He dumped us in his Jeep and took us back. Lee never, ever complained or anything.

RA: Oh, my gosh, you were stranded.

DM: We were stranded, but she loved it. She's a real trouper. She took it very, very well. I was very impressed with her. I felt so awful for her. That's why people were really unfair to her, even her best friends. I couldn't understand this love and hate thing. Mostly Greenberg and Harold [Rosenberg]. The continuation of all these people in her life, and yet they've got all these horrible moments. Just like Willem de Kooning. One minute it was a disaster. and the next minute it was back on top.

RA: I have a letter that she wrote Alfonso that said that she was very upset that he had exhibited Jackson's paintings [in his Executive House Gallery]. She said she never wanted to see him or talk to him again. There's a lot of stuff in there. I felt like she cut herself off from all of her friends, and it must have been even worse as time progressed. As I say, the Littles were the only people that I got to meet.

DM: I don't know.

RA: Betsy Miller? She liked Betsy Miller.

DM: Betsy Miller she liked. I thought she saw quite a few friends. She was certainly invited all the time to go here and [there], she was never without an engagement during my time. I mean, it was just that—she knew some very wealthy people there, at the same time she had a lot of [anger]. One thing about Lee—she was much easier with men and gay men; she adored them. They had a sense of humor. They had the wit. They had the intelligence. John [Bernard] Myers would call her every morning. I called and spoke to her most every day.

RA: You did?

DM: Oh, yes. It was hard, because frankly I did not want to be on the telephone talking to her. I could sell a painting or [something], but I mean, she looked forward to it, it was necessary to her life. She would generally be in good spirits, because she had just spoken to Johnny [John Bernard Myers], and Johnny always told her jokes, and she would repeat the jokes to me.

RA: There's a great article he wrote about naming her paintings. Did you ever name any of her paintings?

DM: That's another thing, all these titles were just titles. They were not [definitive]. People see different titles, it's just what the painting looked like. It had nothing to do with what it was really about, what she was thinking about. Oh, we would do the titles all the time.

RA: Oh, yes?

DM: What do you think? I did a couple of shows, so we'd have to go through all these titles.

RA: I think he even went to the dictionary a couple of times to find titles.

DM: The best was Howard, what's his name?

RA: Richard Howard. He's a poet.

DM: She would listen to him. Richard gave me these names. He is a smart man. I used to see a lot of them, the two of them.

RA: I'm interested in her fashion, this whole thing with her. I think that it's kind of forgotten. There's so much of this, "Ooh, she was so ugly," and really, she had a beautiful mouth.

DM: Somehow she brought herself together and she'd look [great]. I was always pleased to be with her. She had a way, everything she wore. It was beautiful fabric, and her with those amber beads, the amber necklaces. Then . . . she wore her fur coat, and she'd just go all the way.

RA: And her hair by Kenneth [Battelle]. I loved that one.

DM: Kenneth had an influence on those ladies. They just adored him. I was very close with Bunny Mellon for years. I sold the Mellons a lot of art.

RA: So Kenneth did Bunny Mellon's hair?

DM: Yes, Kenneth did.

RA: I think he also did Jackie O's.

DM: Yes.

RA: Barbara Rose did a film about Lee, and in the film, she has a clip of Kenneth doing Lee's hair, and Kenneth says to the side, "I'm scared to death of her." Which is kind of funny.

DM: She loved him. She thought he was great. And her hair looked terrific. It made a difference to her, her hair.

RA: That's so nice. What about her collage work? Can you kind of make a general comment about how she rips things up, throws them on the floor? Even at the Hofmann School? [Hans Hofmann] ripped up some of her drawings and threw them on the floor, and then throughout her whole life, she's ripping [1950s] or cutting [mid-1970s] her old drawings up and putting them back together. What do you think that's all about?

DM: Well, it has happened with artists, you know. It's not necessarily unusual.

RA: Is there anything psychological about that? Is it a rebirth or—?

DM: I'm referring to those charcoal drawings she did with Hofmann, the ones that he ripped up. In fact, she was looking at some canvases to do, for that matter, but all of a sudden, they were rediscovered. She hadn't looked at them for years. Then she does her thing. She had them all cleaned and tissue-papered and all that.

RA: It's so interesting. In terms of tearing and putting back together again?

DM: It's a rebirth. It's a little, I don't call it lazy, but it's just, like, frugal. It's frugal. It's reinventing, that's all. It's reinventing something. It's making use of something old and making it new. That's all it is, for her.

RA: She really took advantage of that. I think some of her best work is her collage work.

DM: Her works-on-paper show was great. [McKinney was referring to the 1975 exhibition, "Lee Krasner: Collage and Works on Paper 1933–74," at the Corcoran Gallery of Art in Washington, D.C.]

RA: It was a great show, wasn't it? Breathtaking.

DM: She did well with her men [those who helped her career], you know? They were devoted to her. They worked hard. Her shows were all successful in a way.

RA: Yes. I actually thought, until I talked to Barbara Rose, that most of the men had dropped by the wayside and that the women like Ellen Landau and Gail Levin [were on board].

DM: They were a different kind of women. When you think about it.

RA: The intellectuals.

DM: When you think of Betty Parsons and you think of Peggy Guggenheim, and those days—the women did not treat her well. They could not focus. They could not see her. It was the men that ended up doing something [for Lee].

RA: That's a good point.

DM: The women's lib thing was a whole rediscovery of her. It's quite obvious that she was being misused and badly treated.

RA: She was also seeing a shrink.

DM: All the time. She would go three times a week, four times a week.

RA: Into the city?

DM: Well, when she was in the city, she would do the shrink. I know that. I don't know what she did out here [in East Hampton].

RA: There was a guy named Len Siegel.

DM: Len Siegel, yes.

RA: Do you remember that name?

DM: I know she talked highly of him. She was very positive. Lee fell in love or was very close to people who were looking after her. Gerald Dickler, her lawyer, but not his wife—

RA: Carol.

DM: Carol. But she loved Gerald. She loved Gene. Gene and Claire Thaw, she liked both. Very rarely did she like the wife. I used to go to the Pollock-Krasner House for the Authentication Committee. They had a lot of problems, and the lawyers and everybody would be there.

RA: Oh, my God.

DM: Of course, I was there for all the fakes. A lot of fakes.

RA: Did you ever feel that the house was haunted?

DM: No. Not really.

RA: Why was she afraid to stay there alone?

DM: She's afraid to stay anywhere alone. She didn't want to be alone.

RA: Even in New York?

DM: Even, yes, New York. That's why I stayed.

RA: Even with the doorman . . .

DM: Yes. She believed in the world of spirits somewhat. . . . She believed that if anything was wrong with her, she would suggest bay leaves or something. You know what I mean? She was into all that.

RA: One other thing I've been working on, but I don't know if I'm going down the wrong path here, but I see a duality in her personality. She can be very angry, I'm sure you've seen her angry.

DM: Yep.

RA: And she can be very pleasant and wonderful and helpful. It's kind of unpredictable. Although maybe you know her so well that you could predict it.

DM: She could go from hot to cold. She could slam a door on you—

RA: And scream.

DM: Well, scream, but also just slam the [door] and cut you off. She could do that. She had that duality.

RA: For me, that was always hard to predict. Living with her was hard.

DM: I know. Oh, yes. . . . I would have a cup of tea, and I would just try to get the tea strong enough, and she would just get [agitated]. . . . I would just pick it up once or twice like that, and [she'd say,] "Put that down." You know, like that. . . . She was always in competition with Jackson's mother. She would always say to me, she always had a hard time because of Jackson's mother. . . . She brought up Jackson quite often. By the way, to sell a painting of Jackson's, it was hard. She didn't want to sell them. Even though we had the right to sell them, to make the deal, if the person bought a Krasner, then we [were] allowed to sell the [Pollock] painting.

RA: After Jackson died, she painted those vibrant, beautiful colored paintings. I wanted to ask you about that. It seems odd that she was painting all those vibrant colors and those beautiful lush paintings that looked very sexual to me, very much like Arshile Gorky. She says that she was crying while she was painting them. Don't they look full of joy to you?

DM: They are. They're celebrations of something.

RA: What are your thoughts on the David Gibbs connection?

DM: [His] influence. Yes. She didn't have too much of that [joy] in her life.

RA: There was this other guy, [George] Mercer, who seemed to be very smitten with her.

DM: Yes, but in a more intellectual way about art and things. It was more in that direction than in a physical [way]. David, I don't think David was that interested in her sexually. He had one goal and one goal only.

RA: This deal.

DM: It's pretty clear, I think.

RA: Part of the Marlborough package would be if they sold a Jackson Pollock, they would have to sell a Lee Krasner?

DM: It wasn't a package. To me, [it was] the only way I could get Lee to release [a Pollock painting]. She gave us the [Pollock] paintings to sell. Not everything, but we always had a nice selection of things, I would say.

RA: Then if they would say, "We like the Pollock," you would say, "Would you be interested in the Krasner?"

DM: Yes.

RA: It's kind of subtle, but yes.

DM: I was subtle with it. I said it was to their advantage, you know? . . . When you think of Lee and all these people—Rosenberg and all of them and Greenberg—she was manipulating. She'd work out something if it was to her advantage.

RA: Exactly what I think, too.

DM: She wasn't just peaches and cream.

RA: It was strategy.

DM: Yes, strategy.

RA: I think that's what James Valliere was pointing out in his talk at the Pollock-Krasner House. They would decide whom they were going to invite for dinner, who would be sitting next to whom, and then they would de-cide what the conversation at dinner would be. I don't know if you were ever pulled into that, but that's part of her strategic planning.

DM: Maybe I was, not knowing what was going on.

RA: Did you ever have to explain her paintings to people who would buy them?

DM: Oh, yes, I tried when I sold something. Everyone sees something different in a painting. Everybody wants it for different reasons.

RA: So, anyway, she loved the Whitechapel Gallery show, I'm sure.

DM: Yes, she did. She had a very good time there, and she was very happy.

RA: I think the tragedy in her life, and she had many, was that she died before she saw the show at MoMA.

DM: Yes. . . . By the way, there's a tragedy there—the whole thing, how that occurred. It was never going to happen until, don't forget, she donated a group of Pollock paintings.

RA: That was part of the deal?

DM: She did make an arrangement, as subtle or as blatant as "When are you going to do my show?" Or "When are you going to do something for me?" Then [MoMA would say,] "It would be nice for us to have large Pollocks. We could have a room of Pollocks." There were ways of handling that that would not make her uncomfortable, but they would get what they wanted, and they did.

RA: Yes. Actually, Barbara Rose did the show from Houston, and I understand it was bigger there.

DM: Yes, it was.

RA: When it came to MoMA, they put it in the basement. It was fewer paintings.

DM: Yes.

RA: Do you think this was one of her goals in life? To have this MoMA show?

DM: Oh, yes. The Museum of Modern Art was everything to her. In fact, Gail [Levin] asked me, "Why didn't Krasner give a painting to the Whitney?" Because the Whitney only collected American paintings. Pollock was not an American painter. He was an international painter. His paintings are all over the world.

RA: Oh, that's interesting. I also heard that she didn't get along with [Whitney director] Tom Armstrong. He came to see her, and she didn't like him.

DM: She went out with Tom many times.

RA: Oh, really?

DM: They went out to dinners. Tom really did a thing on her.

RA: Aha. I didn't know that.

DM: Yes. Tom made a big effort. It wasn't just a one-time-only "Come and see me" kind of thing. They were [often saying], "Come to this opening" or "Come to dinner." Whatever. They worked on her.

RA: They worked on her for one of her paintings? Or one of Jackson's?

DM: Jackson's. [Tom] was a man about town. He enjoyed parties and that kind of world. He was . . . you might say, somewhat superficial, but not saying he's not intelligent, not saying that he [didn't] know what he was doing, but—

RA: He was so well connected. Museum directors need to have those connections. Right?

DM: Sometimes that's more important than the other way. Than the scholar. Connections are extremely important.

RA: Yes.

DM: Lee would be furious today because these Chinese painters are getting thirty million for something like a new artist, and Pollock, I don't know where Pollock would be.

RA: She's doing pretty well, though. I think she's up to five million. Maybe seven. When I left that summer, Lee gave me one of those posters, the Springs Invitational poster with the chevron shape on it. She said, "I'll give this to you, Ruth, but I can't sign it. Then it would be too valuable. I can't allow myself. It's not ethical." So I was furious.

DM: Of course you were.

RA: Furious. I had spent the whole summer [working for her unpaid].

DM: This is what you don't expect her to do. I got a poster from a show at P.S. 1. I don't know if you remember or [saw] that. It's blue and white. Yellow, or cream. The very simple heart shape. She signed it. I didn't even ask her. That's the thing that makes her interesting, to put it that way. I don't know why, she can be very generous, but she was [also] tough to people who worked for her. I just find what we were talking about earlier, about this different kind of personality. Not that she was an angry lady all her life, or like that because she'd been misused. She was very generous and loving, and she did do things for people. She made [an effort with] every artist that she ever knew. . . . She'd go to their openings . . . she'd go and see them. She would do everything. She would also donate money for different things. At the same time, I was surprised that she made a deal with Bill Rubin. She got the cherry on the cake. What she wanted. And she got Pollock, not just one painting, two paintings, but six paintings or eight paintings. [MoMA records show that Krasner gave the museum three major paintings by Pollock in 1980, three years before her retrospective. There was a fourth designated in her will to be donated upon her death.]

Francis V. O'Connor
March 24, 2017

Independent art historian and author of the first doctoral dissertation on Pollock; coeditor with Eugene V. Thaw of the 1978 Pollock catalogue raisonné. With Krasner, Thaw, curator William S. Lieberman, and art dealer Donald McKinney, he served on the first Pollock authentication board. He also served on the second board, after Krasner's death and edited the Pollock catalogue raisonné supplement, published in 1995. He died in November 2017.

FVO: [Lee] wasn't generally concerned about how she, as an artist, was observed. And I guess the swings of pendulum were . . . in fact [between] Picasso and Matisse. They would suggest the structure of [a] work of art and the coloring of a work of art. . . . The most hilarious thing that I saw [was when] I had been invited over for a drink. See, I was living in Washington for many years. So when she found out I was gonna be in New York, she'd invite me to come by. So I came by around five o'clock in the afternoon, and the place was swarming with female artists. A whole crowd of those who were fighting for recognition as women and artists. . . . And so she gave me a drink. I sat down and listened to her. . . . Eventually, they all got up, and she saw them out the door, and she closed the door. And she turned around, she said to me, "Ah, I am glad to get rid of that bunch!"

RA: Well, I know she had mixed feelings about the feminist movement.

FVO: The feminist movement to her was not a great issue, I think. She moved in the art world. You could meet art dealers and artists and people from the art world in her apartment. . . . She always thought she was [a great artist in her own right].

Mark Patiky
November 7, 2017

Internationally known photographer, aviator, aviation journalist, editor, and travel writer. He photographed Krasner in 1969. His sister, Frances, was the wife of Krasner's nephew Ronald Stein.

RA: You took some of the most important photographs that were ever taken of Lee Krasner.

MP: You wanted to hear about my background first?

RA: Yes, please, tell me a little bit about yourself.

MP: I was brought up on Long Island, lived in Huntington in my early childhood. My sister, Frances, my older sister, I have two sisters, but my oldest sister, Frances, was becoming very much involved in fashion. She, in fact, had been fashion editor of *Glamour, Harper's Bazaar, Vogue,* and a variety of other publications, not only here but in Europe. . . . We did a lot of fashion work. One of the shoots that I did was actually right here in the house next door, which is the house that Frances and her husband, Ronald Stein, lived in. Now, Lee—Lee and, I'm guessing, Jackson—originally owned that property, and Frances and Ronald acquired it from her. They were living there, and it was a tiny house, which Ronnie expanded. He built a studio. Then put in a fireplace and extended rooms. It was perfect for photo shoots, so Frances said, "Come on out." We did *GQ* pictures there in the house. . . . I did meet Lee on a number of occasions. She was then with the Marlborough Gallery. I was introduced to a number of the principals of the Marlborough Gallery. Gilbert Lloyd was the son of Frank Lloyd. . . . He was a wheeler-dealer. Frank was just a delightful person, and you could see why he was so successful, because he charmed you instantly, and so did his wife, Gerta. The interesting thing was that I had a chance to meet with him on a regular basis. Of course, when I went back to London after that year in New York, I would bump into Gilbert and his sister on a regular basis. They had a chap working there named Pierre Levai. . . . I found the experience always very intriguing and charming and enlightening. It was great fun being thrown into this milieu. At the time, they represented a lot of [artists], I think Barney [Barnett] Newman was one of the artists they represented. He had an opening, and I believe Lee came to that opening. I seem to recall she was there. He was a character, and his wife was a character. If you met them on the street, you would never think of Barney Newman as this artist type. But I seem to recall he was wearing a tweed jacket and looked like a businessperson. I was introduced through Frances and also Ronald Stein, [for whom] Marlborough had a show. . . . It was intriguing meeting these people and getting a sense of the characters. . . . Ronald Stein said to me, "You know, Lee is having a show in San Francisco [1969], and she needs a photo for the poster. Would you be willing to do the photo?" . . . That's how the opportunity to come out and visit with her and spend time with her evolved. . . . I wasn't sure exactly what kind of portrait I was going to do for her. Lee wasn't the most photogenic person. I thought, "How do I deal with this?" Then Ronald Stein set this . . . event up. He said, "Call Lee." . . . She knew my sister extremely well because they lived next door. . . . I called her up, and she was very pleasant on the phone. She said, "Come out for the weekend and stay in my house, and we'll do the photographs." Again, with fear and trepidation, because I was now going to be photographing an icon of American art. . . . Yes, I did have an art history background, but what do I say? I was just really quite frightened about having this experience with her and came out in the evening. I believe it was a Friday evening. . . . Lee was going to make dinner and showed [me] my accommodation upstairs. . . . In any event, she seemed very pleasant and warm and friendly and just natural—no seeming airs or anything. She was an older woman at the time. She said, "I'm going to make dinner," she said. "You can talk to me while I'm doing this." I thought, yes, but what do I say? I was asking her about the food. My biggest concern was what do I talk about? I thought [at] first, . . . I'll impress her with my knowledge of art history. [Then] I thought, no, no, that's probably not a good idea. Then I thought, . . . just shut up and let her do the talking and then respond. That seemed to work, because Lee liked to talk. . . . She just opened [up at] the opportunity. I thought, it's so marvelous, what one has to realize is that if one can draw a person out, you really get the real person, as opposed to trying to direct them in one way or another. She pretty much talked about ordinary things, the weather and the rising cost of groceries and this and that, and all the basic normal kind of home conversation. . . . I watched as she prepared dinner. This was interesting. She was starting with a pasta, and it was a tagliatelle. I like that type of pasta. I was intrigued by what she was doing. If I recall correctly, she took the pasta, and she mixed it together with cottage cheese and sour cream and dill weed. It was spectacular. I recall taking notes on the recipe so I could reproduce it myself. When I had a dinner party in London after I returned, I called them Jackson Pollock noodles. . . . I remember she had done this extraordinary thing. It was quite simple, but it was so good. I thought, wow. This was 1969. My recollection . . . is a little bit vague about the rest of the meal, but for whatever reason, during the preparation and later when we were eating it, I don't know what it was that caused me to bring up Edward Hopper, . . . I sort of dropped the name, and her eyes lit up. She was very fond of Edward Hopper, it seems. It's good that I picked someone she liked. . . . We chitchatted about that for a while, . . . but I think that she was probably very taken by his light and shadow and the interplay. . . . My personal opinion is that when you start looking at the atmospherics in Hopper's work, it can almost be abstract. It can transition itself to abstraction. . . . I thought, well, I hit a good chord on that one. Then she said, "Would you like a chocolate nut sundae?" I thought, how can you refuse that? But I thought here's the woman in her sixties [sixty-one], she's having chocolate nut sundaes for dessert. She proceeded to scoop the ice cream and used Hershey's chocolate syrup and sprinkled crushed walnuts on the creation. I waited for her to begin, and as I watched the swirls of chocolate rivers form like lava pouring from a volcano punctuated by walnuts . . . I restrained myself from asking whether those chocolate swirls were a Pollock influence or maybe a reflection of Hofmann. . . . The next day, she made coffee, and I believe it was bacon and eggs. Then she said, "I'm going to the studio to paint." She said, "Let's go." She was certainly aware that if I was going to do a portrait, I would have to put her in different situations, but she was intent on starting to paint. . . . We did discuss the photo that we were going to take and what she wanted. I asked her to sit and talk about her work. I thought that would be the best way to get her animated. It was fascinating, because that was one of the photos of her talking about her work. In fact, she was sitting in this chair. I'm not sure that was the picture in the background, but that was ultimately the photo used for the poster. Oh, and they wanted the picture in black-and-white, by the way. That was essentially the poster itself, so I took a lot of black-and-white photos. She said, "I'm going to start working now." I timidly asked her, "Can I photograph you while you paint?" It was a remarkable response. She said yes. She then turned to me, and she said, "You know, you are the first person that has ever photographed me painting in the studio or painting at all." She turned to her yellow cart, and she prepared the colors. . . . Then I did that series in color. [shows a photo] Oh, this was her walking into the studio. I was behind her, and I was following her and photographing her as she walked.

RA: I don't know if that's ever been published. Do you think?

MP: I'm not sure it has. I started doing these in black-and-white, and then I shifted to color. But I was so taken by the way she painted, because she stood back and evaluated. This is *Portrait in Green* (1969) that she's working on. . . . She stood back, and she got her brush with the color that she wanted, [then] she attacked the canvas. She literally ran up to [it] and [made] slashing strokes with the brush. Tremendous energy involved. I thought it's fantastic that she would stand back and evaluate and know exactly where and what she was going to do. I realized that if I did these with somewhat of a motion blur, it would be much more reminiscent of her actual painting. . . . It was extraordinary, because, and I felt it, that sort of thing captured really what it was for her to be painting a particular

Portrait in Green, but in general, I'm sure that's how she dealt with every-thing.... It was just a tremendous blur of motion and action, but with just tremendous sense for what she needed to do. She would stand back and contemplate for a minute, and then launch forward.

RA: Did she have a can of paint in one hand?

MP: No. She would prepare the brush with the paint. She stood back and she ran forward.

RA: The can of paint must have been on the trolley.

MP: Yes, the can of paint was on the trolley. She prepared what she was going to do. That's probably why there was so much paint on the floor.

RA: The nice thing about the studio is that her spilling around the canvas that was tacked to the wall is still there. The floor that she painted on is not there, because that's Jackson's floor. They pulled up her floor. We've got Lee on the walls and Jackson on the floor. That's kind of wonderful.

MP: Right. This went on for some time. I was there taking these pictures. Fi-nally, she stood back, and she stopped. She said, "It's finished." I'm think-ing [to] myself, wait, I'm not sure I get all of this. I don't know why and how, but I blurted out, "How can you tell?" She turned to me, and she said, "I know." In [*Lee Krasner: A Catalogue Raisonné*], they dated this *Por-trait in Green* incorrectly, because I was photographing her in 1969 when she was painting it.

RA: Yes, and they've got it as 1966.

MP: The thing about photographing her was that she just allowed me to be invisible. I didn't say a word while she was working. I was just shooting away.... I just put the camera on a tripod, and I was clicking away and watching all of this. I thought to myself, you know, if I become too ob-trusive, she's just going to throw me out and say, "I can't work like this." ... Apparently, she became quite comfortable with me. I thought, this is marvelous. When I blurted out, "How can you tell?" and she turned to me and she said, "I know," the tone was such that she was explaining to me, as opposed to reprimanding me for asking that question.

RA: That's great.

MP: It was a fascinating experience with her. I must admit that I felt that I drew her out as much as I could in terms of being able to capture Lee Krasner, the artist. I didn't see any other way, other than the motion blurs, to really express what went into those paintings. If those were just frozen stills, you'd see someone applying paint to a canvas, and that would be it. But the real enlightening visual experience for me was the tremendous amount of action that was involved and energy that was involved and foresight. To be able to stand back and say this is where this is going, and to have that sense of where she wanted it to go. I thought because my wife paints in watercolor, and she's certainly very focused, and I thought to myself, this is a totally different way to work, where you stand back and race forward and confront the canvas as opposed to painting the canvas.

RA: Right. How much of it, do you think, came from her unconscious? Can you talk about that a little bit?

MP: I couldn't hazard a guess, other than the fact that it was interesting that the way she approached her work was such that I think a lot of it had to be a subconscious kind of interplay, because I couldn't imagine you could look at that and say, "Well, I'm going to put a little more green here, or this needs a little more white under here." It was just totally spontaneous, and fluid, and it really was. . . . And, I think to some degree, it was very different than Pollock's style. He would drip these things around, but there was so much action involved and so much energy involved [in Lee's work]. That struck me that this was hard work. When she stood back and said it's finished, and that was it pretty much for the day.

RA: Did she tell you what the title of the piece was, or you only learned later?

MP: I don't recall whether she did. I came later to learn it was *Portrait in Green*, but . . . it's interesting because she had all these other pieces in the works as well. I was amazed to see that she was working on multiple pieces at the same time.

RA: I think many of us in the art history world talk about Action Painting and talk about Jackson, but there hasn't been enough in terms of how Lee approached Action Painting and that she actually threw herself into that arena, and really was able to create these spontaneous exercises on the self. . . . There has to be some element that wasn't just about herself but touches us in a universal way.

MP: When I stood there and watched all this happening, and I was thinking to myself, there's no question this is an expression of herself, because she's put [in] such tremendous energy, and her whole being went into producing this work. I thought it was a fascinating opportunity. I wish I had understood more about what she was doing at the time. Then again, maybe that was good that I didn't because I might've imposed some of my own ideas on the photos or whatever or interrupted her freedom to work . . .

RA: Exactly. Because you were the neutral eye.

MP: Right.

RA: But I also think it's important that she must have liked you very, very much to trust you to do that.

MP: No doubt. I was amazed that she had that trust. But again, it probably built up from the moment we got together that Friday evening and we started talking. Maybe it was because so many people try to be very intellectual and talk about art and this and that and impose their ideas and test her. . . . Not only did I approach her with fear and trepidation because I didn't know that whatever I said would be considered an intelligent comment, but the other thing was that I learned from my reportage experience, just let the person be. Then you can draw them out. I guess she felt comfortable because I didn't impose my ideas or will on her to do anything in any particular way.

RA: It was a brilliant, brilliant approach, I must say, because I do think she obviously gave up a lot of her privacy in letting you go to the studio and watch her paint. She never allowed that again, so it was something very special about you. Maybe it was because of Frances, your sister.

MP: She felt comfortable, because she knew my sister, and I was not just a stranger, or a photographer she had no relationship with. . . . I was sort of almost a family member type thing. I was taken by the fact that she was so forthcoming. . . . I kept thinking to myself, wait a minute. you're dealing with an icon of American art.

RA: I'm really interested in Frances, because I think Frances introduced Lee to fashion. In that world, Lee suddenly kind of caught an interest in high fashion and Charles James. She had Charles James, the designer, design some dresses for her. There is a story that Lee had many different fur coats and that all of these were very elegant. In fact, Diana Burroughs, Jason McCoy's former wife, told me that she had Lee's sable coat, that she bought it. But she was very proud to have purchased that and that Lee was so elegant in that coat and that she went to Kenneth [Battelle] to have her hair done. I'm looking at Lee, actually, as having these different personalities at different times. Certainly, around here, she dressed in a housecoat.

MP: Oh, I think [Frances] did influence her with regard to fashion and so forth, because Frances was an icon in the fashion industry.

RA: Right. Yes. I don't think Lee ever had an opportunity to know about fashion. Growing up, she certainly didn't. Living here with Jackson, there was very little opportunity for her to get out. But once she had a chance to meet Frances, I had a feeling she must have really enjoyed that and explored all the different opportunities to be a fashion maven. She really loved that. . . . Didn't you ever see her again after that?

MP: From time to time, I'd see her in New York and also certainly at openings and things of that nature, at the Marlborough Gallery or wherever. I kept myself separate from my sister's life to a high degree. I didn't have the opportunity. I did visit out here on a number of occasions, but I recall the weekends I was visiting with Frances and Ronnie, I don't think Lee was here, we didn't stop by to visit with her. I think they kind of left Lee to her own devices as well. Virtually no other direct interaction with Lee other than that weekend. I perhaps could have pursued a relationship, but I chose not to.

RA: She was very guarded about her own interpretation, her verbal interpretation of her paintings. I think she really was convinced that if you looked at the paintings, you would understand her.

Mark Schlesinger
July 25, 2018

Krasner's studio assistant in 1972; he had participated in the Independent Study Program at the Whitney in 1971. Artist based in San Antonio.

RA: How did you and Lee meet?

MS: I was in the Whitney Independent Study Program in the fall of 1971. What's interesting to me about that moment was that in the spring of 1970, I had asked my art history professor, a man named James Marrow, who was a Northern Renaissance scholar, if he knew the paintings [of Lee Krasner]. And he said he didn't, but his classmate was a woman named Barbara Reise . . . and she was [Barnett] Newman's secretary at the time. . . . Newman agreed to meet with me, and I told him that I would be in New York in the fall of '70. The problem was he died in July 1970. And when I got to New York the following year, I promised myself that I would really take advantage of every opportunity to meet that generation of artists. So when I got to New York, I met with Marcia Tucker, who is a real hero to me. . . . She was a curator at the Whitney. And I said to Marcia, "I would love to go into the racks and see the paintings of the first generation." She said, "Yes, of course." So I went into the racks, and I pulled out this painting, and it was a painting of Lee's, and I thought it was extraordinary. . . . I said, "That painting, I think it should be on view," and there's that little room off of the old Whitney on the first floor. . . . I needed [the director of the Independent Study Program] David Hupert's permission to speak to Marcia, and Marcia was kind enough to meet with me, as was her assistant in those days, a woman named Linda Cathcart. . . . And Marcia said, "Yes, that painting needs to be seen." And so I and some of the other Independent Study Programmers put an exhibition together for that room, virtually in a week or two. . . . What I remember was that the show was one of the first times that students had done something like that and that we were interviewed at a local New York radio station (NPR). The only memory I have of what that painting might be called was that when it was lit, [the] orange on the painting jumped out, and I mentioned that on the broadcast. The day after, I'm living in a single-room occupancy hotel, and Barbara Rose calls the front desk and asks to meet with me since I asked to meet with her. . . . So Barbara agreed to meet with me, and she had heard, I believe, of my interest in Lee. She was working on a project with Lee and asked if I would like to meet Lee. I said, "Absolutely." So we met for lunch with Barbara and we went to Lee's storage, on the Upper West Side. . . . That was '71, '72. . . . And then Lee asked me if I wanted to help her. I didn't even ask what she wanted me to do. I needed money, I wasn't making anything, and secondly, God, are you kidding me? Absolutely. So I worked for Lee on Tuesdays and Thursdays, on 79th Street, late in the afternoon. Here's how kind she was; she knew that I really didn't have enough money for food, so she fed me every Tuesday and Thursday night. Generally, a roast chicken, and it was always wonderful. . . . Soon thereafter she asked if I would like to spend the summer. And I said, "Yes, of course." And so we left . . . and I remember [contemporary-art dealer] Xavier Fourcade picked us up in his car. Lee and I and [Alfonso] Ossorio drove out and stopped at [what Lee called] Ossorio's "Shack." And we walked into Ossorio's mansion. I turn to Lee, and I go, "Nice shack." That's when Ossorio still had [Pollock's painting] *Lavender Mist* (1950) in the living room. Then we went over to Lee's [on Springs Fireplace Road] and had a wonderful summer of working there. . . . The first day, she asked me just to clean out the studio. It was closed for a couple of months, and I walked into it, if you can imagine. I'm sure you had the same reaction the first time you walked into the barn, as just being in a very special place. . . . I asked Lee, "What's behind the wall?" There was a fake wall between the front room and before you stepped up into the studio, there was a fake wall there. I go, "Lee, what's behind this wall?" And she goes, "I don't know." And I said, "I'm gonna take it down." The first thing I did was take that wall down. And if you can believe this, do you know that *Blue and Black* (1953–1954) painting that went to the Houston Museum of Fine Arts?

RA: It was in the show in Houston and then went to New York.

MS: It's a wonderful painting, and if I remember correctly, Barbara [Rose] was the one who got that painting into the Museum of Fine Arts when she was the curator there. . . . I found it behind the wall. . . . Then I cleaned up the space, and Lee had a painting on the wall from the previous summer—that would be the summer of '71—and she asked me to go to the hardware store, buy wood, and to make a stretcher for it. And I looked at her, and I said, "Don't you really want to get a good stretcher for it?" And she said, "Let me think about it." And she got a good stretcher. . . . I stretched canvas on the wall, and she gave me specific instructions [for] how she wanted it sized, by the [Rivet] glue, and that's what I did, and then she started painting. I've heard that no one was ever in the studio with her when she painted. Were you ever in the studio with her?

RA: No, and I've met one other person, Mark Patiky, who was a photographer, and he photographed her in motion. It's not on video film, it's on still film, but it's a great series of shots that he did.

MS: I was in the studio when she painted. . . . And we worked together. I put tape on the paintings, and she said, "No, a little to the left, a little to the right . . ." And that was amazing for me.

RA: You put the tape on them before she actually painted on it?

MS: Right.

RA: To kind of block the paint from sloshing over.

MS: Right. . . . Neither she nor I put it on tightly because she wanted that kind of Mary Heilmann ooze under the tape—so brilliant. And she worked really slow. I'm sure you've heard that, but she did not paint quick. She looked and looked and looked. . . . Lee always waited for the painting to come to her, that was her words. She was waiting for the painting to come to her. . . . I think that there's something really . . . profound in that. . . . Even when she worked at night in the city, I would stay around, and we would talk while she waited for the painting to come to her. . . . I want to ask you a question, and I don't want to be misunderstood, and please don't think this is inappropriate. Do you think you being a woman caused your problems in your relationship [with Lee]? . . . Nancy Graves told me this.

RA: It could have been the case, because, in fact, when I first got to know her, when I would meet her in the city, it seemed very congenial. Then, when I was out here in the country, it got tougher and tougher, so I don't know.

MS: I just always wondered why she responded to people in ways that she didn't respond to me or other men . . . and certainly other gay men. . . . So just to circle back to . . . Marcia Tucker. I go, "You have to get Lee a show, you have to get Lee a show." This was in her office at the Whitney. Linda Cathcart was there. She said, "You're right, I will." And I told that to Lee. I had really just started working for Lee. Lee was, like, "Yeah, I'll believe it when I see it." Do you remember the fall of '73 show?

RA: Yes, the one that Marcia did? It was called "Lee Krasner: Large Paintings."

MS: Marcia told Lee initially that she was going to have the full floor and it was going to be a large retrospective. And what happened was, I go over to Lee one day, and she's really upset. Lee said that she had gotten a call that she's only going to have half the floor, and the other half at some point was going to go . . . to Joan Mitchell in, I think, January or February of '74. So the two women were going to have half the floor, and both were promised full floors. . . . Lee was really upset and wanted to cancel the show. . . . I was extremely surprised, but I remember saying to Lee, "Why? Why would you want to think of canceling it?" And she said, "If I do the show, that's my retrospective, [and] that's it." And I said, "Lee, that's not true, that's really not true. If you do the show, you might still get a retrospective. If you don't do the show, no one's going to know your work. And you're not going to get a retrospective." . . . Richard Howard and Johnny [John Bernard] Myers advised her the same way, and she agreed to do the show. But here's the interesting thing. Marcia was just under the thumb of [Whitney curator] Robert Mac Doty, who was under the thumb of [Whitney director] John Bauer. . . . Marcia said that they were never going to give retrospectives again on the fourth floor. Which was a lie.

John Bauer did not want to give a woman a retrospective. It had nothing to do with Marcia, it was John Bauer. . . . Gail's book [Levin, *Lee Krasner*] said it was Marcia. It wasn't. Marcia is a hero here. . . . She did really great things there. Absolutely. . . . If you hear anything from me today, that's what I want you to hear. . . . Don't you think Lee was right to do the show?

RA: Of course. That's actually the first time I saw her big paintings. That was a gorgeous show.

MS: It was stunning. Absolutely a great show. As was Joan's show. Joan's show was great, too.

RA: I've been wondering about your personal relationship with Lee as well. How did you entertain yourselves? What were her quirks? What did she demand of you? For example, did you drive for Lee when you were in East Hampton?

MS: Very rarely, but I did drive, and she drove. It was up to her. She would say, "Do you want to drive?" And I would say, "Sure." Or else she would just get in the driver's seat and drive the old car. . . . What I remember most was having my first strawberry-rhubarb pie. And this was a specialty, there was this African American woman who made strawberry-rhubarb pie, and Lee made a point of on a certain day going to buy strawberry-rhubarb pie. And I never had that before. It was amazing. . . . It was an African American woman, she was elderly and beautiful and loved Lee. I guess you know, Lee . . . was a different person around different people. She could be incredibly reserved, or she could be incredibly spontaneous, and around this woman she was incredibly spontaneous. And with that wonderful laugh of hers. I mean it was an extraordinary thing to see. As opposed to seeing her around Ossorio, whom she was incredibly sarcastic around. . . . When Ted Dragon walked in, it was like Lee would have nothing to do with him, and I never knew why . . . she absolutely zeroed him out.

RA: Wow, and do you know anything about Ossorio and Lee's relationship? Was it close? Was he buying her paintings at that time?

MS: Oh, here's how naive I was. I didn't know who he was, . . . so I can't answer that, I don't know, I'm sorry. But . . . he was absolutely friendly and in awe of her. Just such a gentleman, that's what I remember.

RA: I heard that Jackson and Lee had their own bedroom at the Creeks [Ossorio's house in East Hampton] so that when they would have dinner at Ossorio's, they could actually crash there, rather than drive home.

MS: I never heard that—that's beautiful, though. From what I've learned subsequently, Ossorio was quite a wonderful and generous man. . . . Did you happen to meet him at all?

RA: No, actually, by the time I got here, she wasn't speaking to him.

MS: What happened?

RA: Well, I found a telegram that she sent to him, telling him to never speak to her again. I don't know why she was upset with him. From what I could tell, he was so generous to her constantly. Buying paintings and helping financially. Oh, it was just amazing. . . . Did she—was she in touch with [Willem] de Kooning then, or no?

MS: Oh, I'll tell you, here's an interesting story apropos. And thank you for bringing up de Kooning. On the ride out, the first ride out, Fourcade was driving, and Ossorio was asking me some not very prying questions but appropriate questions. I told him what I'm interested in, I told him that I worked in a paint factory when I was a teenager and that I'm interested in paint. And Fourcade, I guess, had told that to de Kooning, and de Kooning calls up Fireplace Road and asks to speak to me. Of course, Lee picked up the phone and said, "Mark, come here." And she goes, "De Kooning wants to speak to you, Bill wants to speak to you." And I go, "What?" I thought it was a joke, because Lee knew I kind of like de Kooning's work. So de Kooning gets on the phone and invites me to the studio to talk about paint. . . . And I said, "Let me think about that—let me call you back." I did not know Lee's relationship to de Kooning at that time, and I thought, it'd be horrible for me to leave Lee to see de Kooning if Lee and de Kooning were on the outs. So I asked Lee, "You're not going to believe this," and she goes, "What?" "De Kooning wants to talk paint with me. Would you have any problem with me going over to his studio?" And she said, "No. But just count your fingers when you leave." And I remember that quote, "just count your fingers when you leave." And so I went over to de Kooning's and had, just as you can imagine, an extraordinary afternoon in that room. . . . I have a vague memory that he had a stack of beautiful drawings as you left, and he said, "Mark, take one." And I said, "No way, man, I'm not doing that. I'd rather come back for another conversation." My fear was that it was a test, that if you took a drawing, you would never be invited back. And what was more important to me was being with him, and listening and talking about painting and paint, than about having a drawing. He looked at me, like I guess everybody took one, and I was invited back. I had another afternoon, again with Lee's permission. Starting that summer of '71, he was kind of fragile.

RA: Did any other people stick out in your mind? Was [Robert] Motherwell around?

MS: Oh, God, no. Thank God. No way. No way. Here's a story . . . here's how interesting the art world can be. I skipped a story, after Newman's tragic death in '70, I had looked at Helen Frankenthaler's paintings, and I kind of liked them, and so my intent was, I wanted to meet all of the [first-generation Abstract Expressionist] artists who were still alive. They were all interesting to me. I come from—you have to understand—I come from a place where there was no art. I come from Elizabeth, New Jersey. There were no books in my house, there was never a painting on the wall, there was never music, we never had a television. . . . I basically grew up with a single mother, single-parent home. There was nothing, but I had great teachers in high school. My parents, my friends' parents, were kind to me. I went to the State University of New York at Binghamton; I didn't have to pay a cent to go there. I had great teachers in high school and great teachers at Harper College in Binghamton. And I just wanted to know as much about making paintings, from painters, as quickly as possible. So I wrote a letter to Helen [Frankenthaler]. Helen responded and invited me down. I went down from Binghamton to New York, went to the townhouse on 91st or 92nd Street, and spent the day with Helen. And we became friendly. And that's how I met Barbara Rose, through Helen. . . . Little did I know that . . . Lee hated Helen. She despised her.

RA: They shared a studio at one point, I've just discovered, so they must have been friends at some point. But yeah, I knew that Lee and Helen did not get along. . . . So . . . what did you do in between those two summers, between '72 and '73?

MS: I was in New York . . . and starting to try to have a career and still trying to work for Lee.

RA: Do you remember what series she was working on?

MS: Yeah, this is interesting, because she wanted me to start cutting out those Hofmann drawings. And I couldn't do it. I told her, "Lee, I just think this is wrong, I can't do this." . . . And that's when I pretty much had to stop working for her. . . . She needed someone to help her cut out the paper.

RA: They were actually quite large, and at that time, I understand she had rheumatism or arthritis, and so it was hard for her to stand.

MS: Yeah, [if] my memory was true, even in the summer of '72 . . . her hands had really started to become misshapen. She was able to hold brushes, but I think that I also had to do some painting, because I think on [some] days her hands were really terrible. Then it just got worse until she passed.

RA: So describe to me how your work with her went.

MS: It was basically, we talked about color, and she recognized for some reason that I have a color sensibility. Do you know that Lee had the best eye in New York? Have you heard this?

RA: Yes, yes, I have.

MS: Have you heard that [Clement] Greenberg admitted that her eye was better than his?

RA: Yes.

MS: OK. So Lee and I would go look at paintings. We would go to the museum, and we would talk about paintings. One of the great experiences was . . . looking at paintings with Lee. Looking at paintings with Barbara Rose. Looking at paintings with Charles Stuckey, looking at paintings with Richard Shiff, looking at paintings with Jasper [Johns]. That, to me, was how I learned about painting, [it] was looking at paintings with people who knew a lot more than I did. It turns out I probably have a pretty good eye, [albeit] not as good as Lee, I believe. But Lee and I would go, and we would look at paintings. And we started mixing colors together, and I would put on a color, and we would look at it, and we would talk about how we felt about the color there. . . . And it wasn't anything more than "I like it," or "I can see what that can do." . . . It was not really theoretical at all. . . . When I said that Lee introduced me to my first dealers, you know who [David] Gibbs was? He's passed away—but Gibbs was a Marlborough dealer. And he was an Englishman, and something of a rascal, but he was a great dealer. So the first dealer that Lee introduced me to was David. Now, I had heard that David and Lee had an affair.

RA: And this would have been in the '60s?

MS: Yes. But if you had heard that Lee and David stopped talking to each other, that would be wrong. They were as different as anything imaginable, but there was a bond between the two of them that was very, very strong.

RA: And then, of course, there was this question of who was going to represent Pollock in the States. Marlborough already was representing Pollock in London.

MS: Right.

RA: It looks like Lee then made a deal with them that she would also have [a show], I think she had four exhibitions at Marlborough, and that Ron Stein, her nephew, would also have a show at Marlborough. . . . Tell me about David Gibbs. How do you think he impacted her life?

MS: He was incredibly charming, incredibly good-looking, he was worldly. If you can imagine, the opposite of Pollock, that would be David Gibbs. He was articulate, funny, worldly. He was a war hero.

RA: David Gibbs, I think, was really the catalyst for Lee's coming into her own. You know, after Jackson passes, and many people have told me that David Gibbs was a con artist and maybe he was.

MS: He wasn't . . . I don't think he was the smartest businessman. OK, have you seen the naked photographs of Lee?

RA: Yes, in Provincetown.

MS: When you see those photographs and you see the Lee of the '60s with the glasses and the hair. I think that David and Lee had an incredibly sexual relationship. And I think they really liked each other. And I think she trusted him. . . . That's why she introduced me to him. I worked with David for a number of years. I don't think he was a con artist. . . . I think he was a womanizer, but I don't think he was a con artist.

RA: Do you know about Geraldine Stutz?

MS: I do know about her. . . . She was a tough, tough person. And, of course, she ran the store. Henri Bendel . . . the department store. She had the house in Connecticut; she was a number. David sold a number of my mid-'70 s paintings to friends of Geraldine.

RA: They were married for ten years, and it seems that they were married sometime in the mid-'60s. [1965].

MS: Yeah.

RA: Lee was brokenhearted because he didn't tell her about Geraldine and went off with her and married her. But evidence shows that he was still very much a part of Lee's life right up to the end. . . . I understand that David Gibbs left Marlborough as a consultant, and in fact, Donald McKinney, who was the director of Marlborough during the time that Lee was there, says that David Gibbs was not there for very long. I can't find out exactly how long, but then he went to Pace, and I've interviewed Arne Glimcher, but Arne doesn't remember when David was at Pace. Do you remember that?

MS: Well, I have a vague memory that when David was at Pace, so was Lee.

RA: Exactly. That's what I'm getting at. That's exactly what I'm getting at.

MS: And that's when Lee showed the collages . . . at Pace, and I have a vague memory that that's because of Gibbs, but Gibbs was not at Pace for very long.

RA: Exactly.

MS: And when he left Pace, that's when he formed his other gallery, Gibbs Gallery in SoHo, and that's when I joined him. And that would be around '76 or '77.

RA: It does seem to me, and I asked Arne Glimcher if Gibbs had something to do with Lee being at Pace. Arne doesn't remember.

MS: I agree. . . . I did ask Arne if he felt there was any kind of ulterior motive . . . for him to invite Krasner into the gallery, because, of course I think with Marlborough they were interested in Jackson Pollock. But Arne Glimcher says he had no interest in Pollock at all. Do you think that could be true?

RA: I do.

MS: You know, I loved Lee, but I think Lee really, at times, really made it hard for herself. That there were certain dealers that she could have worked with and it would have been OK, it really would have been OK. Like, why she didn't really want to work with Robert Miller.

RA: Well, she did, finally.

MS: I think she could have worked with him earlier. She knew him, she liked him, there was John Cheim [gallery director at Cheim & Read] working at Miller, and John Cheim loved Lee. The way he loved Joan Mitchell. And he was the best, he was the best with these old, difficult women.

RA: Yeah, I interviewed him, and he said he loved them.

MS: I'll tell you one story. . . . I'm curious about this 9th Street studio with Frankenthaler and Lee. I got married in '75. Lee was going to come to the wedding—it was just a small [ceremony], not a big thing. And she heard from someone that Helen was coming to the wedding, and she called me up and said, "Is Helen coming to your wedding?" And I said, "Yes, she is." And she said, "Well, then I'm not." And I said, "OK, I'm gonna call you right back." I called up Helen, and I said, "You can't come to the wedding." She said, "No, Mark, I love you, I'm coming to the wedding." I said, "You can't." She said, "You're just being difficult, I'm gonna come." And she came, and Lee didn't. That to me is indicative of Lee's sensitivity, not wanting to be around certain people. Knowing that those people really bring out bad sides of her. And Helen believing that the whole world exists for Helen, and Helen not taking no for anything. Qualities that I admire in both, by the way.

RA: Now, speaking of personalities, I've tried to do some research on Lee and her psychoanalyst, whose name was Len Siegel. He evidently lived out here, maybe on Three Mile Harbor Road, and also had an office in the city. It seems that she started going to him before Jackson died. Then, after he passed, she continued on with him. Do you know anything about her analysis?

MS: No, only stressing how important it was that I get into analysis. . . . Which I did. It's just what New York Jews do.

RA: Well, did she recommend an analyst?

MS: She did not. She did not venture that far into that suggestion. It took a while, I finally found an analyst, but it was not someone that Lee would know.

RA: But what about her personality? Can you describe, you know, she's so friendly and open with you, then with other people she's so angry? I mean, what happened to her in those moments?

MS: Believe me, I've thought about it, and I recognized that for years I judged people the way Lee judged people. And that . . . was not a good thing to do. . . . But Lee was incredibly competitive and incredibly insecure at the same time. I don't know if you ever were invited to one of her evening dinners to talk. So when you met her, you arrived at, like, four, five o'clock in the afternoon, and you would sit in the room. You might have a Campari and soda, there might be some nuts. Then you'd talk and then you'd go and sit in the dining room and have a roast chicken dinner or a pot roast dinner—whatever she cooked or bought around the corner. And one time a young art historian came and was talking. [She] was talking to Lee about Lee, then it was getting close to dinner. I was there, and I was sitting to Lee's left, and the young art historian, a female art historian, sitting to Lee's right. Lee's about to serve them food, and the art historian asked Lee a personal question about Pollock. . . . So Lee looked at her. . . . that was the trigger. If you're there to talk to Lee, talk to Lee about Lee. You don't set Lee up and ask her about herself and then ask the Pollock question. So I get served chicken, and she doesn't. She's not served anything. And she tries to talk to Lee and apologize. Lee absolutely—the way she did with Ted Dragon—Lee absolutely zoned this young art historian out. And she got up, and I walked her to the door, and I came back, and I looked at Lee, and Lee was almost in tears. . . . So when artists of a generation older than me would refer to her as Mrs. Pollock, can you imagine? Can you imagine a painter of the '60s referring to her as Mrs. Pollock? And I would say, "You mean Lee?" And he goes, "Yes, Mrs. Pollock." There was never an end to it, and to me that was really heartbreaking.

RA: Yeah, that was a tragedy. Really for her. She tried so hard. I was told by Cindy Nemser, who warned me that Lee would be difficult—she said never mention Jackson. So going into it, I never mentioned him, and she never mentioned him, either. Did she talk to you about Jackson?

MS: She actually did. . . . You know there's that really beautiful front room? We would sit out there; it was so quiet. . . . I'd never been in any place like that. I don't know if you have, but I really thought it was . . . as peaceful a place that I had ever been. And I treasure those memories . . . it's sort of like . . . the sunlight on my body. I just treasured that quietness that Lee gave me. And she would talk and reminisce, not often, but she would bring up Jackson, and I never asked, either. I was never warned, but I knew that was not the thing to do. First of all, I adored her, and I adored her paintings, and I just respected her. . . . One time we were sitting, maybe it was [at the] Guild Hall, actually. I'm sitting with Lee, and Nancy Graves walks over, and Nancy had on a kind of really beautiful big beret. I liked Nancy a lot, I thought she was really a first-rate person. And Lee looked at her and said, "Who do you think you are, Rembrandt?" And Nancy, being Nancy, just was able to parry that into "It's nice to see you, Lee, I hope you're well." And just walk away with some dignity. And I looked at Lee, and she said, "Pretentious bitch."

RA: Yes.

MS: And that's another trigger. Have you ever experienced if someone acted pretentious in front of her, that was it?

RA: I didn't, but John Cheim told me that he had that experience when he was with Lee in Houston at the exhibition ["Lee Krasner: A Retrospective," 1983–1985]. And people would come over and say, "Oh, what a great show." You know, "This is so wonderful." And Lee would turn her back on them and, you know, make them feel like they were insulting her in a way. He said it was very heartbreaking to see that.

MS: Yeah, [but] I would not be; I would not have the career that I have had if it wasn't for women. I know that. I know that in my soul. I had great male friends, I had great female friends. But I once witnessed at a dinner, a dinner for Joan Mitchell after an opening at Fourcade. Fourcade placed two paintings [which he'd] sold to one man, and at the dinner he was sat next to Joan. And Joan turned to him and blasted, "Just because you bought my paintings, don't think you fuckin' own me."

RA: Oh, my God. I heard she was difficult.

MS: Yeah, so he just . . . again, he just excused himself and exchanged places with a younger person who sat next to Joan. . . . And they could feel the vibration in the room. . . . And her paintings are that way. . . . And when I introduced [Lee] to the woman I was going to marry, [Lee] wasn't calm.

RA: Was she happy for you?

MS: I think she was happy about my making paintings that she liked; I don't know if she was ever happy that I got married. It never came up. Other than she wouldn't come to the wedding, but that was not because of the woman I was marrying but because she . . . did not want to be around Frankenthaler.

Jason McCoy
September 13, 2017

Krasner's nephew by marriage and son of Pollock's broth-er, Sanford (Sande) McCoy.[366] He and then-wife, Diana Bur-roughs, spent summers in the mid-1970s near Krasner in Springs. Director and owner of the Jason McCoy Gallery in New York since 1982.

RA: I understand that you and your former wife, Diana, helped Lee in her last years.

JM: Well, I certainly do have powerful memories of Lee, and I will start, I guess, by saying that she was with Jackson [and was] a part of my life from as far back as I can remember. Yes, but after my father's death in 1963, . . . Lee, who had been very close to my father, took a much great-er interest in me than she ever had directly as a younger person. I don't think she really knew what to do with young people, necessarily. Jackson had an inner warmth that extended to children quite naturally. But Lee . . . it didn't come naturally to Lee. That being said, when I was sixteen, and I'm fond of remembering, because I could drink, drive, and smoke, I became much more interesting to her, and I began to spend summers with her because she loathed [spending] nights alone in the house.

RA: What year was that?

JM: 1964. . . . The relationship developed as I got older, too. I moved to New York, and I would see her once a week, at least. . . . I had a constant and long relationship [with her] from, let's say, 1964 to 1984. That was the year that she died. . . . My ex-wife, Diana, and I tried to see her once a week, and sometimes it worked and sometimes it didn't. But Diana and I met in 1975 and married in 1977. One of the nice things in my life that I'm pleased to have shared with Lee was Diana, and I have three children. Our first son was born in 1982, and we called him Sanford Roy, actually, after both

. . . Diana's dad's name, Roy, and my father's name was Sanford. . . . Our second child was born two years later in 1984. His name is Jackson. . . . We knew we were having a boy, and I asked Lee if it would be all right to name him Jackson. I think she was happy. She died, of course, before Jackson was born, but she knew, as we knew, that it would be a boy.

RA: So what was your first real memory of Lee?

JM: My first . . . Well, I have . . . I don't know where it sits in my memory, but one of the associations I have is her cooking and something about fish for dinner and . . . I associate this with Lee and always have, but the decision was for a fillet of sole, and I had no idea what that meant. . . . Of course, I have a memory that Jack and Lee gave me my first bicycle. . . I don't know, my parents may have bought it. I don't know, but . . . the bike was a Humber, which is an unusual English bike at that time. It was sort of the Bentley of [bicycles], the Rolls-Royce in the branding way. . . . But it had narrow tires, and it was orange and [had] white fenders. I learned to ride a bicycle, and it was hell, because everybody else had wide tires and streamers on their [handlebars]. . . . I went on to master riding it eventually, because the tires were so narrow and skinny and my dad used to take us . . . across the street to the parking lot of a factory, which is nothing but two inches of gravel. I fell so many times, because it was soft and [the tires were] narrow. Of course, training wheels were out of the question. I don't think I was ten years old. . . . It was a big bike. . . . But I'm saying, [it was] also typical of Lee [and] Jack, in a certain way, generosity, and in another way, not having any idea how old I was. That really was something else that was about Lee. Because when my dad died in December, when Lee saw me and we began . . . to see each other, and I started to spend time in the Springs, she never, ever considered me anything other than an equal.

RA: So what did your mom and dad think about Lee?

JM: I think . . . my dad and Lee were very close. . . . Sometimes there were summers or periods of time that [my mother, Arloie] would go over and they'd . . . babysit [for Krasner].

RA: OK. I am discovering that there are a whole bunch of us who spent summers with her.

JM: And my mother was one of them. Depending on, and I really don't remember the schedule of who was where when . . . but in spring, it was always an issue. I remember when Diana and I were married, or at least together for, I guess, two years before we got married, '75 and '76, and were married in '77. But around that time I began renting the studio, the apartment that John Little had in his barn.

RA: Do you think your mom and dad both really loved Lee?

JM: They were sisters-in-law. I think Lee . . . tolerated my mother, but I wouldn't say that they were close. I think she loved my father, and I think she respected my father. I think she respected them both for the time that they lived with Jackson, or Jackson lived with them. In fact, Lee and Jackson stayed on [in their New York apartment when] my parents left and moved to Connecticut. . . . But at that time . . . it was my mom who I know Lee didn't [like very much]. . . . She tolerated her. And she would use her, of course.

RA: Lee was upset about Bob Friedman's book, *Jackson Pollock: Energy Made Visible*, published in 1972.

JM: Yes, she was.

RA: Probably because of the references to Ruth Kligman. Do you think?

JM: I think Lee knew full well who Ruth was, and in a curious way, Lee . . . was terribly honorable. She never talked about Ruth. She never talked about Jackson in disparaging ways. I can't say that she didn't like gossip, because I know she would [gossip] with Josephine [Little]. She would [gossip] with Ted [Dragon]. . . . Part of the style of life then was, if you came . . . home, wherever you came from, after dinner, you'd spend an hour, maybe, rehashing what Edward [Albee] said or Alfonso [Ossorio] said. But there was a lot of meditation about everything. From making a salmon to making a chicken. . . . If she was making a salmon, it would be very specific. I picked up all of those kinds of trademarks, so as not to lose my own head. I remember, I'm sure it was me, coming down and saying, "What a nice day." Lee was at the table with a cigarette and tea, and all that, saying, "What makes you think it's a nice day? Why? What's so nice?"

RA: I know.

JM: A mistake. You know? And if you ever saw Lee in an interaction with Frances Stein, her nephew's wife until they divorced, they would really fight. . . . My mother was unequipped to deal with anything [negative]. That time when Diana was breaking down—this was in New York. It was a Sunday night, and Lee turned on her and reduced Diana to tears. It was some feat. Diana said, "Why are you being so mean to me?" Lee said she couldn't explain it. . . . But, you know, Diana would bicycle over from the Littles' to stay with Lee, because Lee was alone . . . but usually, there was one . . . person, usually a woman, who might get picked on or couldn't do anything right.

RA: How about reading? I'm very interested in whether you saw her reading or not.

JM: Lee, I don't think, read at all. I don't know whether she may have been dyslexic. . . . I have no idea. She liked to be read to . . . I don't recall her ever with a book herself. . . . She would stew. There were times she wasn't working, she didn't paint. She might go to the studio and sit. . . . Then she'd talk to me. The most difficult times for her [were] not when she was working, but when she was not. . . . I think she had more book learning in the sense of what she took from Hofmann. Her ideas were structural, more Hofmann-esque. Although, I think she admired Matisse more than Picasso. Jackson, in a sense, was more intuitive in his need and reasons to paint. I think Lee's ambitions were initially more structured. She focused on . . . the Cubism and Hofmann's lessons, and the way that she looked at art history was, I don't want to say more traditional, but maybe, more analytical in a way. . . . And she brought that to Jackson, as she brought Hofmann to Jackson.

RA: I never met this David Gibbs. What do you know about him? . . . I've read that they were engaged.

JM: Never saw the ring.

RA: OK. But they did go to Bermuda together.

JM: I don't remember that, either.

RA: Yes. Anyway, he was persuasive in getting her to Marlborough Gallery?

JM: Lee really liked Frank Lloyd . . . because he was direct. He was direct about money.

RA: What stands out in your mind about Lee that others have overlooked?

JM: At this point in time, I don't know that Lee is overlooked.

RA: Yes. Well, I don't mean to say that she's overlooked, but . . . is there something about her? Something about her talent or her artwork?

JM: She was authentic to herself . . . I think uncompromising, difficult, she had no need to curry favor with anyone. I think that there are a lot of things that, even since her death, come to [mind]. . . . She was the equivalent of my Picasso. Someone who was so big in my life, and she was incredibly generous . . . I guess, [by] treating me as an adult. Lee was a great, great lady.

RA: Do you know about her psychoanalysis with Dr. Leonard Siegel?

JM: Sure. Yes, she saw him.

RA: She's talked about the swing of the pendulum, kind of a yin and yang in parts of her life or paintings. Did you see that?

JM: I wouldn't think of a pendulum. I think I knew John Little was involved with the I Ching, and she was, I don't know, I wouldn't say fascinated, but she was interested. And she's interested in Catholicism. Alfonso's Catholicism, Josephine's Catholicism. . . . There's so much about Lee that makes sense, but it's hard to describe. . . . The considered way that she dealt with her art, with her life, and of course, towards the end of her life, how she meticulously planned a studio and recycled all [her work] . . . looked at every picture and either destroyed it or changed it.

RA: At the end of her life she did this?

JM: Well, the last ten years. The suite of collage paintings, when she no longer had the physical energy to paint.

RA: The Hofmann drawings.

JM: And she recycled them. . . . And she discovered them, of course, with Bryan Robertson, in the attic of the house in Springs. But she looked at every drawing, and one pile was to keep and then one pile was to destroy. She didn't destroy that pile. Immediately she remade a series of collages, using, as she had in the '50s, the piece of drawing that Jackson had discarded, rice paper, and whatnot, and her own paintings. What all that means about a gesture or imitation, she thought a great deal about what she was doing. For all of the business of abstract art and the meaning, nothing was ever arbitrary. Although everything was from nature. I think that that was who she was. You know, she was certainly full of passion . . . and held a grudge.

RA: She had a strong sense of her own right and wrong.

JM: And her glamor. But it's Frances Stein who gave Lee her style. Frances would introduce Lee to Kenneth [Battelle, the first celebrity hairstylist], who cut her hair, to Charles James, who [designed her] wardrobe, . . . the Ritter Brothers [furriers, then located at 32 East 57th Street]. Lee's first ever passion, if she was said to have a passion for something, it was for fur coats.

RA: Yes, I didn't know that, though. She had leopard? I knew about the fur coats, but I actually didn't know what. . . . She had sable?

JM: She had sable. When she died, we bought her sable coat for Diana. It was great. . . . But that is also kind of the way Lee was. She wouldn't have cared about a [car]. She had a Ford convertible, a 1960, that Ronny must've encouraged. Then she got that [Mercury] Comet, which she was probably still driving in 1974.

RA: She wasn't driving anything when I knew her. You drove her around in a Comet?

JM: It was a two-door Comet. Huge engine. It sounded like grumbling power, no muffler. . . . Diana would also help. She loved Lee, too. Lee . . . tolerated her, but Lee can be so mean. She was never mean to me, and if she was, I didn't call for a couple of weeks. There's no point in engaging. There's nothing to fight about. Yes, but I loved her.

Diana Burroughs
September 20, 2017

Formerly married to Jason McCoy, Krasner's nephew by marriage. She first visited East Hampton with McCoy in summer 1975 and returned over the next nine years. She lived near Krasner, in John Little's barn at Duck Creek, and would often spend the night at Krasner's. Currently director of prints at the Marlborough Gallery, New York.

DB: The first time I met Lee was the first summer I was with Jason. It was 1975, and Jason had rented the apartment in John Little's barn. . . . I was twenty-seven years old. I wanted to be very polite, and I said, "Can I help you?" Lee said, "Yes." She was making a fish dish, and she wanted me to seed the cucumbers. Now I know how to seed a cucumber, but at that time I had no idea. Now obviously, you cut it in half lengthwise, and you take a spoon, and you just scrape out the thing. She said, "Seed the cucumbers." I cut it in half, and I'm taking one seed [at a time], and she never said anything to me. Ordinarily, what you would do is say, "Here, let me show you how to do it." She just let me suffer. . . . She was such a difficult woman. I think Jason was her want-to-be son, she was his want-to-be mother, so they had a relationship of mother-son that was wonderful because they weren't mother and son. They didn't have the stuff that comes in between. They genuinely loved one another. . . . I was the not-wanted extra person. She tolerated me, but if you went to her house for dinner, and we used to go once a week in the city, there was always somebody . . . it was like Russian roulette, there was always somebody who was "It." Nine times out of ten, I would say I was "It." I probably exaggerate; maybe it was seven times out of ten. When you're "It" most of the time, you think you're "It" all the time. When that was the case, then I could say, "Oh, it's windy out." Like we're looking right now. She'd say, "Who are you to talk about the wind? Are you the weather?" . . . You know the voice. . . . There was no winning. I was always so tremendously relieved when somebody else was "It." I remember that poor person opened their mouth and was yelled at. I went, "Oh, my God, I can get through the evening and I'm going to be OK." I really found it hard, but she was a great artist. You forgive genius because, for whatever it was, there are other people who are just horrible and have no redeeming qualities. She had the most beautiful arms—I don't know if you remember—the most beautiful arms of anybody I've ever seen. That's not something you say, "Oh, they've got great legs" or "beautiful hair." She had such beautiful arms, and if you look at pictures you'll see. She was a great artist, so I tolerated it up until she died, in June of 1984, and my second child was born in October '84. The spring before she died, she was in and out of the hospital. I remember visiting her, and I was three months pregnant or something like that, and she was horrible to me. I said to myself, "I'm not subjecting myself to this, I'm not subjecting my child to this, I'm out." I said to Jason, "I'm out. I refuse to do it." . . . I did not see her from that moment, let's just say, March, until June when she died.

RA: Who asked her if it was all right to name this child Jackson? Was it you or Jason?

DB: Nobody asked her. It was none of her business.

RA: I've had several people say that they saw Lee as very glamorous. My experience was that she was very plain, in a good way, a strong way.

DB: I think that by the time you and I met Lee, she had become not glamorous and kind of frumpy and dowdy. Jackson died in '56, and I met her twenty years later. She clearly went through a period; she had all the fur coats. She got, I think, five fur coats. I still have her sable.

RA: Do you wear it?

DB: I do. I had to buy it from the estate for three thousand dollars. The rest were stolen by the help. When she was dying, she had nursing care from New York Hospital. They stole her gray pearls and her Fischer coat. All her good things. It was the sable; she must've bought it either in the '50s or the '60s. [It was] voluminous. By the time I got it—probably in '85— there was all the anti-fur [atmosphere]. This was, like, you couldn't escape the coat because there was so much [of it]. I think in terms of glamor, she had . . . the designer, Charles James. She apparently went through a phase where she did Charles James clothes. I have a dress of hers that was beautiful. I wouldn't wear it now because I'm too old; this is for a younger person to wear, but it's spaghetti straps, like a flapper dress, chiffon, those layers. Fabulous. It fits me—I have to be no heavier than I am now. Lee, when you and I knew her, could never have worn that dress, but it was her dress. She clearly was glamorous in that period, but not when you and I knew her. She always wore those smocks.

RA: What about the intellectual side of Lee? Would you consider her an intellectual?

DB: Would I say she's intellectual? No, I never would have called her an intellectual. She was clearly very smart. She was clearly curious. She had very interesting friends. I always felt that when we went to her house in New York, because that's when she entertained, there were always interesting people. . . . Well, she was friends with Edward Albee. She didn't suffer fools, and she was smart. Was she an intellectual? I wouldn't ever have [said that]. She was incredibly competitive with women. I never heard her say a nice thing about a woman artist, [especially] Louise Nevelson. [Krasner was jealous of Nevelson, who was the most prominent woman artist at Pace when Krasner joined it.]

RA: Yes, that was not a good topic.

DB: She wouldn't say, "Helen" [for Helen Frankenthaler]. It was always, "Hel-en!" and "Dorothea!" Actually, I think she might've liked Dorothea Rock-burne. She was very disparaging about women artists. . . . Loie [Arloie McCoy, Jason's mother] was an incredibly difficult, passive-aggressive woman. . . . I don't think Loie liked Lee, and Lee really didn't like Loie. I don't ever remember Lee saying disparaging things about Sande [McCoy, Jackson Pollock's brother]. I really think he gave his life over to helping Jackson.

RA: I wonder, how did you feel about taking care of her? You bicycled over from the little barn to spend the night with her?

DB: I did that because of Jason when I was young. I'd have to go and spend the night, and I was young and in love. Oh, my God, spending the night with Lee . . . I stayed in the one [bedroom] in the back. I got to the point that I would go there at like nine o'clock or ten o'clock at night, when I didn't have to deal with Lee, and I'd leave first thing in the morning. She just needed a body there.

RA: Did you have a chance to meet Lee's brother, Irving?

DB: No. No, she kept her family [away]. . . . She had a strange relationship with Ronnie [Stein, Krasner's nephew] by the time I came into the picture in '75.

RA: Lee got Rusty [Kanokogi, Krasner's niece] and her husband a job in a judo school.

DB: That was the only person that she seemed to have any decent relationship with.

RA: Did you hear anything or know anything about Jackson's mother, Stella?

DB: I think she was a very, very strong force in the family. . . . Loie, Jason's mother, I think really liked her and admired her. It's sort of like the alpha dog. Stella was the alpha woman in the orbit of the Pollock family. I just have images in my mind, having never met her, but she'd be in the kitch-en making the dough for the pies, and she was the alpha woman. Loie accepted it, and I always sensed that Lee probably did not.

RA: Did you meet de Kooning?

DB: No, I didn't meet de Kooning. No, because Lee couldn't stand Elaine de Kooning, so that was that. . . . Lee did not like women, basically, except for Nancy Graves.

RA: Nancy Graves, the artist?

DB: Right. [She also liked] Barbara Rose and Susan Sontag. . . . I think she suffered from being a woman and under Pollock. She was very smart, because she used Pollock to her advantage, in that she never would have gotten a show at MoMA if she hadn't parlayed a gift of Pollock's [paint-ings] to MoMA. They gave her a show in exchange at MoMA in 1984. You can corroborate that with Jason. I thought, "Good for her. She should do that." . . . Well and good for her to parlay getting something in exchange.

I think that the other thing I respect her for is that there's not a lot of Pollocks in the estate, and she built the market. She built the market, and she insisted that the work go to museums and not just be sold to people. She kept her head up. As difficult as she was, she was a great woman. She was somebody that I admire. I'm very happy I had her in my life. I couldn't keep it up, but I'm very happy that she was part of my life while she was.

RA: Did you see, maybe like sometimes with Jason, she would be loving and tender, and at other times she would be cruel?

DB: I think it was more, [as] with creative people, she went through periods that were dry. Not every artist can go into the studio every day and create, and she would go through a period where she worked really hard and created a body of work, and then it would be fallow for a year or a year and a half. I think part of Lee's personality was around her either being creative or being fallow.

RA: She said that if you took the time to look at her paintings, you would understand her personality. Of course, her style does change, but certainly there were these different periods.

DB: Look at the "Little Image" paintings of Jackson's and her work side by side. There were several paintings I absolutely had no idea whether it was Jackson or Lee. They look exactly alike.

RA: Lee loved to tear up her work. But then she'd paste it all back together again and make collages out of it. There seemed to be this destruction and then this rebirth.

DA: I think there were all the charcoal drawings. She had a whole stack of those charcoal drawings.

RA: I was with her then. In fact, I think she did most of them [the "Eleven Ways to Use the Words To See" series (1976–1978)] here in the city. . . . I understand that you and Jason helped her in her last days and were there for her.

DB: As I said, the last two or three months, I refused to see her because I couldn't deal with it. Jason was there, and he was very, very caring and wonderful to her. I believe he was with her the night that she died and everything. I was seeing Laurie Anderson at BAM [Brooklyn Academy of Music] the night that she died. I think it was June 19, actually.

RA: Last question: Where do you think Lee stands in the galaxy of Abstract Expressionist artists?

DB: I think she's certainly one of the great women artists in the Ab Ex field. I put her on par with Joan Mitchell. Was she one of the best Ab Ex artists? I don't know. . . . You have to understand that it was hard because she was a woman in a man's world. It was a man's world, and Ab Ex was all about the macho.

Darby Cerrone Cardonsky
December 8, 2017

Worked as Krasner's assistant in New York from 1976 to 1984 and with the Pollock-Krasner Foundation in its first year. Co-owner and director of the Bachelier Cardonsky Gallery in Kent, Connecticut, 1988–2009. Currently associate professor and coordinator of the MFA in Visual Arts program at Western Connecticut State University.

RA: When did you meet Lee?

DC: I met Lee on this interview in her apartment on 79th Street . . . sometime in 1976. . . . I was twenty-five. I was just naive. I only knew I wanted the experience of working with such an extraordinary artist and, in my mind, such a strong woman. I have always carried two things that Lee said to me in those years. The first thing was in that interview, and I think of myself as having been a fairly, and still am, quiet, polite, trying-not-to-bother-anybody person, and I remember about halfway through the interview, she just very directly and fiercely said, "Stop clicking your pen," and it was such a simple, silly thing, but it has stayed with me forever. Absolutely stayed with me forever. . . . It clearly bothered her so much . . . I assumed I wasn't going to get the job. It set up or it underlined the difference in our temperament, personalities, stature. I match that with my memory of Lee because it was so authoritative. It was so bold. It was just a simple thing. It bugged her, and she just told me. I did get the job. I was surprised.

RA: What was the job? Was the job every day?

DC: Nope. It was established that I would go once a week to her, . . . working with her in her apartment. . . . I would take care of primarily correspondence for her and keep up her records that she kept very well. She had her own very little office in a closet, but she wanted me to keep all of her records updated.

RA: What was the gallery then?

DC: She was with Pace. She had been with Marlborough, but she had a few shows at Pace before she then left to go to Robert Miller. My own sense of it was that she certainly knew how much commitment [Arne Glimcher] had to her work and how much he did love her work, but I think she felt that he was so commercially involved with so many stars, big names. I think she was looking for something that was a little bit more personal. I always felt that that's why she did go to Robert Miller. . . . I did meet Edward Albee. They were very close friends, and she was incredibly fond of him.

RA: And Jason McCoy [Jackson Pollock's nephew]? Did you meet Jason?

DC: Oh, many times. Jason and Diana. In fact, I did a show in my gallery of Pollock-Krasner prints. Then [I did one with] just a few of Pollock's works. . . . He and Diana were so movingly sweet with Lee, particularly as she started to decline. They were there all the time.

RA: What stands out in your mind about Lee?

DC: I think the humor. I really do. . . . I thought she had an incredibly brilliant sense of humor. That really is the one thing that I find myself saying when people ask me about Lee. That, I do think, was something about her that most people don't remember. She was so fierce to me. I'm saying that in a complimentary way. I loved her fierceness. I loved her bold outspokenness.

RA: Did she help you with your career?

DC: She helped me immensely. I quote her. I think of her all the time. I say that genuinely. Really, she had such an impact on me. I think it was because I started working with her [when] I was so young—maybe twenty-five. I was very attracted to her strength and to someone who had fought so hard, worked so hard, not only for herself but for Pollock.

RA: How long were you with her?

DC: Nine years. I worked up until she got sick, which was, I believe, part of '84, I guess.

RA: But in the '80s, she had arthritis, and I think she had diverticulitis.

DC: I used to take her to her acupuncture appointments, which, I know, were of great relief to her in those later years.

RA: I mentioned to you the "swing of the pendulum," and I'm very interested in how that is seen by different people who knew her.

DC: Again, [I viewed her] with great admiration, because I always thought it was quite extraordinary that Lee could go from one series of work to a very different series of work and they'd be equally powerful. [There was] the work that I thought was the most extraordinary, at least to watch, to kind of be around the studio and to see the work she cut up ["Eleven Ways to Use the Words To See" series (1976–1978)].

RA: Gorgeous. I think a lot of artists, certainly established artists, don't always have the courage to do that.

DC: Yes. Well, she said to me that she didn't understand artists that just have one image. She said their brains were dead, and she was always going to be changing and evolving. I think that that is all part of her intelligence and her wisdom that she was always looking for something to ignite her. I loved watching her work in the studio, and the studio was connected to this little office. So I was often sitting there, and she was certainly someone who did not want to talk while she was in the studio, so it was really just observing, and she didn't want someone helping her, either, unless it was something physically difficult for her to do. But I admired that also. I often wish I could have nine more years with Lee now when I am more sensitive or more introspective. I would love to go back and not be so naive with her or in my relationship with her. But at the same time, I guess she seemed to be so self-aware of the swings and of the cycles of life and, particularly, I do think in tune so much with nature and seasons. I felt that she understood herself so thoroughly that she knew how to get out of the dark places when she needed to but also understood the need to be in them, maybe, sometimes. I just think, like most artists, that's what keeps them going. That's what keeps them alive. I don't think it's an exaggeration at all, and I work with so many students now who say that art is what has saved their lives, or art is what gives them a safe place. That's where they go to rescue themselves. I believe in that thoroughly, and I think that that was her path. . . . Certainly, Lee's absolute necessity was to do her work.

RA: I think that makes a lot of sense. What do you think inspired the "Eleven Ways to Use the Words To See" show?

DC: It's an interesting question. I would love to sit with a group of people who knew her at that time to try to figure that out. I do know that she did go through, and I remember watching her go through her drawings. She had so many of them, and then she decided that some of them really weren't that good. . . . She made decisions about what drawings to cut up and what drawings to save. I'm not sure what inspired that thought to cut them up, but it sure was a beautiful thought. And to take something that was so figurative and turn it into something entirely abstract and subjective. . . . Lee, to me, was such a conceptual thinker. The idea of that, I thought, was just beautiful. I don't know if it came from some practical thought that she had all these drawings—what was she gonna do with them? I don't know. She was pretty practical, too. She used to dry her paper towels. She would use paper towels, and she would dry them out all over her studio.

RA: Obviously, you were inspired by her.

DC: One of the things she said is almost a mantra for me . . . two words. I had done something at some point that was . . . a mistake. It wasn't a big mistake, but it was a mistake . . . in communication or in something I wrote or something I translated. . . . She said, "Why did you do that?" And I said, "I assumed that . . ." and she just looked at me, and she said, "Assume nothing." And I hear that. Again, it was kind of like that "stop clicking your pen." It was this really forceful command, and it was far enough into our relationship that I wasn't intimidated by it, but I loved what it said. I loved what she said. I love what that whole sentence said. "Assume nothing." . . . I think . . . we didn't need a lot of words to understand each other. . . . I guess that is why I stayed with her for nine years. It wasn't always easy. . . . She wasn't a hugger. I did feel that she really cared about the people, the people that you've been meeting.

Lisa di Liberto
December 6, 2017

A Krasner "summer sitter" in 1980 while a student at State University of New York Purchase. Currently an art teacher and freelance designer.

RA: When and how did you meet Lee?

LdL: I was an art student at SUNY Purchase, and my father is a photographer. He was photographing artwork at a gallery in Manhattan, and there was a woman by the name of Darby [Cerrone Cardonsky]. Darby was [Krasner's] personal assistant. Darby was going to be away and needed someone to fill in for her, so they were looking for a student, and my dad asked me, and of course, I jumped at the opportunity because I was an art student and that was a dream come true. I met with Lee at her apartment in Manhattan, and she interviewed me, and she told me what I would be doing. I was going to be a companion for her, driving her around, helping her cook, and living in the house with her.

RA: Did you meet her at her apartment in New York?

LdL: Yes, I did. That's where she interviewed me initially. I believe the semester hadn't ended yet. My dad drove me out. I had my bike with me. I had never come out to East Hampton before. It was 1980. . . . I was just about to turn nineteen. . . . When I first met [Lee] in the city, she seemed great. She was very excited, she told me exactly what I would be doing and [asked] if I was OK with that. I said, "Absolutely." . . . I would basically be her companion. I wouldn't be so much a personal assistant. I would be driving her, I would be helping her shop, and she would always be there with me, but she couldn't drive. I would be taking her to the store, to the farmers market, picking up food with her, and then coming home. She would largely do the cooking. Sometimes I would do some cooking. . . . When I arrived, I was just in love, because, first of all, it was very beautiful. I could see the studio in the distance, and it was amazing. She showed me my room, she showed me around the house, and then we got down to business. The first memory, after I had been given the tour of the house, I asked her if I could sit in the library and look at the books, and I could do that anytime, which was a really nice thing. I had a lot of down time, and so I really wanted to talk to her about her artwork, about Jackson Pollock. I remember in the house, there was one Pollock hanging up, a very small painting, and the rest of it was her work or the work of others, from what I recall. She didn't really want to talk to me about art, but she did allow me to go into the library and read and look around. I felt like the house was very accessible. The studio was not; that was off limits. I was not allowed to go anywhere near the studio. I was a little disappointed, but I would go around and peek through the windows. We definitely got off to a good start. We did have lots of conversations, because there were lots of things that were so new to me. . . . I'm living there with this woman who is entrenched in the community. I remember when we went shopping, she wanted me to get new potatoes, and I said, "I don't know what new potatoes are." She said, "They're these red potatoes." I said, "I've never seen those before." To this day, I eat those.

RA: What was each day like? You'd eat breakfast and lunch.

LdL: I think it was very simple. I really don't remember dinners at all. I was mostly in my room. I had to go to my room because company would come over, and she didn't want me to be present. I had no place to go, because I couldn't drive the car without her.

RA: She would have company almost every night?

LdL: Alfonso [Ossorio] would come to dinner often at the house, but I never met him. . . . I think she was really tired and would go to sleep early. My bedroom was upstairs, and now, in retrospect, I realize that there were waves of bugs, so I had beetles in my room. Every night, I would hear them. I also remember in the morning, once she asked me to help her zip something up when she was getting dressed. Her room was opposite mine off to an angle, and the sunlight was coming in from her room, and so she was standing there in her nightgown. The sun is beaming on her, and I walk in, [and it] just seemed like this very angelic moment. It was very beautiful. It was like a beautiful photograph. I walked in the room to help her, and there on the dresser was this box covered with seashells. . . . I said, "What is this, Lee?" She said, "This is my homeopathy." I said, "What is homeopathy?" I really was bright-eyed. She opened it up, and she explained to me what homeopathy was, and she showed me all the tinctures that she used. I was, like, "This is amazing. This is so cool." That was my goal, was to learn as much as I could, because I was going to be her companion. I wasn't there to assist her in the studio. It had nothing to do about art, except on my part. Maybe I was a little too eager, thinking what it might be like, but there were these other moments of learning about who she was as a person. This is a part of what she does. She had this homeopathy. It was this whole creative process, and I thought that was a very cool thing. Later in life, I also tried homeopathy, again because of her. . . . The next time I had heard it, I was like, "Oh, homeopathy. Oh, my God, I know all about that. Lee did it. At that point, she felt like my grandmother, and it was this familial thing, and it was about healthcare, but in a more alternative way.

RA: What else stands out in your mind about Lee?

LdL: I would say I felt it very telling . . . when I entered the house, and I saw [a] small piece [by Pollock], I didn't even know he did small pieces like that. It was the only one, and it was off to the side. Everything else in the house was either hers or a few pieces by other people. To me, that was very telling, that perhaps whatever happened didn't end well. . . . She didn't want to tell me too much or share too much, but she was willing to share other things about who she was as a person, not so much as an artist. . . . I think that there was sort of an employer-employee relationship already established by her, and for me, it was a little bit more romanticized. There's this book, a child's book, one of the characters is a thorn mallow. It's somebody that's very hard on the outside but very soft on the inside. I felt like that is similar to who she was.

RA: Did she ever lose her temper with you?

LdL: In the end.

RA: What happened then?

LdL: In the end, I had to put something in the oven. We were having lunch together. I had to put something in the oven, so I turned the oven on, and then I went upstairs, and then I heard a crash, so I ran downstairs, and I said, "Lee! Lee! Are you OK? Are you OK?" She's standing there in the kitchen, livid, and she said, "The stove wasn't lit." I said, "What do you mean? I turned it on." She said, "It wasn't lit. Don't you know how to turn on an oven?" She was screaming at that. Her personality had already kind of switched, because when she wasn't really wanting to talk to me that much anymore, there was no one to talk to, even though there was somebody in the house. I was like a caretaker in a way, just following directions. It had dissolved in that way. I was there, so I think she went on automatic. . . . There was not a lot of communication. I turned on the stove like I would turn on my stove at home. That's what I told her. She said, "You have to light the pilot." I said, "I'm sorry. I don't understand." She said, "You have to light the pilot." She showed me, and she said, "Don't you do this at home?" I said, "No. We just turn on the oven, and it goes on." She just kept screaming at me, and I said, "Lee, no more. We have to stop. I can't work for you anymore."

RA: Did you ever notice a duality in her personality?

LdL: Yes, I did.

RA: That sweet person and then that angry person.

LdL: Yes.

RA: Do you have any idea why she was like that?

LdL: I don't, except I think that she may have been . . . just like the house, like those paintings hanging up . . . under Pollock's shadow or his presence. Now he's gone, and only one thing is hanging up, and all of her stuff is there. It's like she was free. That's what that middle room reminded me of, like some kind of oppression, because there wasn't a lot of sunlight in there, and it just happened to be where the Pollock painting was hanging up. Her stuff was there, too, but it was larger, and it had more of a presence, so it really felt like, "This is my space now." I could understand a bitterness and an anger from that kind of thing. I totally can. Perhaps as a student and knowing I wasn't going to be there next year, it wasn't like she could form that much of a relationship. Maybe she wasn't capable of forming a relationship with somebody on a very temporary basis like that. . . . I do really think that the personality thing was her defense mechanism. Don't get too close. Don't ask too much. I learned that midway through, because, when we had these other moments, it was really very genuine. . . . At one point, I felt like she could be a mentor, if nothing else, just in conversation . . . this whole period of the arts, really important part of history. It felt kind of sad for me that we couldn't have a communication of some sort to that effect.

RA: Those were the highlights.

LdL: They were the highlights, and they were the distraction to the bigger things. "You're here to do a job, but you're not here to learn about me," is I think kind of what it is in a nutshell. . . . It felt very weird. . . . I do remember we were picking raspberries. She had all these guys come to the house that were doing her lawn and we were all out front. She showed me where the raspberry bushes were. Again, it was one of those moments, and I thought, "If it could just be like this all the time. I'm not trying to get anything from you." It was too bad. I, as a person, didn't feel like I could be treated that way, either.

John Post Lee
September 13, 2017

Krasner's personal assistant in 1981, in East Hampton and New York City. Cofounder of Bravin/Lee Programs, which specializes in works on paper and offsite visual arts projects. Gallery owner, adjunct instructor, film producer, and curator.

RA: When and where did you meet Lee Krasner—in the city or in Springs?

JPL: I had the interview in her apartment [in New York in 1981].

RA: OK, so you interviewed her for your senior paper at Vassar at that time.

JPL: I didn't know who Lee Krasner was. . . . I was finishing my junior year, and I ran into someone at Vassar who had graduated the year before, Harlan Meltzer. He's a director in Mystic, Connecticut. Shakespeare director. And he goes, "What's going on?" And I'm, like, "I dunno, I have to go back to Philadelphia for the summer. I think my father's gonna make me work [for the] stock exchange." And he said, "My girlfriend is

Carrie Bartram, and she's Lee Krasner's secretary. And they need someone to work in East Hampton for Lee Krasner." At the time, I thought
that Lee Krasner was Lee Strasberg. And it triggered in my mind, this
acting coach person who needs an assistant. "Oh, I'll do that." And that's
how it started. . . . Carrie got me an interview with her. And of course, I
went to the library to find out who Lee Krasner was, and I was, like, oh,
it's this artist. And I memorized all her paintings, which is part of the
reason why I got the job.

RA: When you walked into her apartment, you said, "Oh, my gosh. Great
painting."

JPL: It kind of blurts out the way that a student remembers stuff.

RA: Were there any other people you've talked to or met who were "summer
sitters"?

JPL: Yes. They didn't tend to last all summer. . . . I lasted all summer.

RA: And then what about her nephew and next-door neighbor, Ron Stein?

JPL: I really liked him in a certain way. I was fascinated by the fact that he was
a pilot. He had great stories. There was one little vignette where he started talking about Harold Rosenberg basically trying to run over his wife
and driving the car through the back of the garage, through the wall, and
the car ended up in the swimming pool.

RA: Now, whose wife? Harold Rosenberg's wife?

JPL: Yes. Harold Rosenberg tried to run over his [own] wife and . . . so what
happened is that Harold Rosenberg and the car, going through the back
of the carport, and rolls into the swimming pool. So Lee says, "You
know, Ronnie," talking about me, she says, "He's gonna go back to the
shed, and he's writing down everything we say."

RA: Talking about you.

JPL: And Ronnie says, "Lee, so what? It's part of art history." She said something like, "He doesn't need to know that art history."

RA: Oh, I can hear her voice.

JPL: [Regarding a visit to the Creeks.] I had never met any people like that.
I think that I was astonished by the land. And I think there's something
about the chopping down of trees and turning them into sculptures that
really offended me. And I remember writing something negative about
them. And I'd had a lovely day, but there was something about the landscape, the way that they chopped down trees and turned them into art,
that seemed funny to me, like something appalling in a way.

RA: Was the house then painted black on the inside? Do you remember that?

JPL: I just remember nautical themes, and very fantasy-like, and amazing.
There were [Alfonso] Ossorio paintings and a lot of Ted Dragon's mon-
tage areas. Like episodes of interior design, in a way. But the lunch was
amazing, and it was this really privileged feeling. . . . That summer . . .
one of the other things that we did is, we edited Barbara Rose's text for

the *Krasner/Pollock: A Working Relationship* [exhibition] catalog.[367] I would read her sentences and paragraphs, and then it was very contentious with Lee. Barbara Rose wasn't there. But I think she was in a persistent state of feeling that, probably in many cases, and with good reason, people were getting things wrong. That there were inaccuracies. And there were times where, in reading this thing, I had to sort of stand up to her and say, "This is an opinion. This isn't stated as a fact. It's not a fact. And I don't think Barbara had a mind for you to change her opinions." She wanted to fact-check certain things. So I stood up to her, to some extent.

RA: Do you remember anything specifically? Did she take notes, or were you taking notes?

JPL: She didn't . . . her arthritis was [bad] . . . she could sign her name, but she wouldn't have been able to take notes or whatever. So what I was doing was, I had a manuscript. Yes, I was working on the manuscript.

RA: And then sent it back to Barbara.

JPL: She knew her art history. And I think that . . . everyone agrees that without Lee, Jackson wasn't going to be introduced. She knew that she was not the better artist, but, as she said to me, "I wasn't the better artist. But neither were fifty-five of these other jerkoffs." She said, "I wasn't as good as Jackson, but who was? . . . I'm the only one that gets compared to him." And in a way, it does go back to Hillary [Clinton] in the way that women are treated. Women of great substance are treated in the way that their society creates a referendum on them that they would never, ever do to a man.

RA: I couldn't agree with you more. Do you remember anything specifically when you were reading to her, that she would say, "That's not true"?

JPL: No . . . but I do remember that a lot of times, it was very semantic. And I had to figure out how to rewrite something that Barbara Rose had written. I'm, like, "Who the hell am I?"

RA: How old were you then?

JPL: Twenty-one or twenty-two. And she'd be, like, "Just do it!"

RA: What stands out in your mind about Lee?

JPL: First of all, I think she was a very erotic person. I think that possibly my reason for getting along with [her] so well is [that] I treated her like a lady. I would open the door for her, and I would close the door for her, and I was deferential. . . . And there was a level at which, once you got in, you were in. So she was loyal. And she became a good friend, and of course, I still, even afterwards, didn't realize that I was rubbing elbows with art history, in a way. But I would usually help her open the house. I don't think she lasted more than a couple of years after me.

RA: She died in '84.

JPL: For a couple of years, I would drive around and open the house in Springs. . . . [I remember] one telling incident, when this French curator was staying there, from the Pompidou or something. He was gay. He came to my bedroom in the middle of the night. Another time I did try to sneak out. I was unsuccessful, though. . . . Here's what I did. I ran into this girl in town from Vassar, and she goes, "Come over tonight!" And I'm, like, "OK. How am I gonna do this?" So I go, it's nine o'clock or something, "I'm gonna go to bed and I'm gonna turn in, Lee." I always had to turn in. I read to her. I would read the *New York Times* or something like that. So I went upstairs, and I went into my room, and then I closed the door, made a noise, and then I went into the guest room, which had the two beds in it. So that room, that big room, was sort of in between her room and the bathroom. She had to walk down the hall to go to the bathroom. And so I was dressed, and I had my shoes in my hands. And I went and lay down [on the floor] on the far side of the bed. . . . Now I'm able to look under the beds at the hallway, with the light on. So [she] comes up very plodding, getting up the stairs. She goes into her room, she goes back and forth a couple of times, and then I'm lying there, and she walks to her bedroom, but then she walks back. So I see her feet.

RA: Under the door!

JPL: Like, in the doorway. And they're now facing in. And all of a sudden, she walks in the room. [I'm thinking,] "What the fuck? Why is she walking in the room?" And the way the bed was constructed, you couldn't get under the bed. It had a low-hanging bed frame that I couldn't fit under. . . . then she comes over, [and I'm thinking,] "I'm dead! I'm dead!" And I put my head under. That's the only thing that would fit. . . . I'm on the floor, but I put my head in, like that's gonna help. So she comes over, and she sees me, and she almost has a heart attack. She screams. She sits down, and she goes, "What were you doing there?" Because I startled her. And she'd gone over to close the window, which had been opened, because she thought it was gonna drizzle that night. . . . So what happened is, I said, "Aaah. Oh! I fell asleep! I came in here to get a book, and I must have fallen asleep! Good night!" Next day, [in the car,] she says, "What were you doing lying on the floor?" And I was thinking to myself, "This is my conversation where I'm gonna tell her off in a way. And say I need to have a night off." And I turned to talk to her, and a bird hit the windshield of the Subaru. And it was like from the Bible. The bird hitting the windshield. And it was so startling . . .

RA: She forgot she'd asked what you were doing!

JPL: That was it. It never came up again.

RA: Unbelievable.

JPL: And I mean, this bird burst. There was blood and feathers [everywhere]. So it never came up. But what I think it speaks to is the fact of my desperation and her control. . . . I think her determination is like a bootstrapped Jew . . . they're willing to throw down for themselves. They're gonna work hard, and they're talented. They win a lot of Nobel Prizes. She was clever, and she probably got herself out of Brooklyn into Manhattan to go to the Museum of Modern Art. . . . I think that generation of Jews are tough.

RA: Did you notice a duality in her personality?

JPL: Kind of a binary, with polarity. I would say that her personality, and those people that also grew up in the Depression, Jews, immigrants . . . she's the child of an immigrant, she was born here, right?

RA: She was born here.

JPL: Sometimes, when you know them, or you know people who come out of that set of conditions, sometimes their personality [makes] you sometimes think you're being attacked or insulted or [they're] being aggressive. But it's just the way that they communicate. And I don't think she was always necessarily aware that her matter-of-factness, her quickness to be able to put someone down or whatever, that it was negative. I don't think she really understood it was negative. In that world, she would [go on] insulting or whatever, it wasn't really necessarily because you were angry at the person or something. It was just part of that generation. I'm not trying to explain it away. . . . I think she treated me fairly, and at the same time, it was seventy-five straight days or whatever of working. Of not working but what I call "hurry up and wait." Hurry up and wait, when you might be doing nothing, but you had to do it there. And I would go to the shed after dinner. She didn't feed me enough food, because she couldn't—

RA: You went to the pizza place [Springs Pizza]?

JPL: Yes. So I don't think that it was possible for anybody to understand how much a twenty-one-year-old [eats]. . . . And so . . . after dinner, I would go out to the shed and type, and I had an IBM Selectric. And then I would basically go through the woods—this is before Lyme disease. And I would go behind the shed and then go through the woods. I wouldn't just walk down. I would go over there, and I would get a sub, and I would get a six-pack of beer. And then I would drink the six-pack of beer, and eat the sub, and type in the shed. And then come back in at around nine or ten and start reading to her. I would have articles from the *New York Times* and stuff that I found. There were no computers, so I had things to read to her. Mostly I would read to her stuff about [Ronald] Reagan. And she hated Reagan, of course. I would read the newspaper to her. And I was kind of buzzed, 'cause I had six beers. And I always thought, kind of funny, it's like Jackson drank his face off, and I drank my face off. I get it.

RA: I see that there is a yin and yang, a swing of the pendulum, in those works. And I'm wondering, I don't know what you said in your thesis, but I'd love to know.

JPL: I think . . . she had a strong interest in saving things. There were these bottles, these jars with acorns in them or pine cones. She saved stuff, and the idea of taking older lithographs and older materials, drawings from her time at Hans Hofmann, really is sort of revolutionary when you think about it, in terms of how art has turned towards appropriation, about self-appropriation. Even the fact that she thought it would be OK to basically start painting or putting collage elements on a painting from 1963—everything was material. . . . She's obviously very interested in nature. I used to garden for her. . . . Do you remember that rock garden?

RA: Oh, sure. It's still there.

JPL: So she would sit on the back porch, and she'd look at it, and she'd say, "Which one do I pull?" And I'd be, like, "This one?" "NO!" She'd get frustrated. "This one?" "NO!" Then I would start to . . . find something that I knew she didn't want to pull. "This one?" "NO! NO!" "THIS one?"

RA: That is so funny. Oh, my gosh. So those are my questions. I did actually want to ask one more about collage. How do you think collage, which she used throughout her career, helped her express herself?

JPL: Well, when you talked about the personal nature of the work, her collage elements were not . . . the Nouveau Réaliste idea of a package of cigarettes like Gauloises or whatever. They were her own work. And so she was cannibalizing her own work, and what's more autobiographical than that kind of cannibalizing, and destroying and creating? Which is what we all do every day.

RA: Right. I see that as being one of the swings of the pendulum.

JPL: OK. So when I was leaving my last day, it was in the afternoon. And I said goodbye, and she said, "Wait, wait, come back!" We kept wishbones. When I would take the wishbone out of whatever little things we got, bones in fishes. And she goes, "Let's do the wishbone." And she won. We made a wish, and then she won. I said, "You won, Lee." And she goes, "No, you won, because I was wishing for you." . . . Anyway, that's the whole story.

D. Terrance Netter

January 4, 2018, telephone

A longtime friend of Krasner. She and he met with a group of students from Georgetown University who were visiting artists in the area in 1965.[368] A former Jesuit priest who left the priesthood to marry. Artist and founding director of Stony Brook University's Staller Center for the Arts; he promoted Stony Brook's acquisition of the Pollock-Krasner House in East Hampton. He stayed with Krasner in 1982 to help with the editing of the Barbara Rose catalog for Krasner's retrospective exhibition. Below are my notes from a telephone conversation with Netter, who declined to be recorded.

When I spoke to Netter, he recalled one incident in particular late in their friendship. Netter said, "I stayed with Lee one week in 1982." He read to Krasner the essay that Barbara Rose was writing about her for her retrospective in Houston. He said that Krasner would question practically every other sentence and call Rose about it. Krasner and Rose were close, so this was always a welcome exchange of information. And he recalled that once they had finished reading the catalog, which took, he said, "one long week," she invited him to dinner out in East Hampton as a thank-you.

"Oddly enough," he said, "she paid for the dinner by check." And at the dinner, she asked him about giving the Pollock-Krasner House to Guild Hall. But it was soon discovered that Guild Hall would require an endowment to go with the house. So she suggested that Stony Brook University might possibly take the responsibility.

Netter, as it turned out, was teaching at Stony Brook and was a very good friend of Jack Marburger, who was the president of Stony Brook. Marburger said that he was interested and that he wanted to meet with Krasner; he said he would make sure that the house would become the responsibility of Stony Brook. He also nominated Krasner for an honorary doctorate from the State University of New York, which was awarded in June 1984, shortly before her death.

Just before Krasner died, Netter said, he was asked to stay with her for a week. Evidently, a number of Krasner's close friends and family were asked to do this one week at a time at the end of her life.

Netter recalled that at the end of that week, he said to her, "You know I love you." And she said, "I never doubted it." When I asked him, "Well, wouldn't it have been nice if Lee had said, 'I love you'?" he said there was no need, that he knew she did.

As a thank-you for Netter initiating the agreement between Krasner and Stony Brook, the university honored him with a doctoral degree in 2013. He spoke highly of Helen Harrison, the director of the Pollock-Krasner House and Study Center and said with pride that it was he who was instrumental in hiring her.

CHAPTER SIX

Conclusion: The Monster Becomes the Magician

Just as the Western world was reacting to the horrors of World War II, it was also experiencing a dramatic cultural shift, whereby artists no longer focused primarily on the external world but its interior workings, looking toward psychological abstraction. And the artists, many of whom had recently arrived on American soil, found themselves caught up in its turmoil. Redirecting attention from the external, unpredictable, and unstable activities in the environment to the psychological and spiritual life of the individual seemed a logical step toward embarking on a new, more relevant way of expressing oneself.

A handful of artists at the time, many affiliated with the WPA, began to explore what could only be called a radical form of expression—challenging the traditional as well as the modernist modes of art making and ripping open the arena of the unconscious. Lee Krasner was one of these artists. Her participation as a member of the first generation of Abstract Expressionists gives her a special place in the hierarchy. Certainly, there have been a number of investigations into her work and her life, beginning with the insightful writings of Robert Hobbs, Gail Levin, Barbara Rose, and Ellen Landau.

My study is a more personal one, aimed at unveiling the woman who was often regarded by many as difficult and angry but was at the same time deeply revered by others. Her early, groundbreaking contributions led the art world into the realm of the unconscious, drawn to the power of the spiritual and nature at its most palpable. While artists around her, most especially her husband, Jackson Pollock, were investigating many of the same new artistic directions, Krasner, from the start, had her own approach.

The many faces she projected leads us to wonder who she really was. Her circle of friends—artists, dealers, collectors, and museum professionals—were willing to share their thoughts about her powerful presence. I am grateful for their candid points of view and believe that they, together with my own interviews with Krasner during the summer of 1974, offer glimpses into her true nature.

205

I found several themes that recurred in these discussions, as well as in her work, and considered how, on occasion, they resonated in my own life.

Not least was Krasner's constant visual reference to nature. While she was often ambivalent about it, she acknowledged, "There's nothing that I can think of, including spirit, that I conceive away from nature. I do not think I can separate myself from nature."[369] Her most successful paintings underscore this preoccupation.

A second theme was her involvement with psychotherapy and analysis. Much has been written about Pollock's long and arduous relationship with psychoanalysis, but little is known about Krasner's fragile mental state and her investigations into the Jungian theories of the Sullivanians.

Another avenue of exploration is the influence Krasner's colleagues, friends, and family had on her life. We know she'd spent eleven tumultuous years with Pollock, but we are less likely to be aware of her whirlwind affair with David Gibbs. We've learned that other figures, such as artist-collector Alfonso Ossorio, writer B. H. Friedman, and gallerists Donald McKinney and Arne Glimcher, generously supported Krasner, but she was not consistently loyal to them.

Krasner's story also opens a window onto the feminist movement of the time and onto Krasner's reluctance to participate in that revolution. However, her example of independence and courage represents a paradigm for women who continue to suffer under the threat of misogyny through misalliances and political inequity. Her chosen path tells us a great deal about the avenues available to talented women then and now, inspiring personal confidence in the face of a world full of hazards and roadblocks.

Perhaps most interesting to me is the long line of people whom Krasner invited, after Pollock's death, to stay with her in Springs over the summers. These people, known as her "summer sitters," myself included, who were admitted into Krasner's private world of art insiders, provided firsthand accounts of her behavior. Krasner often spoke of her paintings reflecting the "swing of the pendulum" between Matisse and Picasso. My interviews with "summer sitters" revealed that her personality itself paralleled these swings. While there is reason to suspect she may have been bipolar, as suggested by the extent of her mood swings and her severe insomnia, there is no clear evidence to confirm such a diagnosis. However, throughout her life, Krasner was clearly undergoing emotional struggle.

Biographers and critics have viewed Krasner as a complex woman who was her own creation—a Hamptons "local," a sophisticated Bohemian from New York City, and a woman of taste and authority, in areas ranging from food to fashion to her life's work as a leading artist in the Abstract Expressionist movement.

Looking back on my years as director of Guild Hall, I feel deeply grateful for Krasner's invitation to visit her in 1974. She changed my life in various ways, not least by enabling me to move from a teaching post at a two-year college in upstate New York to become the chief curator at the Joe and Emily Lowe Art Gallery at Syracuse University. It was her letter of support, when I applied to the Whitney Museum of American Art's Independent Study Program in 1980, that opened the door onto the national stage. Of course, it was also my privilege to devote myself to women artists who, like her, were thirsting for recognition and to have been part of the contemporary art world, having directed four museums around the country, organized numerous exhibitions, including as guest curator at the National Museum of Women in the Arts in 1999, and finally, served for seventeen years as the director of Guild Hall, a major cultural center in the Hamptons. Guild Hall is considered home to most of the first- and second-generation Abstract Expressionists. As a result, many people in this community and in the New York City art world were sources for this book, through audio and video tapes and in-person interviews.

Guild Hall

Guild Hall, a regional museum and theater in the heart of East Hampton that opened to the public in 1931, provided a haven for Krasner. The small but significant locale offered her the opportunities she sought in the art world. Here she was recognized for her own accomplishments in the Hamptons Abstract Expressionist circle and never had to play politics or the "widow card" to be recognized.

Guild Hall often exhibited Krasner's work, beginning with "Seventeen Eastern Long Island Artists" in 1949. The show had been suggested by

Fig. 27
Left to right:
Lee Krasner,
Robert
Motherwell,
and Willem
de Kooning at
the opening
of Guild Hall's
Fourth Annual
Invitational
Exhibition
for Regional
Artists, 24 July
- 12 August
1952. Behind
the artists: de
Kooning's *Town
Square* (1948).

Krasner and was organized by artist John Little and the Guild Hall director Enez Whipple.[370] It was seen by many in the community as a protest against the conservative watercolor artists patronized by the exclusive Maidstone Club. As Whipple later wrote: "With board permission, the committee removed the staid memorial oil portraits and most of the furniture from the galleries to install recent work by Jackson Pollock and Lee Krasner among others." Despite condemnation by the white-gloved ladies, *Guild Hall News* reported that attendance at the opening was "the largest on record and the crowds attending the exhibition daily were further evidence of the increasing interest in contemporary art being created in the area."[371]

However, like many of the indignant Maidstone crowd, Mary Woodhouse, the founder of Guild Hall, was outraged. She requested that her portrait be sent to her home in Palm Beach, but, upon being reassured that this was only a temporary installation, she relented, allowing the portrait to be kept on the premises and out of view, but only temporarily, during the exhibition's run.

The following summer, Little, who was Krasner's neighbor, organized the first all-abstract exhibition at the museum, titled "Ten East Hampton Abstractionists," with Krasner, Pollock, Little, Robert Motherwell, James Brooks, and others.[372] As a response to some conservative members of the board who questioned the validity of this exhibition, Motherwell wrote a statement in the *Guild Hall News*: "What the public means by art is representation of an object that it can recognize . . . what an artist means by art the public cannot experience without long training and an adventurous mind." He went on, urging the broader acceptance of efforts by those who wished to do "something else."[373] More regional exhibitions ensued. In 1966, the "Artists of the Region" show included only six artists, Krasner being one of them.[374] The important point is that Krasner was not simply included in these exhibitions but was consistently recognized as a central figure in the selection.

Seven years later, in 1973, Krasner played with the idea of suggesting an exhibition. She said she was tired of hearing so much about younger artists and therefore proposed a show devoted to the "old guard." Guild Hall's "Twenty-One Over Sixty" show in 1973 included herself, at age sixty-four, plus many of her friends—among them Perle Fine, Ilya Bolotowsky, James Brooks, Costantino Nivola, Willem de Kooning, Adolph Gottlieb, Ibram Lassaw, and Esteban Vicente. Although she said she regretted taking on this responsibility, her point was that good, older artists who had "a lot of mileage" should not be overlooked.[375]

One of the most controversial and significant exhibitions in Guild Hall history was the 1981 "Krasner/Pollock: A Working Relationship," organized by Barbara Rose, which traveled to the Grey Art Gallery at New York University.[376] The exhibition was conceived by Whipple and was to be the major show of the season on the occasion of the fiftieth anniversary of the museum-theater complex. The premise behind the exhibition was to compare works created by Pollock and Krasner through 1956, when Pollock died. Rose was determined to show their relationship as one of give-and-take rather than one in which Pollock consistently dominated.[377] John Russell, the critic for the *New York Times,* wrote: "It documents a partnership that will always be important to the history of American art in the 20th cen-

Fig. 28
Krasner and Barbara Rose at preview of Guild Hall exhibition "Krasner/Pollock: A Working Relationship," East Hampton, NY, 1981.

tury. It also documents, by implication, what may now be called the heroic period of East Hampton." He went on to say: "Lee Krasner is accepted in her own right as a painter of the first rank and as one who has gone on growing in the 25 years since Pollock's death. But there remains a historical injustice in the way that she was treated in the 1950s and '60s, and it is one of the merits of the Guild Hall that it sets the record straight in that regard."[378] Another review was titled "Bombshell of a Sleeper," by William Pellicone for *Artspeak*. It took an even more passionate stand for Krasner:

> Hardly anyone seemed the least perturbed at the glaring revelation hanging on the walls . . . the fact that Lee Krasner gave Pollock everything because of her superior talent and he eventually destroys her future path with his superior barbaric, macho strength. . . . In much of Pollock's [early] work the handling is amateurish, loaded with unsuccessful and literal over dramatization of his figurative groupings. A pompous, journalistic thirties type W.P.A. mural storyline prevails throughout. Krasner's work, on the other hand, is more sophisticated and years in advance of Pollock at subduing and transcending illustrative/literary impediments. . . . Where Pollock is flat footed—Krasner is a knowledgeable ballerina.[379]

Poets and Artists

It was artist and community activist Jimmy Ernst, son of the Surrealist Max Ernst, who suggested an exhibition in 1982 titled "Poets and Artists."[380] In her Guild Hall history, Whipple wrote: "[Jimmy's] spirit was as generous as his ideas were expansive, and in 1980 he came up with a new way for us to express our commitment to showing area artists to 'pay decent attention to a group of human beings [poets] . . . whose pride is the free spirit.'"[381] Lillian

Braude, art collector and sponsor of poets, was asked to organize the show, pairing off the poets with painters and sculptors. The rules for painters were to make a painting five feet by seven feet and have some or all of the poem appear on the canvas.

The *New Yorker* poetry editor Howard Moss was paired with Krasner, who adored Moss. His writing was well known and admired across the country. His poem "Morning Glory" was the inspiration for the image and was perfect for Krasner, full of allusions to sex and nature. Her painting, which incorporates the poem's first four words, responded accordingly. The pistil, erect in the center of the flower, gives off droplets of pollen, while petals, or corolla, enclose the reproductive organs. Sadly, this was one of Krasner's final paintings.

The poem "Morning Glory" reads:

How blue is blue, its membrane-fine
Water mark of spiral hairline lines
Faintly showing through each trumpet flower
From the lighted tent of the corolla.

That blue is never seen again in nature,
No, not even in the sea, its silky,
Wrinkled foreskin twirling open, open
Among green hearts diagonally placed.

In a matching, alternatively rising pattern
On the wiry, overreaching stem, and up
A string that's trying to ensnare the sky
Or anything else—as long as it's above:
Chicken wire, trellis, fence rail, nail . . .
As if transcendence were simply a matter
Of going up, and up and up, until
There's no place left in the world to go.[382]

A professional photographer from the area, Ann Chwatsky, was hired to take portraits of some of the artists in the show. She captured Krasner's still-powerful personality in her picture, giving us a poignant record of the artist just two years before she died. Chwatsky portrayed her in a magenta scarf (Krasner's favorite color), which she'd brought to the shoot, thrown over her drab navy-blue housedress. The photographer applied some make-up to her face. She looks even somewhat pleased while she continues to exude her iron will.[383]

Krasner was recognized in this important show, along with other major artists and writers from the community, including artists Elaine de

Kooning, Willem de Kooning, Jimmy Ernst, Audrey Flack, Franz Kline, Alfonso Ossorio, Philip Pavia, Syd Solomon, and Hedda Sterne and poets Kenneth Koch, Robert Long, Frank O'Hara, Harold Rosenberg, Harvey Shapiro, and Grace Schulman.[384]

Eleven years following Krasner's death in 1984, Guild Hall's curator, Christina Strassfield, organized an exhibition of her paintings. Titled "Lee Krasner: The Nature of the Body, Works from 1933–1984," it focused on nature as the single most important influence on Krasner. In the *New York Times*, Phyllis Braff wrote that "the thematic handling [of nature] increases awareness of podlike forms and their relationship to the curving shapes of the human body. These shapes are sometimes echoed by arcs that transform themselves." Braff further observed: "The bulbous forms emphasized throughout the show tend to make Krasner's work seem more sensuous than that of her Abstract Expressionist colleagues."[385]

Guild Hall has a number of significant prints and paintings in the permanent collection, among the most important of which are Krasner's "Little Image" painting *Shattered Color* (1949), and *Untitled* (1963) purchased in 1972 with funds from the National Endowment for the Arts.[386]

In sum, the spirit of Abstract Expressionism has remained at the center of the East Hampton art community from the mid-1940s until today. Largely rural, isolated from city life, the region continues to stand as a home for artistic innovation and originality. Much of its reputation is traceable to Krasner and her tenacity, as well as to Guild Hall, the institution at the heart of her art community.

Alfonso Ossorio

Alfonso Ossorio and his partner, the ballet dancer Ted Dragon, were close friends of Pollock and Krasner. They often entertained the couple and would purchase works by them to hang in their mansion. Additionally, in 1950, Ossorio's city apartment on MacDougal Alley became a second home for the Pollocks when Ossorio left to create a mural for the interior of a Roman Catholic chapel commissioned by his family in the Philippines. Ossorio was an important artist in his own right, best known for his brilliantly colored assemblages of found objects, such as deer antlers and vivid glass eyeballs, that inhabit his crammed picture surface.

As a major collector of the couple's work, Ossorio might well have been the first to purchase a work from Krasner, and it could have been a "Little Image" painting.[387]

The Ossorio-Dragon collection contained altogether eight Krasner works, including four "Little Image" paintings, among them *Untitled* (1948–1949), which she created in her upstairs bedroom by dripping thinned pigment from a can; as well as the dense, calligraphic *Untitled* (1949), now in

MoMA's collection; and the larger-format *Continuum* (1947–1949), in which the "writing" has dissolved into tiny overall pointillist gestures. The last of this series, *Untitled (Little Image)* (1950), is a vertical canvas with symbols reflecting an article by Kurt Seligmann, titled "Magic Circles," in the Surrealist magazine *View*.[388] The magazine, published in 1942, was in the Pollock-Krasner bookcase. Seligmann wrote: "The creative work of the artist is perhaps also a magical act, whose purpose is to recognize the soul of the world and to create through this knowledge in the same manner as the *magician* who creates disturbances by means of a few scribbled signs."[389]

Ossorio's collection also contained the important work on paper, *Black and White* (1953), her first fully developed composition that includes collage. Its references to Picasso's *Girl before a Mirror* (1932) are obvious and reflect back to another, more realistic self-portrait by her from 1928, when she caught her image in a mirror tacked to a tree. Also among Ossorio's holdings was *Prophecy* (1956), a work she created just before Pollock's death. Relating to her lifelong fear of her own "monster," she titled this work after her return to the States from abroad. As she said to Richard Howard, "the painting becomes an element of the unconscious—as one might bring forth a dream."[390] Another from this "humanoid" series is *Four* (1957), a pastel-hued composition of abstract circles/eyes. Finally, there was a gouache on paper, *Untitled (Metamorphosis)* (1965) depicting Surrealist symbols of good and evil spirits.[391]

In 1957, ever the generous philanthropist, Ossorio partnered with John Little and Elizabeth Parker to establish East Hampton's Signa Gallery, a summer exhibition space that lasted for four years. Mike Solomon, son of Syd Solomon, told me, "It was probably the most avant-garde art gallery on the planet" at the time. "It was all because of Alfonso, because he knew everybody on the planet. And he reached out, and he could afford to help. . . . So Lee was the one, even though Alfonso and my dad were friends, it was Lee's prodding and urging—this is what my father told me—that got him included in two of those shows at the Signa Gallery."[392]

Beginning in 1956, Ossorio was responsible for exhibitions in the lobby gallery of the Executive House, a New York City building owned by Hamptons philanthropist Evan Frankel. Located at 225 East 46th Street, the Executive House often exhibited artists from the Hamptons. In his book on Ossorio, Friedman speculates that the artist's involvement in these galleries was not just to help promote the Hamptons artists but also "to get his [own] work seen."[393]

Ossorio's first show at the Executive House was "An Exhibition of Painting and Sculpture," November 8 to December 4, 1956. It included three of his Pollocks: *Lavender Mist: Number 1, 1950, Number 10, 1949,* and *Number 5, 1948,* in addition to works by John Little, Raoul Hague, and himself.

All three of the Pollock paintings also went to the MoMA memorial exhibition, which followed just two weeks later, on December 19.[394] Krasner believed the Executive House show would undermine the MoMA memorial. Furious that he had preempted MoMA, she sent Ossorio a telegram on November 8:

> i feel your act of showing jackson's paintings at this time and in this place so brutal that i must ask you not to speak to me or see me
> lenore pollock[395]

Thus, while Ossorio was a huge figure in acknowledging and supporting both Pollock and Krasner and other artists from the area, his own role as both artist and philanthropist in the Abstract Expressionist movement was not without controversy. It seemed his and Krasner's on-and-off feud explains why she would not allow me an introduction to Ossorio in order for me to see her pivotal painting *Prophecy* (1956), although it hung only a few miles away.

B. H. Friedman

During the period just before Pollock's death and for a few years after, Krasner had developed new friendships. In 1955, B. H. Friedman and his wife, Abby, came out to East Hampton to visit, and immediately thereafter, Friedman wrote to Pollock to ask him to introduce him to Ossorio: "It was nice meeting you last week. We are planning to be in East Hampton the weekend after next—that is July 22–24 [1955]. We would like very much to see you then if it is convenient for you. Also, if it is not too much trouble, we would be interested in seeing Ossorio's house."[396] In 1958, Friedman, in his desire to help Krasner, commissioned her and her nephew Ron Stein to create two monumental mosaic murals on the exterior of the Uris Building at 2 Broadway. Collage was always a favorite medium for Krasner. While at the Hofmann School in the late 1930s, she had used small pieces of colored paper to create abstract images, and on the WPA, she worked with Harry Bowden on a similar project.[397] Friedman, from a prominent New York City real estate family, was always more passionate about writing than about business, but he found it difficult to leave the security of the company.[398] Even as a member of the Whitney Museum

Fig. 29
Mural, No. 2 Broadway (Broadway Entrance), 1959.

board of trustees and a published author, he longed to be more at the center of the art world.[399] Still, his insightful essay on Krasner in the catalog for the Whitechapel retrospective exhibition in 1965 and his critical biography on Pollock published in 1972, as well as the monograph on Ossorio in 1986, testify to his passion and commitment to the artists in the Abstract Expressionist movement, especially those who lived in East Hampton.[400]

In the early 1990s, I was fortunate enough to meet Abby and Bob Friedman at the home of Jeanne Bultman, the widow of the Abstract Expressionist artist Fritz Bultman. Jeanne had been kind enough to invite me to stay in her husband's New York City attic-studio while I was doing research on him for an exhibition I had organized as director of the art museum in Roanoke, Virginia. Bultman, one of the Irascibles, made remarkable collages in vivid colors, some of them eight to ten feet tall.[401] Of course, at dinner at Jeanne Bultman's, we discussed Krasner. It was a jolly group, including Francis V. O'Connor, the coeditor with Eugene V. Thaw of the Pollock catalogue raisonné, and there was much laughter. Little did I know that even before this dinner party and well before my stay with her, Krasner had fallen out with Friedman. It may have been that his groundbreaking book on Pollock, *Jackson Pollock: Energy Made Visible*, offended her because of the references to Ruth Kligman that appeared toward the end of the text.[402] In his journals, which are now at the Archives of American Art in Washington, D.C., he wrote candid personal notes that offer insights into the East Hampton art scene of the late 1950s and '60s. While he went on to write art criticism, novels, and plays, it was obvious that he was heartbroken about his relationship with Krasner. He questioned why Krasner had at first been thrilled to coach him during the writing of *Energy Made Visible*, asking him to read it to her over one weekend, and then abruptly changed her mind.[403]

The tragic rift between Krasner and Friedman led to her threatening to sue him to stop publication and ending their friendship, but the book was finally published in 1972. Unfortunately for me, it was the basis of most of my 1974 interview with Krasner. She knew it but never said a word and refused to allow me to meet with or interview Friedman—or, for that matter, anyone else.

I again met Bob and Abby Friedman when I accepted the position of executive director at Guild Hall in 1999. The Friedmans were devoted patrons; in fact, Guild Hall presented a staged reading of his play *Married Moments*, at its John Drew Theater in June 2001, the second summer I was there. Toward the end of their lives, while still living in their home on Georgica Pond, Bob Friedman called me to come over and choose whatever art I thought Guild Hall would like for its permanent collection. I remember meeting their son Jackson in the kitchen and talking briefly to Abby, who was very ill.[404] Bob Friedman took me into every room, pointing out various works, always encouraging our acceptance of his proposed donation. Thanks to their generosity, Guild Hall now has fourteen works donated by Abby and B. H. Friedman, thirteen of them given in 2003 and one in 2004. All are exceptional examples by area artists, including Miriam Schapiro, Ted Dragon, Paul Brach, Paul Jenkins, Howard Kanovitz, Ibram Lassaw, Stephanie Brody Lederman, Conrad Marca-Relli, Hans Namuth, and David Slivka.[405]

The 1983–1984 Krasner Retrospective

According to Gail Levin, the Krasner retrospective emerged in a discussion among Ellen Landau, Barbara Rose, and Krasner as they drove with Bill Rubin to Charlottesville, Virginia, in 1979 for a symposium. It seems that Harry Rand, curator of twentieth-century painting and sculpture at the National Museum of American Art at the Smithsonian in Washington, D.C., had already written to Rubin in August 1979 to tell him that he was organizing a Krasner retrospective and he wanted it to travel from D.C. to MoMA. This letter went unanswered. However, on the drive to Charlottesville for the symposium, Krasner and Rose insisted on stopping at a restaurant to use the ladies' room, leaving Rubin alone with Landau in hopes that she might persuade him to hold the show at MoMA. In early 1980, Rubin replied to Rand to say he looked forward to working on the retrospective.[406]

Rand recalled that he had originally initiated the idea of the Krasner exhibition while speaking to Eugene Thaw at the opening in December 1978 of Pollock's "New-Found Works" exhibition at the National Collection of Fine Arts in Washington and that Thaw "called over Lee who seemed more than agreeable."[407] When he learned that Rose was going to take control of the exhibition, he said, "It felt like a betrayal of all of Ellen's [Landau] hard-won scholarship, and I knew very well what Lee was doing. Barbara Rose had a high public profile, and Ellen Landau didn't. When push comes to shove, I said we can't override Ellen's contribution, and Lee said, 'No. It's got to be this way [with Barbara Rose].' I also knew they [MoMA] couldn't back out because what they cared about is that they owed Lee Krasner a tremendous amount." In addition to Pollock's *Gothic* (1944), which was a bequest, Krasner donated three other Pollock paintings to MoMA in 1980— *Easter and the Totem* (1953), *Circle* (ca. 1938–1941), and *Bird* (ca. 1938–1941)—an act that would support the theory of a payback, since it would have been at around this time that Krasner (along with Rand, Landau, and Rose) was trying to persuade MoMA to give her a show. It is interesting that three of these paintings not only were donated in the same year but also have the same credit line, "Gift of Lee Krasner in memory of Jackson Pollock," whereas other works she donated to MoMA have "Gift of Lee Krasner Pollock" as the credit line. Krasner rarely used "Lee Krasner Pollock" as her name, and the absence of "Pollock" in the credit line for the 1980 donations could show her growing independence.

Rand said, "Whatever form this show took, they [MoMA] would do it."[408] I asked Donald McKinney if he believed the donation was meant to "grease the skids," so to speak. He responded, "I think so . . . but she was embarrassed and did not elaborate too much on this other than to imply that she was planning to do that, and which paintings, and that sort of thing."[409]

However, it was Rose who actually fulfilled Krasner's final wish, the dream of her lifetime: the Museum of Modern Art retrospective.

Barbara Rose

It was 1963 when Barbara Rose was introduced to Krasner by their mutual friend, art dealer John Bernard Myers. Rose soon became a close friend and confidant of Krasner. Because her children were away, spending their summers with their father, Rose was free to spend hers in Springs. Rose was totally committed to this friendship with a woman she found enormously talented and deeply compassionate, and she brought with her the professional reputation that Krasner required to reach her goal.[410]

"Lee and I had been talking [about a] retrospective at MoMA from the '60s when I first met her," Rose commented. "It was her obsession. Bill Rubin [director of painting and sculpture] was a very close friend because he was a fan of Frank Stella, to whom I was married. We talked about everything. He drove me up to Sarah Lawrence, where I was teaching. I considered Bill my teacher of modern art, which I never studied. My field is Renaissance and Baroque Spanish painting and archeology."[411] She continued, "Despite the enormous misogyny in the museum world, he saw Lee as high up in the Abstract Expressionist roster, along with the big boys."[412]

To conclude, it was Rose who finally secured the recognition of Krasner's major contributions in the visual arts, who rediscovered her and put her back on the map. She wrote, produced, and directed the film *The Long View* (1978) and organized the artist's 1983 retrospective, which began in Houston before finally arriving at the Museum of Modern Art in 1984.[413]

Rose told me, "Both Bill [Rubin, at MoMA] and [Bill] Agee [at the Houston Museum] understood Lee's work and appreciated it as part of high modernism. Agee bought the large painting [*Blue and Black* (1953–1954)] very early. Bill [Rubin] was very aware of Lee's contribution to Jackson and discussed it with many.

I could never have done the MoMA retrospective without Bill's approval, as he was the director of painting and sculpture. He had the utmost respect for Lee."[414]

Rose took charge and was able to arrange for the retrospective to go to various other venues, from the originating Houston Museum to San Francisco, Norfolk, Phoenix, and, finally, New York. At every venue, the reviews were more than positive. Rose succeeded by organizing a show that reached the entire nation, Landau went on to write the catalogue raisonné for Krasner published by Abrams in 1995, and Gail Levin, her biographer, gave Krasner the academic credibility she deserved in her 2011 Harper Collins publication.

The Robert Miller Team

In Houston, at the Krasner exhibition, the handsome young John Cheim squired seventy-five-year-old Krasner around in a wheelchair. The first time he met the artist was at Robert and Betsy Miller's mansionette at 120 East End Avenue with her nephew Jason McCoy in 1981, at which time they proposed that Krasner join their gallery.[415] It was the last gallery to represent her before her death. Robert Miller, who met Krasner through Ron Stein at Rutgers, had been her studio assistant in 1963, and he and his soon-to-be wife, Betsy Wittenborn, actually lived with the artist on Springs Fireplace Road that summer. Betsy Miller and Krasner were very close. Both were Scorpios (they shared the same birthday, October 27), and Miller was a promising ceramist.[416]

Cheim was enthralled with Krasner. He spoke to me of her appearance, remarking that she had an "erotic undercurrent. She had a very artistic free spirit, and there was a natural eroticism in her work." At the exhibition's opening, despite the fact that she was in considerable pain, suffering from arthritis, his awe and sense of responsibility for her were inspiring. "I was thrilled to meet her and be involved in any way."[417] He remembered people coming up to her in the galleries and kneeling at her feet to wish her congratulations. He also recalled her snapping back at her well-wishers, responding angrily that this honor had come "too late."[418]

Another of the Miller team from 1979 to 1994, Nathan Kernan, told me he was "thrown into" the planning of the retrospective with Rose and Krasner. As the registrar, he often went with them to the Morgan Manhattan warehouse at Third Avenue and 82nd Street. He admitted being "intimidated" by Krasner and remembered her suite at the Wiltshire Hotel (now the Zaza Hotel) in Houston, where she welcomed various art-world VIPs and was surrounded by flowers and champagne. Krasner's dear friend from the Hofmann years, Ray "Buddha" Eames, arrived from California with a bouquet of roses from her garden. Eames wore a long dress with an attached panel, which, much to everyone's chagrin, kept getting entangled in Krasner's wheelchair. In the elevator, Krasner said to her, "Watch the skirt, Buddha!" Kernan remembered, "She told me, if someone boring stopped her to say hello—keep pushing." Because it was her seventy-fifth birthday, the museum turned out the lights, and everyone sang "Happy Birthday." Krasner appeared annoyed that the focus shifted from the paintings to her personally.[419] A lavish dinner at the Houston Country Club followed. Fortunately, Krasner didn't know that the club at that time was restricted against Jews.[420]

Jeffrey Potter

Jeffrey Potter's book *To a Violent Grave* is a remarkable snapshot of the people and events that marked the life and death of Jackson Pollock. He was a neighbor and friend of Krasner and Pollock, an intellectual who chose to work out of doors with big machinery moving earth and rocks. Not an artist himself, he fixated on Pollock as a fascinating but unlikely companion. Potter, often while in the midst of moving earth, enjoyed Pollock's unannounced visits. His fondness led to a book of reminiscences that brings a sense of reality to Pollock's sad tale. He dedicated the book to her—"In Memory of Lee Krasner"—but, in fear of possible retaliation, admitted he never allowed her to read drafts of the text, and she died before it was published.

Months after Krasner's death, Potter was asked to speak at the unveiling of her gravestone on June 23, 1985, at the Green River Cemetery in Springs. An excerpt of his comments follows:

> It wasn't until after Jackson's death that I appreciated Lee as a person and artist. In her becoming Lee Krasner, the basis of her being did not change; her focus changed, and that vast intelligence and energy were channeled into two remarkable and unparalleled creations: her growth as a painter to become of the first rank, and her handling of his estate with a brilliance that has made it as historic an achievement as is the acceptance of his work and the record of his life. There have been other "Pollocks" whose fame rests on personal notoriety and creative breakthroughs. But there have not been other Lees, nor will there be.[421]

It is worth noting that her gravesite is adjacent to Pollock's but not side by side with it. Her stone is located behind his, apparently at his feet but actually at his head. It came originally from the Pollock-Krasner property and had previously been used for Pollock until Krasner found a bigger stone to use in its place. Willem de Kooning and Franz Kline had helped Krasner decide where to place the final Pollock boulder, with Wilfrid Zogbaum and his wife looking on. Riding his huge backhoe, Potter placed it on top of the knoll at the rear of the cemetery, at Pollock's feet. Unfortunately, after Krasner's death, Ron Stein learned that she gave the larger share of her fortune to create a foundation to support artists. It was he who chose to use Pollock's original gravestone, already in place, as Krasner's marker.[422]

It reads today, "Lee Krasner" in her handwriting and, below that, "Lee Krasner Pollock, October 27, 1908–June 28, 1984." The top of the stone is covered with tribute rocks from admirers, as this is considered a sacred place by women artists, a sanctuary for her thousands of admirers.[423]

The Pollock-Krasner Foundation

Finally, it is important to consider the Pollock-Krasner Foundation, for which Krasner provided in her will. She was able to give back—and generously. She could enable so many passionate, creative people, young and old, to pursue a career in the arts under her inspiration. She wanted to create a foundation that would assist artists and arts organizations, while at the same time perpetuating her and Pollock's memory and legacy. In 1985, the Pollock-Krasner Foundation was established primarily for the purpose of providing financial assistance to working artists of established ability. Krasner left approximately $23 million in cash, securities, and art to the foundation to set this very generous granting organization on its path to fostering the arts in significant ways. Today the market value of the foundation's assets is roughly $80 million, and it has given more than 4,500 grants totaling $76 million in seventy-eight countries.[424] As a result, scores of underrecognized but committed artists continue to pursue their careers each year. In 2018–2019, the Pollock-Krasner Foundation awarded $3,168,000 to 111 artists and twelve organizations. The 123 grants provided support for national and international artists and not-for-profit organizations. Krasner left this enduring legacy for future generations, recognizing the need for the financial support that she herself had been denied.

Krasner also had another legacy in mind, and she turned for advice to Terry Netter, a close friend and a professor at Stony Brook University. She invited him to dinner in the Hamptons. Netter remembered the dinner for two reasons: first, Krasner paid for it with a check, and second, and most important, she asked him to help her preserve the home and studio in Springs where she and Pollock had created their most important works. Netter proposed it to the university's president, John H. Marburger III, who was interested. Three years after Krasner's death, her estate deeded the property to the Stony Brook Foundation, which operates it as a historic site and research center for the study of modern American art in the global context. It was designated a National Historic Landmark in 1994.

Krasner's life ended with her knowing that her long-awaited retrospective at the Museum of Modern Art and her works-on-paper exhibition at the

Brooklyn Museum would open in just a few months. Accompanying the MoMA show was "Lee Krasner: The Education of an American Artist," an exhibition of some of her books and memorabilia, which opened one month later at the Cooper Union, where she studied in the 1920s.[425] Her sister Ruth Stein summed up her accomplishments by observing, "At the very end, she got everything she wanted in life. The success in the end was that the whole world acknowledged her."[426]

Years earlier, at the Pollock-Krasner home, while sitting around the kitchen table with his wife Janice van Horne and Pollock, Clement Greenberg told Krasner "that the 'monster' no doubt represents the concealed part of herself—concealed not just from others but from herself—that had finally revealed itself."[427]

While she was always fearful of her internal conflicts, as reflected in her volatile work, Krasner was able to harness her anxieties and turn her "monster" into the "magician." With her unparalleled courage, she crystallized her creative process into a union of canvas and psyche. Her creative path was an agonizing journey between destruction and rebirth, "the swing of the pendulum." Thanks to the 2019–2020 retrospective tour throughout Europe, organized by Eleanor Nairne at the Barbican Art Gallery in London, the artist's life story, detailing her courage and tenacity in the face of art world misogyny, along with her explosive paintings, will be a source of inspiration for new audiences worldwide.

This book, *Lee and Me*, has been especially liberating. It is the tale of my journey toward understanding Krasner's legacy, her personal history, and her work, in addition to understanding my own strangely similar stories of failure, setbacks, hurt, and a few successes. The power Krasner held over me for decades has finally been exercised, and it is my pleasure to share her compelling story with the world.

"When we have the courage to walk into our story and own it, we get to write the ending."[428]

NOTES

Chapter One.
Driving Miss Krasner

1. Lemke was an associate professor in the School of Library Science and chairman of the Publications Committee of Syracuse University Library Associates; *Courier*, Syracuse University Library Associates *Courier* 9, no. 4, and 10, no. 1: 27.
2. Linda Nochlin, telephone interview with author, October 24, 2017. Pollock-Krasner House and Study Center, East Hampton, NY.
3. Gail Levin, *Lee Krasner: A Biography* (New York: William Morrow, 2011), 275.
4. Levin, *Lee Krasner*, 449–450; Pollock-Krasner House and Study Center, "Last Will and Testament of Lee Pollock," January 10, 1979, 7.
5. Levin, *Lee Krasner*, 249–250.
6. Levin, *Lee Krasner*, 241.
7. Lee Krasner, taped interview with author, East Hampton, NY, summer 1974. Pollock-Krasner House and Study Center.
8. Levin, *Lee Krasner*, 329.
9. Krasner, interview.
10. James Valliere, email to author, March 14, 2018.
11. Valliere, email.
12. Krasner, interview.
13. Helen Harrison, *East Hampton Avant-Garde: A Salute to the Signa Gallery, 1957–1960* (East Hampton, NY: Guild Hall Museum, 1990), 13; Levin, *Lee Krasner*, 321.
14. James T. Valliere, *Lee Krasner and Jackson Pollock's Legacy* (Stony Brook, NY: Stony Brook Foundation, 2009). Valliere observed that Krasner was often confused about the locations of Gerard Point and Louse Point.
15. Levin, *Lee Krasner*, 232.
16. Krasner, interview.
17. The Founders Monument is in the center of Montauk Highway and was unveiled on July 4, 1910, as part of Bridgehampton's 250th-anniversary celebration.
18. Victoria Barr, telephone interview with author, May 14, 2018.

Chapter Two.
The Tapes: Guarding Her Myth

19. In regard to the "French painting" show at MoMA, there was an exhibition in 1929 that displayed French artists ("Cézanne, Gauguin, Seurat, van Gogh," November 7–December 7, 1929). However, this was the one that included van Gogh and not Matisse or Picasso, so it probably isn't the one to which Krasner was referring. I suspect the exhibition she was speaking of was "Painting in Paris," which opened in the temporary MoMA space in 1930 (January 19–March 2) and featured twenty-five artists, including many works by Matisse and Picasso. The archive of this exhibition (including a list of works on display) is available online at https://www.moma.org/calendar/exhibitions/2024?locale=en. Krasner was probably confusing these exhibitions, particularly as they occurred in such quick succession.
20. Arthur Rimbaud, *Une saison en enfer* (*A Season in Hell*), 1873, translated by Delmore Schwartz (Norfolk, CT: New Directions, 1939).
21. Levin, *Lee Krasner*, 139; Robert Hobbs, *Lee Krasner*, exhib. cat. (New York: Independent Curators International and Harry N. Abrams, 1999), 32.

Chapter Three.
The Plan

22. Levin, *Lee Krasner*, 106.
23. Alicia Longwell, chronology, in William C. Agee, Irving Sandler, and Karen Wilkin, *American Vanguards: Graham, Davis, Gorky, de Kooning, and Their Circle, 1927–1942* (New Haven: Yale University Press, 2011), 225.
24. Lieberman was MoMA's head of the prints department (which later expanded to include drawings) between 1949 and 1967, following which he was concurrently appointed head of the painting and sculpture department from 1967 to 1971, and finally, he was the founding director of the drawings department from 1971 to 1979; Barbara Rose, *Lee Krasner: The Long View*, film (New York: American Federation of Arts, 1978).
25. Levin, *Lee Krasner*, 68–69.
26. Levin, *Lee Krasner*, 69. Lee Krasner, interview with Cassandra L. Langer, March 1981.
27. Levin, *Lee Krasner*, 124.
28. Helen Harrison, email to author, January 13, 2018. The Pollock-Krasner House and Study Center has bank statements and canceled checks. Pollock's name was not on the account until after he quit drinking in 1948. The Pollock-Krasner House and Study Center does not have the mortgage contract, but it was paid monthly from the bank account.
29. Steven Naifeh and Gregory White Smith, *Jackson Pollock: An American Saga* (London: Barrie & Jenkins, 1990), 541.
30. B. H. Friedman, *Alfonso Ossorio* (New York: Harry N. Abrams, 1973).
31. Levin, *Lee Krasner*, 337–338.
32. Levin, *Lee Krasner*, 338.

33. Ellen G. Landau, *Lee Krasner: A Catalogue Raisonné* (New York: Harry N. Abrams, 1995), 317.

34. It traveled to the Pennsylvania State University Museum of Art and the Rose Art Museum at Brandeis University.

35. Kenneth Polinskie, telephone interview with author, May 2, 2018.

36. Polinskie, interview.

37. Roy Slade, telephone interview with author, October 12, 2018.

38. "Ex-Corcoran Gallery Chief Vincent Melzac Dies at 75," *Washington Post*, October 13, 1989.

39. Roy Slade website, http:// www.royslade.com/web/ resume.html. After leaving the Corcoran, Slade became the director of the craft- and design-oriented Cranbrook Art Museum in Michigan.

40. John Russell, "Gene Baro, 58, Organizer of Art Exhibitions," *New York Times*, November 16, 1982, p. 84; Roy Slade website, accessed January 11, 2019. http:// www.royslade.com/web/ corcoran.html.

41. Gene Baro, *Lee Krasner: Collages and Works on Paper 1933–1974*, exhib. cat. (Washington, D.C.: Corcoran Gallery of Art, 1975).

42. Roy Slade, telephone interview with author, October 12, 2018.

43. Roy Slade, telephone interview with author, December 14, 2018.

44. Landau, *Lee Krasner*, 146. They are made up of large, torn sheets of paper and canvas pasted on her paintings from the 1951 Betty Parsons Gallery exhibition.

45. Benjamin Forgey, "Three Decades with Lee Krasner," *Washington Star News*, January 10, 1975; Lee Krasner Papers, Archives of American Art, Smithsonian Institution, Washington D.C., Box 12, Folder 31.

46. Barbara Rose, quoted at

"Women Artists: Reshaping the Conversation," Long House Reserve, East Hampton, NY, August 26, 2017.

47. Amei Wallach, "Lee Krasner: Out of Jackson Pollock's Shadow," *Newsday*, 1981; Robert Hughes, "Bursting Out of the Shadows," *Time*, November 14, 1983, 92.

48. Ann Pringle, "Modern Houses Inside and Out," *New York Herald Tribune*, September 20, 1948, 22. Lee Krasner Papers, Box 12, Folder 26.

49. Harrison, email: Pollock's mosaic (glass set in cement, 54 x 24 inches, CR1048) was made for the WPA Federal Art Project ca. 1938–1941 but was rejected by the project. It is still in the Pollock-Krasner Foundation estate and is similar in composition to *Birth* (ca. 1941), the painting he put in the 1942 McMillen show.

50. Stuart Preston, "Modern Work in Diverse Shows," *New York Times*, October 2, 1955, section X, 15.

51. B. H. Friedman, quoted in Levin, *Lee Krasner*, 323.

52. Stuart Preston, "The Week's Variety," *New York Times*, March 2, 1958, 391. Lee Krasner Papers, Box 12, Folder 26.

53. Clement Greenberg, quoted in Bryan Robertson and B. H. Friedman, *Lee Krasner: Paintings, Drawings and Collages*, exhib. cat. (London: Whitechapel Art Gallery, 1965), 4.

54. Greenberg had also attended Syracuse.

55. Ruth Appelhof, "The Swing of the Pendulum," master's thesis, Syracuse University, 1975.

56. Greenberg refused to speak at Pollock's funeral (Levin, *Lee Krasner*, 312), but then, in 1959, he offered Krasner an exhibition at French & Co., which offer was subsequently withdrawn.

57. Grace Glueck, interview with

author, New York, April 10, 2017. Pollock-Krasner House and Study Center.

58. Levin, *Lee Krasner*, 340.

59. Levin, *Lee Krasner*, 275.

60. Mark Schlesinger, email to author, November 17, 2018.

61. Landau, *Lee Krasner*, 105, 110, 112.

62. Levin, *Lee Krasner*, 340.

63. Levin, *Lee Krasner*, 340.

64. Mike Solomon, email to author, May 31, 2018. The bedroom at Ossorio's was originally "set aside" for Pollock and Krasner.

65. Levin, *Lee Krasner*, 340.

66. David Gibbs, letter to Lee Krasner, postmarked December 21, 1959.

67. Krasner, interview.

68. Levin, *Lee Krasner*, 135.

69. Daniel-Henry Kahnweiler, "Picasso: Massacre of the Innocents," 1956, reprinted in Ellen C. Oppler, *Picasso's Guernica: Illustrations, Introductory Essay, Documents, Poetry, Criticism, Analysis* (New York: W. W. Norton, 1988), 219.

70. Ad Reinhardt, "How to Look at a Mural: Guernica," 1947, reprinted in Oppler, *Picasso's Guernica*, 235.

71. Richard Howard, "A Conversation with Lee Krasner," in *Lee Krasner Paintings 1959–1962*, exhib. cat. (New York: Pace Gallery, 1979). Lee Krasner Papers, Box 10, Folder 3.

72. Howard, "A Conversation."

73. This will be discussed in chapter 4.

74. Landau, *Lee Krasner*, 314, 315.

75. Levin, *Lee Krasner*, 340.

76. David Gibbs, letter to Lee Krasner, April 6, 1960. Pollock-Krasner House and Study Center.

77. Donald McKinney, telephone interview with author, February 28, 2019.

78. Glueck, interview.

79. "Atticus among the Art Dealers," London *Sunday Times*,

May 15, 1960, 9.

80. Photograph held at the Pollock-Krasner House and Study Center

81. McKinney, interview. McKinney thought the contract was signed in 1963, when Krasner was recovering from a broken arm, but Levin, *Lee Krasner*, 347, says it was November 1960. It was not until November 12, 1963, that the Marlborough-Gerson Gallery opened in New York. Pollock's exhibition was in January–February 1964.

82. Landau, *Lee Krasner*, 180.

83. David Gibbs, letter to Howard Wise, December 22, 1960.

84. Levin, *Lee Krasner*, 356.

85. *Art in America* 50, no. 2 (Summer, 1962): 20.

86. Gerald Dickler, letter to David Gibbs, February 12, 1962.

87. David Gibbs, letter to Lee Krasner, August 11, 1962.

88. Landau, *Lee Krasner*, 361.

89. Landau, *Lee Krasner*, 361.

90. Valliere, interviewemail to the author.

91. Valliere, *Lee Krasner and Jackson Pollock's Legacy*.

92. Krasner and Pollock's dog was named Ahab, from Melville's *Moby-Dick*.

93. Helen Harrison, email to author, July 2, 2019. There are two El Greco books on Valliere's list: Maurice Legendre and A. Hartmann, *Domenico Theotocopuli dit El Greco* (Paris: Hyperion, 1937) and Ludwig Goldscheider, *El Greco* (London: Phaidon Edition, 1938). His list was made in 1963. Neither book has any marginalia. The Legendre and Hartman book may be a replacement. It has a price of $6 penciled on the fly leaf and a note that it belonged to someone else. That note could have been there when Pollock bought it, but the price looks more recent.

94. Her New York apartment, where, as Glueck told me, Gibbs also had a room or rooms. Krasner went there to recover following her brain hemorrhage. Levin, *Lee Krasner*, 360; Schlesinger, email to author; Valliere, email to author, March 14, 2018. According to Valliere, she resided at the Adams in 1963, and he visited her there in 1971–1972.

95. Valliere, email.

96. Helen Harrison, taped interview with author, East Hampton, NY, April 20, 2017. Pollock-Krasner House and Study Center.

97. Levin, *Lee Krasner*, 361–362.

98. Gerald Dickler, letter to David Gibbs, March 9, 1964.

99. McKinney, interview.

100. *Brian Robertson*, Jackson Pollock (London: Thames and Hudson, 1960).

101. Ronald Stein, video interview with Molly Barnes and Gaby Rogers, broadcast September 1, 2001, LTV, East Hampton, NY.

102. Diana Lurie, "Living with Liberation," *New York Magazine*, August 31, 1970, 34; Judith A. Leavitt, *American Women Managers and Administrators: A Selective Biographical Dictionary of Twentieth-century Leaders in Business, Education, and Government* (Westport, Conn.: Greenwood Publishing Group), 360.

103. Stein, interview

104. Levin, *Lee Krasner*, 370.

105. Robertson and Friedman, *Lee Krasner*, 2.

106. Molly Barnes, interview with author, New York, March 10, 2017. Pollock-Krasner House and Study Center.

107. Stein, interview.

108. Levin, *Lee Krasner*, 361.

109. Stein, interview; Levin, *Lee Krasner*, 362.

110. McKinney, interview.

111. Stein, interview.

112. Arlene Bujese, taped interview with author, East Hampton, NY, January 11, 2018. Pollock-Krasner House and Study Center.

113. Stein, interview.

114. Paul Rickenbach Jr., interview with author, East Hampton, NY, April 14, 2018. Pollock-Krasner House and Study Center.

115. Bujese, interview.

116. Glueck, interview.

117. Levin, *Lee Krasner*, 363.

118. Krasner, interview; John Bernard Myers, "Naming Pictures: Conversations between Lee Krasner and John Bernard Myers," *Artforum* 23, no. 3 (November 1984): 69–73.

119. Myers, "Naming Pictures," 69–73.

120. Levin, *Lee Krasner*, 376.

121. Landau (*Lee Krasner*, 92) cites this work as ca. 1943; however, Levin (*Lee Krasner*, 195) writes that it is more likely to have been completed in late 1942.

122. Schlesinger, email.

123. Stein, interview.

124. Levin, *Lee Krasner*, 340. Levin writes that the weekend Gibbs and Krasner met in the summer of 1959, "his marriage was disintegrating as he began dividing his time between New York and London." Gibbs was still married at this point, to someone in London.

125. Arnold Glimcher, taped interview with author, New York, February 7, 2018. Pollock-Krasner House and Study Center.

126. Stein, interview.

127. McKinney, interview.

128. McKinney, interview.

129. Elizabeth Walter, telephone interview with author, June 7, 2018; Levin, *Lee Krasner*, 380.

130. Nancy Callahan, *The Freedom Quilting Bee: Folk Art and the Civil Rights Movement* (Tuscaloosa: University of Alabama Press, 1987), 60.

131. Rachel Dobson, email to

author, June 11, 2018.

132. Jackson Pollock and Lee Krasner Papers, ca. 1914–1984, bulk 1942–1984, Archives of American Art, Smithsonian Institution, Washington, D.C.; David Anfam, *The Umber Paintings, 1959–1962*, exhib. cat. (New York: Kasmin Gallery, 2018), 120.

133. McKinney, interview.

134. Diane McWhorter, *Carry Me Home: Birmingham, Alabama: The Climactic Battle of the Civil Rights Revolution* (New York: Simon & Schuster, 2001).

135. Rachel Dobson, "Art Chair Marched in First Selma to Montgomery Marches," *Loupe* (University of Alabama), 2015.

136. Rita Reif, "Quilting Co-op Tastes Success, Finds It Sweet," *New York Times*, April 18, 1969, 47; Jeri Richardson, "The Freedom Quilting Bee Cooperative of Alabama: An Art Education Institution," Ph.D. dissertation, Indiana University, 1970, 94.

137. Walter, interview.

138. Callahan, *The Freedom Quilting Bee*.

139. Callahan, *The Freedom Quilting Bee*, 35.

140. Callahan, *The Freedom Quilting Bee*, 61–62.

141. Walter, interview.

142. Rachel Dobson, "Exhibition Brings Back Alumni Memories of the Civil Rights Era," *Loupe* (University of Alabama), 2012.

143. Callahan, *The Freedom Quilting Bee*, 61.

144. Reif, "Quilting Co-op Tastes Success."

145. Levin, *Lee Krasner*, 406–407.

146. Levin, *Lee Krasner*, 406.

147. McKinney, interview; Lee Seldes, *Mark Rothko* (New York: Da Capo Press, 1996).

148. Glimcher, interview.

149. "Art—Museums," *New York Times Index*, 1975, 123; Donald Blinken, telephone interview with author, September 25, 2017. In my conversation with Blinken, he said he had no recollection of the event.

Chapter Four.

Beauty and the Beast

150. Quoted in Cindy Nemser, "A Conversation with Lee Krasner," *Arts Magazine*, April 1973, 47. Krasner, interview.

151. Helen Harrison, interview with author, East Hampton, NY, December 21, 2018. Pollock-Krasner House and Study Center.

152. Krasner, interview with author.

153. Landau, *Lee Krasner*, 169, 174, 189, 292.

154. Gail Levin rejects the catalogue raisonné's date for this, saying it was probably done in late 1942, not 1943; Levin, *Lee Krasner*, 195.

155. Landau, *Lee Krasner*, 292.

156. Carol S. Pearson, *The Hero Within: Six Archetypes We Live By* (San Francisco: Harper, 1986), 37.

157. Levin, *Lee Krasner*, 27.

158. Levin, *Lee Krasner*, 31.

159. Levin, *Lee Krasner*, 32.

160. Quoted in Eleanor Munro, *Originals: American Women Artists* (New York: Simon & Schuster, 1979), 104.

161. John Graham, *System and Dialectics of Art*, annotated and introduced by Marcia Epstein Allentuck (Baltimore: John Hopkins University Press, 1937)

162. Author unknown, *Silver Voices: A Fairy Tale*, Leadenhall Press Series, (London: Field & Tuer, no date)

163. Marie Louise von Franz, *The Interpretation of Fairy Tales* (Boston: Shambhala, 1996), 1–4.

164. Von Franz, *The Interpretation of Fairy Tales*, 4.

165. Myers, "Naming Pictures," 69–73.

166. Levin, *Lee Krasner*, 63.

167. Levin, *Lee Krasner*, 137.

168. Levin, *Lee Krasner*, 137.

169. Levin, *Lee Krasner*, 450.

170. Agee, Sandler, and Wilkin, *American Vanguards*.

171. Krasner worked for the Public Works of Art Project (which later became the Federal Art Project under the WPA) from January to March 1934, assisting a geology professor with a book about rocks (see Levin, *Lee Krasner*, 87). However, she began working for the WPA in August 1935 (see Levin, *Lee Krasner*, 93), and her last assignment was from January to April 1943 (Levin, *Lee Krasner*, 159).

172. Krasner, interview.

173. Eleanor Nairne, ed., *Lee Krasner: Living Colour*, exhib. cat. (London: Barbican, 2019), 69. There is some discrepancy between scholars regarding the number of window displays; Landau writes in the catalogue raisonné (*Lee Krasner*, 93–96) that there were twenty-one window displays, while Levin states that there were nineteen in her biography (*Lee Krasner*, 189). I have decided to go with the most recent scholarship.

174. Ann Bowen Parsons, "Interview with Lee Krasner," August 23, 1967. Lee Krasner Papers, 1.

175. Landau, *Lee Krasner*, 93.

176. Landau, *Lee Krasner*, 93–96.

177. Levin, *Lee Krasner*, 50.

178. Levin, *Lee Krasner*, 50.

179. Krasner, interview.

180. Levin, *Lee Krasner*, 190.

181. Krasner was not included in this exhibition, but Pollock was. For more information on the exhibition, see https://www.moma.org/calendar/exhibitions/1990.

182. Levin, *Lee Krasner*, 138.

183. Levin, *Lee Krasner*, 90–91.

184. Levin, *Lee Krasner*, 138.

185. Rimbaud, *Un saison en enfer*, quoted in Levin, *Lee Krasner*, 138.

186. Poetry Foundation, "Arthur Rimbaud," https://www.poetryfoundation.org/poets/arthur-rimbaud.

187. Quoted in Landau, *Lee Krasner*, 260.

188. Paul Jenkins, interview with Deborah Solomon, New York, January 12, 1984, 13. ©Estate of Paul Jenkins, from the unpublished personal papers of Susanne Donnelly, widow of Paul Jenkins.

189. Munro, *Originals*, 104.

190. Munro, *Originals*, 104.

191. Munro, *Originals*, 104.

192. Munro, *Originals*, 104.

193. Jenkins, interview.

194. Janice van Horne, *A Complicated Marriage: My Life with Clement Greenberg* (Berkeley: Counterpoint, 2012), 134–135.

195. Van Horne, *A Complicated Marriage*, 134–135.

196. Grace Glueck, "An Artist Finds New Favor," *New York Times*, November 11, 1984, 29.

197. Longwell, chronology, 183.

198. Jacqueline Dector, *Nicholas Roerich: The Life and Art of a Russian Master* (London: Thames and Hudson, 1989).

199. Betsy Bradley, Jay Shockley, Elisa Urbanelli, eds., "New York City Landmarks Preservation Report on the Master Apartmentes" (PDF). Masterr Building, 310-312 Riverside Drive, Borough of Manhattan (New York: New York City Landmarks Preservation Commission).

200. Glueck, "An Artist."

201. Glueck, "An Artist." John Graham, *System and Dialectics of Art*, annotated and introduced by Marcia Epstein Allentuck (Baltimore: Johns Hopkins University Press, 1971).

202. Helena Blavatsky, *The Key to Theosophy, Being a Clear Exposition in the Form of Question and Answer* (Los Angeles: United Lodge of Theosophists, 1920).

203. Graham, *System and Dialectics of Art*, 8.

204. Between 1983 and '84, the exhibit traveled from the Museum of Fine Arts in Houston to the San Francisco Museum of Modern Art, the Chrysler Museum in Norfolk, the Phoenix Art Museum, and then in 1985, it went to the Great Hall Lobby of the Cooper Union.

205. Krasner, interview with author.

206. Landau, *Lee Krasner*, 35.

207. Hobbs, *Lee Krasner*.

208. Robert C. Hobbs, "The Visionary Impulse: An American Tendency," *Art Journal* 45, no. 4 (Winter 1985): 302. Robert Hobbs, interview with author, New York, October 23, 2018. Pollock-Krasner House and Study Center. Robert Hobbs, email to author, February 27, 2019.

209. Hobbs, interview.

210. Polly Young-Eisendrath and James A. Hall, *Jung's Self Psychology: A Constructivist Perspective* (New York: Guilford, 1991), 43.

211. Young-Eisendrath and Hall, *Jung's Self Psychology*, 116–117.

212. Young-Eisendrath and Hall, *Jung's Self Psychology*, 160.

213. Joseph Campbell, *The Hero with a Thousand Faces* (Princeton: Princeton University Press, 1949), 12.

214. Campbell, *The Hero*, 13.

215. Levin, *Lee Krasner*, 149–153. Krasner, interview.

216. The Riverside Museum, formerly the Roerich Museum until the Depression in the early 1930s, when it was renamed, was built especially for Nicholas Roerich in 1929, was located in the Master Apartments at 103rd Street and Riverside Drive, and it moved in 1949 to 319 West 107th Street.)

217. See Levin, *Lee Krasner*, 153, for a full account.

218. Juan-Eduardo Cirlot, *La pintura moderna v. la pintura abstracta*, trans. Frank Elgar (Barcelona: Editorial Gustavo Gilli, 1966), 60.

219. Kirk Varnedoe and Pepe Karmel, *Jackson Pollock* (New York: Museum of Modern Art, 1998), 327.

220. Quoted in "Pollock's Studio: Interview with Lee Krasner by Barbara Rose," in Barbara Rose, ed., *Pollock Painting* (New York: Agrinde, 1980), n.p.

221. Naifeh and Smith, *Jackson Pollock*, 651–655.

222. Levin, *Lee Krasner*, 266.

223. Levin, *Lee Krasner*, 266.

224. Bruno Alfieri, "Piccolo discorso sui quadri di Jackson Pollock," *L'Arte Moderna* (Venice), June 8, 1950.

225. Tessa Namuth, interview with author, Wainscott, NY, April 22, 2018. Pollock-Krasner House and Study Center.

226. Anonymous [Dorothy Seiberling], "Jackson Pollock: Is He the Greatest Living Painter in the United States?" *Life*, August 8, 1949, 42–45.

227. Varnedoe and Karmel, *Jackson Pollock*, 325.

228. Lee Krasner, video interview with Hermine Freed, East Hampton, NY, 1973. Pollock-Krasner House and Study Center.

229. Levin, *Lee Krasner*, 279.

230. Paul Brach, interview with Jeffrey Potter, 1982. Pollock-Krasner House and Study Center.

231. Marquis, *Art Czar*, 145.

232. Levin, *Lee Krasner*, 307; Audrey Flack, quoted in Potter, *To a Violent Grave*, 228; Will Blythe, "The End of the Affair," in Helen A. Harrison, ed., *Such Desperate Joy: Imagining Jackson Pollock* (New York: Thunder's Mouth, 2000), 288.

233. Zacharias, interview.

234. McKinney, interview.
235. Irving Sandler, "The Club,"
Artforum, 1965, republished
in David Schapiro and Cecile
Schapiro, *Abstract Expressionism:
A Critical Record* (Cambridge:
Cambridge University Press,
1990), 50–52.
236. Lee Krasner, interview with
Barbara Novak, Boston, October
1979. Lee Krasner Papers, Box
10, Folder 5.
237. Levin, *Lee Krasner*, 306.
238. Philip Pavia, quoted in Levin,
Lee Krasner, 260; Natalie Edgar,
*Club without Walls: Selections
from the Journals of Philip Pavia*
(New York: Midmarch Arts,
2007); Philip Pavia, telephone
conversations with author,
March 2019.
239. Parsons, "Interview.".
240. Krasner, interview with
Novak.
241. Levin, *Lee Krasner*, 272.
242. Denise Lassaw, email to
author, February 20, 2019.
243. Sandler, "The Club," 52.
244. Krasner, interview with
Novak.
245. Siegel, email to Harrison.
246. Levin, *Lee Krasner*, 497.
247. M.-L. von Franz, Joseph L.
Henderson, Jolande Jacobi, and
Angiela Jaffe, *Carl G. Jung: Man
and His Symbols* (New York:
Doubleday, 1964).
248. C. L. Wysuph, *Jackson Pollock:
Psychoanalytic Drawings* New
York: Horizon Press, 1970).
249. Hobbs, *Lee Krasner*, 108, 116.
250. C. L. Wysuph, *Jackson Pollock:
Psychoanalytic Drawings* (New
York: Horizon, 1970).
251. Levin, *Krasner*, 207–208. Jeffrey
Potter, interview with Violet
Staub de Laszlo, June 18, 1980.
252. Dates vary: Hobbs said
Krasner began treatment with
Sullivanian psychiatrist Leonard
Seigel in 1952, while Levin said
she began analysis in 1955 (see
Levin, *Lee Krasner*, 295).
253. Celia Siegel, email to Helen

Harrison, August 5, 2008.
254. Marcia Tucker, *Lee Krasner:
Large Paintings*, exhib. cat. (New
York: Whitney Museum of
American Art, 1973), 16.
255. Siegel, email. There is no
evidence to date to indicate
whether Krasner did this before
or after Pollock's death in
August of that year.
256. Ralph Klein, interview with
Jeffrey Potter, May 18, 1982.
257. Violet Staub de Laszlo,
quoted in Jeffrey Potter, *To a
Violent Grave: An Oral Biography
of Jackson Pollock* (New York:
Pushcart, 1987), 75.
258. Violet Staub de Laszlo, *The
Basic Writings of C. G. Jung* (New
York: Modern Library, 1959).
259. Alice Goldfarb Marquis, *Art
Czar: The Rise and Fall of Clement
Greenberg* (Boston: Museum of
Fine Arts Publications, 2006),
145–146. Levin, *Lee Krasner*,
295–296.
260. Levin, *Lee Krasner*, 296.
261. McKinney, interview.
262. Levin, *Lee Krasner*, 295.
263. Levin, *Lee Krasner*, 296.
264. Athos Zacharias, interview
with author, East Hampton, NY,
September 15, 2017. Pollock-
Krasner House and Study
Center.
265. Munro, *Originals*, 104.
266. Levin, *Lee Krasner*, 19. Barbara
Rose, email to author, February
17, 2019.
267. My grandfather, who was
for many years the head of
periodicals at the Library of
Congress, created a genealogy
that is now corroborated by
the Latter-Day Saints website.
Richard Parsons—a Mormon
and my cousin—found this
information.
268. "Martha Carrier (Salem witch
trials)," https://en.wikipedia.
org/wiki/Martha_Carrier_
(Salem_witch_trials)
269. "Martha Carrier (Salem witch
trials)."

270. Levin, *Lee Krasner*, 25.
271. Krasner, interview.
272. Levin, *Lee Krasner*, 122.
273. McKinney, interview.
274. June Weir, "Fashion Profile;
Carrying On," *New York Times*,
November 1982: D92.
275. R. Couri Hay, interview with
author, New York, January 9,
2018. Pollock-Krasner House
and Study Center.
276. Elizabeth Strong-Cuevas,
interview with author, New
York, September 28, 2017.
Pollock-Krasner House and
Study Center.
277. Bujese, interview. Diana
Burroughs, interview with
author, New York, September
20, 2017. Pollock-Krasner House
and Study Center.
278. McKinney, interview.
279. Helen Harrison, conversation
with author, East Hampton,
NY, 2017.
280. Gail Levin, "Making Art
History in Springs: 1975," *East
Hampton Star*, July 26, 2011: C1
281. Joan Semmel, interview with
author, Springs, NY, August 10,
2017. Pollock-Krasner House and
Study Center.
282. The Signa Gallery, founded
in East Hampton by John Little,
Alfonso Ossorio, and Elizabeth
Parker, was open between 1957
and 1961.
283. Levin, "Making Art History."
284. Despite not participating in
all-female exhibitions, Krasner
was involved with the fight
for greater inclusion. For
example, on April 12, 1972, she
protested with the Women in
the Arts organization outside
the Museum of Modern Art for
more female artists in museums.
285. Semmel, interview.
286. Women's Caucus for Art,
Views by Women Artists (New
York: New York Chapter of
Women's Caucus for Art, 1982).
287. McKinney, interview.
288. Robert Goldwater,

"Reflections on the New York School," *Quadrum*, no. 8 (1960): 26.

289. Lucy Lippard, *From the Center: Feminist Essays on Women's Art* (New York: Dutton, 1976), 4.

290. Lucy Lippard, quote from talk at Women's Caucus for Art, New York, 1980.

291. Hobbs, interview; Levin, *Lee Krasner*, 52–53, 245–246.

292. Levin, *Lee Krasner*, 19, 27.

293. Hobbs, *Lee Krasner*, 121.

294. National Institute of Neurological Disorders and Stroke, "Dyslexia Information Page," https://www.ninds.nih.gov/disorders/all-disorders/dyslexia-information-page.

295. Valliere, *Lee Krasner*, 14.

296. Valliere, email to author, March 27, 2018.

297. Krasner, interview.

298. Bultman interview, Potter, *To a Violent Grave*, 65.

299. Levin, *Lee Krasner*, 54–55.

300. Campbell, *The Hero*, 42.

301. Campbell, *The Hero*, 43.

302. Lee Krasner quoted in Landau, *Lee Krasner*, 26.

303. Krasner, interview.

304. Nemser, "A Conversation."

305. Levin, *Lee Krasner*, 68–69.

306. Levin, *Lee Krasner*, 24, 58. MoMA, https://www.moma.org/calendar/exhibitions/1767?locale=en.

307. Landau, *Lee Krasner*, 25.

308. Levin, *Lee Krasner*, 292–293.

309. Potter, *To a Violent Grave*, 198.

310. "Often such massive sacrifice, if not a result of cowardice, comes from an inability to discriminate between giving that is necessary and life-giving and giving that brings death to the Martyr and hence to those around him or her." Pearson, *The Hero Within*, 106.

311. Levin, *Lee Krasner*, 122.

312. Levin, *Lee Krasner*, 128.

313. Landau, *Lee Krasner*, 143–145. *Bald Eagle* was not in the Stable Gallery exhibition.

314. Pearson, *The Hero Within*, 77.

315. Pearson, *The Hero Within*, 51.

316. Landau suggested that the "Earth Green" series (which is not necessarily a definitive series) was 1957–1958; see Landau, *Lee Krasner*, 160. However, Hobbs included works from 1956 and 1959 in his discussion of the series; see Hobbs, *Lee Krasner*, 138–151.

317. Pearson, *The Hero Within*, 52.

318. Pearson, *The Hero Within*, 56.

319. Howard, "A Conversation."

320. Richard Howard, conversation with author at the memorial service for Charles Bergman, 2018.

321. John Russell, "Gallery View; Delights, Surprises—and Gaps," *New York Times*, March 8, 1981, D31.

322. David Anfam, in *The Umber Paintings*.

323. Levin, *Lee Krasner*, 363, 369–370.

324. Landau, *Lee Krasner*, 230.

325. Graham refers to *automatic écriture* in *System and Dialectics of Art*, 135; Landau, *Lee Krasner*, 230.

326. Pearson, *The Hero Within*, 77.

327. Landau, *Lee Krasner*, 181.

328. Campbell, *The Hero*, 337.

329. Jenkins, interview with Solomon.

330. Claude Cernuschi, "The Politics of Abstract Expressionism," *Archives of American Art* 39, no. 1–2 (1999): 30–42.

331. Howard, "A Conversation."

332. Levin, *Lee Krasner*, 350.

333. David Anfam, "Mood Umber," in *The Umber Paintings*, 10.

334. Levin, *Lee Krasner*, 332–333, 345–355.

335. Pearson, *The Hero Within*, 79–80.

336. Van Horne, *A Complicated Marriage*, 140–141. Van Horne's account of Krasner is brutally honest; she found her extremely difficult.

337. Quoted in, Howard, "A Conversation.".

338. Gibbs, letter to Krasner, April 6, 1960.

339. Howard Wise, letter to Lee Krasner, June 20, 1963. Lee Krasner Papers, Box 8, Folder 10.

340. McKinney, interview. McKinney concurs that Marlborough paid for some, if not all, of the expenses.

341. Landau, *Lee Krasner*, 316.

342. Krasner, interview.

343. Anfam, "Mood Umber," 14.

344. David Anfam, ed., *Abstract Expressionism*, exhib. cat. (London: Royal Academy of Arts, 2016); David Anfam, conversation with author, Barbican Art Gallery, London, May 29, 2019.

345. Pearson, *The Hero Within*, 116.

346. McKinney, interview.

347. Landau, *Lee Krasner*, 278.

348. Landau, *Lee Krasner*, 278.

349. Glimcher, interview.

350. Landau, *Lee Krasner*, 278.

351. Joseph Campbell, *The Masks of God: Creative Mythology* (London: Penguin, 1968), 124, 503.

352. Glimcher, interview.

353. Tucker, *Lee Krasner*, 14.

354. Hilton Kramer, "Lee Krasner's Art—Harvest of Rhythms," *New York Times*, November 22, 197: 50.

355. Ruth Appelhof, "Nature as Image and Metaphor: Works by Contemporary Women Artists," in Women's Caucus for Art, *Views*. Lucy Lippard, Linda Nochlin, Ann Sutherland Harris and Sabra Moore, among others from the Caucus, led this citywide effort.

356. Pearson, *The Hero Within*, 129.

357. Pearson, *The Hero Within*, 120.

358. Barbara Rose, email to author, December 17, 2018.

359. Pearson, *The Hero Within*, 121.

360. Person, *The Hero Within*, 116.

361. Pearson, *The Hero Within*, 125.

362. Campbell, *The Hero*, 333.

Chapter Five.
Summer Sitters

363. Levin, *Lee Krasner*, 277.

364. www.aaa.si.edu/collections/jackson-pollock-and-lee-krasner-papers-8943/series-1.

365. James T. Valliere. "El Greco's Influence on Jackson Pollock's Early Works." *Art Journal* 24, no. 1 (Autumn 1964): 6–9.

366. Jackson Pollock's father LeRoy was born McCoy but took on the name of his adoptive parents, which was Pollock.

367. Barbara Rose, *Lee Krasner/Jackson Pollock: A Working Relationship* (East Hampton, NY: Guild Hall Museum, 1981).

368. Netter says 1964, and Arlene Bujese, who was on the trip, says 1965 in an email to author, July 1, 2019.

Chapter Six
Conclusion: The Monster Becomes the Magician

369. Krasner, interview with Novak.

370. Enez Whipple, *Guild Hall of East Hampton: An Adventure in the Arts: The First 60 Years* (East Hampton, NY: Guild Hall of East Hampton, 1993), 36.

371. Whipple, *Guild Hall*, 36.

372. Levin, *Lee Krasner*, 261.

373. Whipple, *Guild Hall*, 37.

374. Levin, *Lee Krasner*, 377.

375. Whipple, *Guild Hall*, 38.

376. Levin, *Lee Krasner*, 435.

377. Jackson Friedman, son of B. H. and Abby Friedman, said in an interview with me that while trying to make her own art, Krasner "drew [Pollock's] potential out of him . . . really brought him alive, and helped him to be himself, helped him to be comfortable, provided him with food and shelter and love, let him create. I'm quite sure

that I understood my father did not think he would have evolved to the creative master that he became without that nurturing."

378. John Russell, "Lee Krasner and Jackson Pollock Painting Show in Hamptons," *New York Times*, August 14, 1981, C1.

379. William Pellicone, "Bombshell of a Sleeper," *Artspeak*, August 1981, n.p.

380. Levin, *Lee Krasner*, 440.

381. Whipple, *Guild Hall*, 42.

382. Howard Moss, quoted in *Poets and Artists*, exhib. cat. (East Hampton, NY: Guild Hall Museum, 1982), 20. A second iteration of this poem is in the archives of the New York Public Library in the Howard Moss Papers.

383. Ann Chwatsky, interview with author, East Hampton, NY, November 28, 2018. Pollock-Krasner House and Study Center. The photo is on the front jacket of this book. Chwatsky was delighted to be invited by Krasner for lunch prior to the photo shoot but was surprised that she was served only a meager plate of potato salad.

384. *Poets and Artists*, n.p.

385. Phyllis Braff, "Lee Krasner's Use of Figure and Her Treatment of Nature," *New York Times*, August 27, 1995, 16.

386. Guild Hall Archives, 2019, East Hampton, NY.

387. Mike Solomon, public talk on Alfonso Ossorio at the East Hampton Library, summer 2018. Helen Harrison, email to author, June 18, 2018. Ossorio and Dragon owned seven paintings, four drawings, and a collage by Pollock, including his magnificent *Lavender Mist: Number 1, 1950* (with Ted Dragon). Also *Number 5, 1948* (with Ted Dragon); *Number 19, 1949*, *Number 10, 1949*; *Number 8, 1950*; *Number 10, 1951*, and *Number 3, 1952*. Ted Dragon owned

Dancing Head, 1938–1941, *Number 30, 1949* (*Birds of Paradise*), and *Number 18, 1951*.

388. Landau, *Lee Krasner*, 116.

389. Kurt Seligmann, "Magic Circles," *View*, 1942, 3; emphasis added. This reference was found in the MoMA Library and is no longer in the Pollock-Krasner House.

390. Howard, "A Conversation."

391. Seligmann, "Magic Circles," 3.

392. Mike Solomon, telephone interview with author, May 31, 2018. Pollock-Krasner House and Study Center.

393. Friedman, *Alfonso Ossorio*.

394. Helen Harrison, email to author, May 23, 2018.

395. Lee Krasner, telegram to Alfonso Ossorio, November 8, 1956. Lee Krasner catalogue raisonné archives, Pollock-Krasner Study Center, University of Stony Brook, Southampton, NY.

396. B. H. Friedman, "Lee Krasner: An Intimate Introduction," in Hobbs, *Lee Krasner*, 14. B. H. Friedman, letter to Mr. and Mrs. Jackson Pollock, July 12, 1955, Archives of American Art, Friedman Papers.

397. Landau, *Lee Krasner*, 58.

398. Jackson Friedman, telephone interview with author, May 27, 2018.

399. B. H. Friedman, *Jackson Pollock: Energy Made Visible* (New York: McGraw Hill, 1972); B. H. Friedman, *Gertrude Vanderbilt Whitney: A Biography* (New York: Doubleday, 1978).

400. Jackson Friedman interview; Daisy Friedman, taped interview with author, New York, February 7, 2018. Pollock-Krasner House and Study Center.

401. The exhibition, "Fritz Bultman: A Retrospective," was held at the New Orleans Museum of Art (August 7–October 3, 1993). A portion

of it then traveled to the Greenville County Museum, South Carolina (November 9, 1993–January 2, 1994); the Art Museum of Western Virginia, Roanoke (April 29–July 10, 1994); and the Provincetown Art Association and Museum (September 9–October 30, 1994). Although Bultman was not in the Nina Leen photograph in *Life* magazine of the Irascibles, his signature is included on the 1950 letter sent by them to Roland L. Redmond, president of the Metropolitan Museum of Art, objecting to a national competitive exhibition of "American Painting Today 1950."

402. Friedman, *Jackson Pollock*.

403. B. H. Friedman, letter to Lee K. Pollock, November 30, 1970; B. H. Friedman, letter to Charles Bergman, January 9, 1996.

404. Jackson Friedman interview; Daisy Friedman.

405. Jess Frost, email to author, June 2, 2019.

406. Levin, *Lee Krasner*, 423–429.

407. Harry Rand, email to author, July 3, 2019. "Jackson Pollock: New-Found Works" (October 5–November 26, 1978). traveled to National Collection of Fine Arts, Washington, D.C. (December 22, 1978–February 11, 1979); David and Alfred Smart Gallery, University of Chicago (March 12–May 6, 1979). The catalog contains essays by Eugene V. Thaw, Francis V. O'Connor, Andrea Spaulding Norris, and David Bourdon. Harry Rand, email to author, February 28, 2018.

408. Harry Rand, telephone interview with author, March 6, 2018.

409. McKinney, interview.

410. Barbara Rose, interview with author, New York, April 10, 2017. Pollock-Krasner House and Study Center.

411. Barbara Rose, email to Barbara MacAdam, May 23, 2019.

412. Rose, interview.

413. Barbara Rose, email to author, July 7, 2019. Rose credits Lana Jokell, who was the editor and "was very helpful."

414. Barbara Rose, email to author, June 9, 2019.

415. Cheim was part of the Robert Miller team, having spent nineteen years there not only organizing exhibitions but also designing catalogs, such as Bryan Robertson and Robert Hughes, *Lee Krasner: Collages*, exhib. cat. (New York: Robert Miller Gallery, 1986); Edward Albee, Lisa Liebmann, and Stephen Westfall, eds., *Lee Krasner: Paintings from 1965–1970*, exhib. cat. (New York: Robert Miller Gallery, 1991); John Cheim, ed., *Lee Krasner: Umber Paintings, 1959–1962*, exhib. cat. (New York: Robert Miller Gallery, 1993).

416. Betsy Wittenborn Miller, interview with author, New York, April 17, 2017. Pollock-Krasner House and Study Center. While doing my research in 2018–2019, I found a unique coil pot in the pantry of the Pollock-Krasner House that Betsy Miller identified as her work—no doubt a gift to Krasner.

417. John Cheim, interviews with author, Amagansett, NY, March 26, 2017, and April 1, 2018. Pollock-Krasner House and Study Center.

418. Cheim, interviews. Cheim also designed the catalog for "Lee Krasner: The Nature of the Body, Works from 1933 to 1984," organized by Christina Strassfield at Guild Hall in 1995.

419. Nathan Kernan, Telephone interviews with author, June 19, 2019, and June 25, 2019.

420. Barbara Rose, email to author, June 22, 2019.

421. Jeffrey Potter, as transcribed by Patsy Southgate, a recapitulation of remarks at the Lee Krasner gravestone inscription unveiling, June 23, 1985, Green River Cemetery, Springs. Lee Krasner biographical archives, Pollock-Krasner Study Center, Stony Brook University, Southampton, NY.

422. Helen Harrison, emails to author, April 21, 2019, and July 2, 2019.

423. Krasner is buried with many other famous artists and writers, including her husband (the first of the artists), Stuart Davis, Ibram Lassaw, Jimmy Ernst, Alfonso Ossorio, Harold Rosenberg, Frank O'Hara, and Perle Fine, among others.

424. Kerrie Buitrago, email to author, May 16, 2019.

425. Barbara Rose also organized this exhibition, which also originated in Houston.

426. Candace Leigh, "Honoring the Artists of the Hamptons: Lee Krasner," *Dan's Papers*, July 1, 1988, 2E.

427. Van Horne, *A Complicated Marriage*, 135.

428. Brené Brown, *Dare to Lead* (New York: Random House, 2018), 240.

INDEX

LIST OF PLATES

1. *Self-Portrait*, c. 1929-30, oil on canvas, 30 1/2 × 32 1/2 in. (77.5 × 82.6 cm). The Metropolitan Museum of Art, New York: p. 113.

2. *Self-Portrait*, c. 1928, oil on linen, 30 1/8 × 25 1/8 in. (76.5 × 63.8 cm). The Jewish Museum, New York: p. 114.

3. *Untitled (Surrealist Composition)*, c. 1935-36, mixed mediums on blue paper, 12 × 9 in. (30.5 × 22.9 cm.) Pollock-Krasner Foundation, New York. Courtesy of the Pollock-Krasner House and Study Center, East Hampton, NY: p. 115.

4. *Untitled*, c. 1940, oil on canvas, 30 × 25 in. (76.2 × 63.5 cm). Private collection. Courtesy of the Pollock-Krasner House and Study Center, East Hampton, NY: p. 116.

5. *Igor*, c. 1943, oil on canvas, 18 × 24 7/8 in. (45.7 × 63.2 cm). Private collection. Courtesy of the Pollock-Krasner House and Study Center, East Hampton, NY: p. 117.

6. *Mosaic Table*, 1947, mosaic and mixed mediums on wood, 46 in. diam. (116.8). Private Collection. Courtesy of the Pollock-Krasner House and Study Center, East Hampton, NY: p. 117.

7. *Shattered Color*, 1947, oil on canvas, 22 × 26 1/8 in. (55.9 × 66.4 cm). Guild Hall Museum, East Hampton, NY. Courtesy of the Pollock-Krasner House and Study Center, East Hampton, NY: p. 118.

8. *Blue and Black*, c. 1953-54, oil on canvas, 57 3/4 × 82 1/2 in. (146.7 × 209.6 cm). Museum of Fine Arts, Houston, TX. Courtesy of the Pollock-Krasner House and Study Center, East Hampton, NY: p. 119.

9. *Lame Shadow*, 1955, oil on canvas, 82 × 57 3/4 in. (208.3 × 146.7 cm). Private Collection. Courtesy of the Pollock-Krasner House and Study Center, East Hampton, NY: p. 120.

10. *Bald Eagle*, 1955, oil, paper and canvas collage on linen, 77 × 51 ½ in. (195.6 × 130.8 cm). Audrey and Sidney Irmas, Los Angeles. Courtesy of the Pollock-Krasner House and Study Center, East Hampton, NY: p. 121.

11. *Milkweed*, 1955, oil and paper collage on canvas, 82 ½ × 57 ¾ in. (209.6 × 146.7 cm). Albright-Knox Art Gallery, Buffalo, NY. Courtesy of the Pollock-Krasner House and Study Center, East Hampton, NY: p. 122.

12. *Prophecy*, 1956, oil on cotton duck, 58 1/8 × 34 in. (147.6 × 86.4 cm). Private Collection. Courtesy of the Pollock-Krasner House and Study Center, East Hampton, NY: p. 123.

13. *The Seasons*, 1957, oil and house paint on canvas, 92 3/4 × 203 7/8 in. (235.6 × 517.8 cm). Whitney Museum of American Art, New York: p. 124-125.

14. *Cool White*, 1959, oil on canvas, 72 × 114 in. (182.9 × 289.6 cm). National Gallery of Australia, Canberra. Courtesy of the Pollock-Krasner House and Study Center, East Hampton, NY: p. 126.

15. *The Eye is the First Circle*, 1960, oil on canvas, 92 ¾ × 191 7/8 in. (235.6 × 487.3 cm). Glenstone, Potomac, MD. Courtesy of the Pollock-Krasner House and Study Center, East Hampton, NY: pp. 126-127.

16. *Cosmic Fragments*, 1962, oil on cotton duck, 69 7/8 × 123 1/8 in. (177.5 × 312.7 cm). Pollock-Krasner Foundation, New York. Courtesy of the Pollock-Krasner House and Study Center, East Hampton, NY: p. 128.

17. *Happy Lady*, 1963, oil on cotton duck, 58 × 75 ¾ in. (147.3 × 192.4 cm). Flint Institute of Arts, Michigan: p. 129.

18. *Right Bird Left*, 1965, oil on canvas, 70 × 135 in. (177.8 × 342.9 cm). Ball State University Museum of Art, Muncie, IN: p. 130-131.

19. *Palingenesis*, 1971, oil on canvas, 82 × 134 in. (208.3 × 340.4 cm.). Pollock-Krasner Foundation, New York. Courtesy of the Pollock-Krasner House and Study Center, East Hampton, NY: pp. 132-133.

20. *Rising Green*, 1972, oil on canvas, 82 × 69 in. (208.3 × 175.3 cm). The Metropolitan Museum of Art, New York: p. 133.

21. *Imperative*, 1976, oil, charcoal, and paper on canvas, 50 × 50 in. (127 × 127 cm). National Gallery of Art, Washington DC. Courtesy of the Pollock-Krasner House and Study Center, East Hampton, NY: p. 134.

22. *Butterfly Weed*, 1957-81, oil on canvas, 70 × 44 in. (177.8 × 111.8 cm). Pollock-Krasner Foundation, New York. Courtesy of the Pollock-Krasner House and Study Center, East Hampton, NY: p. 135.

23. *Untitled*, 1982, collage on canvas, 46 × 58 in. (116.8 × 147.3 cm). Private Collection. Courtesy of the Pollock-Krasner House and Study Center, East Hampton, NY: p. 136.

PHOTO CREDITS

The images appear courtesy of the following sources. Every effort has been made to credit the photographers and the sources; if there are errors or omissions, please contact Officina Libraria so that corrections can be made in any subsequent edition.

p. 4, Fig. 1, 2, 30: Photographs courtesy of Ruth Appelhof; Fig. 3, 5, 7, 8, 11, 13, 19: Photographs by Ruth Appelhof; Fig. 4, 6: Lee Krasner Papers, Archives of American Art, Smithsonian Institution, Washington DC. Courtesy of the Pollock-Krasner House and Study Center, East Hampton, NY; Fig. 9: Photograph by Martha Holmes. New York: Museum of Modern Art Archives; Fig. 10, 18, 28: Photographs courtesy of The East Hampton Star, East Hampton, NY; Fig. 12: Photograph by Richard Lewin, with permission by the John Noble Foundation; Fig. 14: Courtesy of the Pollock-Krasner House and Study Center, East Hampton, NY; Fig. 15: Photograph by Hans Namuth. Lee Krasner Papers, Archives of American Art, Smithsonian Institution, Washington D.C. Courtesy of the Center for Creative Photography, University of Arizona, Tucson, AZ; Fig. 16: Modified from "Atticus Among the Art Dealers," *Sunday Times* (London). Courtesy of the Pollock-Krasner House and Study Center, East Hampton, NY; Fig. 17: Photograph courtesy of Molly Barnes; Fig. 20: Image courtesy of the Pollock-Krasner House and Study Center, East Hampton, NY. Gift of Ronald J. Stein; Fig. 21: *Lee Krasner, The Nature of the Body: Works from 1933-1984*, exhib. cat., East Hampton: Guild Hall, 1995; Fig. 22: Jackson Pollock and Lee Krasner Papers, Archives of American Art, Smithsonian Institution, Washington DC; Fig. 23: Photograph courtesy of R. Couri Hay; Fig. 24, 25: Photographs by Mark Patiky; Fig. 26: Photo by Arnold Newman. *Art in America* cover, Nov-Dec, 1973. Courtesy of the Arnold Newman Foundation; Fig. 27: Photograph courtesy of Guild Hall; Fig. 29: Modified photograph by Helen A. Harrison. Courtesy of the Pollock-Krasner House and Study Center, East Hampton, NY.